Elizabeth Taylor

Quixstar

A Novel

Elizabeth Taylor

Quixstar
A Novel

ISBN/EAN: 9783337028091

Printed in Europe, USA, Canada, Australia, Japan

Cover: Foto ©Thomas Meinert / pixelio.de

More available books at **www.hansebooks.com**

A NOVEL

BY

THE AUTHOR OF "BLINDPITS"

NEW YORK
G. P. PUTNAM'S SONS
4TH AVENUE AND 23D STREET
1873

QUIXSTAR.

CHAPTER I.

It is a pretty little town Quixstar, and knows it—or at least if you could suppose a town guilty of affectation, you could easily think that Quixstar sometimes tried to look more than usually interesting. If you looked out in the morning, for instance, and caught all the eastward windows flashing back the sun's rays like the eyes of a young beauty, while the buildings in grey shadow looked on with a kind of quiet wonder, as a timid chaperon might do, alarmed as to what would happen next; or at twilight of a summer's day, when the town folded its hands and lay back in its arm-chair; or by moonlight, when its very smoke seemed to be etherealized, and its steeple went right into the sky, one bright particular star standing by it, so near that the weathercock might have scorched his wings; or in winter, when it wrapped itself in ermine to the throat—if you watched—but, indeed, if you begin to watch any person, place, or thing, you will soon get more interested than you are aware of, and Quixstar was really an interesting town, worth watching at almost any time. It combined compact tidiness with old-fashioned picturesqueness, and its inhabitants took a pride in it, a pride which threatened the stability of the last-mentioned quality; but happily it is easier and cheaper to keep things going as they are than to make sweeping changes, so that a native of Quixstar, though he may have been absent half a lifetime, on returning will see little difference, except that the clock in the steeple has had its face and hands washed. This may be an improvement; but he will miss with a pang the familiar old weather-beaten visage that so often told him whether he was too late for school or not.

The town is small—so small that every inhabitant might know every other inhabitant, might know of his business, his habits, his affairs, and everything that is his. Whether this is to be reckoned an advantage or a drawback depends on taste and temperament. However obscure you are, you may be somebody in Quixstar, and that is something; better be first in—what was the place?—than second in Rome; but if you have no fibre of Julius Cæsar in your nature; if you would like to slip through life like a knotless thread; if you have the weakness to shrink from being the subject of critical dissection, then give Quixstar and its co-towns throughout the empire a wide berth.

It is to be doubted if any one ever gets to such a pitch of apathy as to take absolutely no interest in his neighbor's affairs; but when you have arrived at the knowledge that men and women in civilized life wear much the same sort of garments, differing a little in texture; that what is in one man's dining-room is in another man's; that your neighbor's closets are filled with duplicates of what is in your own, and that ten to one the people round you are as well-behaved as yourself, with probably a sprinkling of rogues to carry off the vices of the community, as the lightning-rod conducts the dangerous fluid to the ground,—when you have a conviction of all this, your are apt to get out of bed in a lazy fashion; you dress, saying, *Cui bono?* you look at the sun in the heavens, and say there is nothing new under it; in short, you are prepared for everything; the emotion of surprise you have put away in your mental garret among other obsolete lumber, and if you ever look at it you say, " Oh, that reminds me of long ago." It is very satisfactory to know that no one in Quixstar had got into this melancholy state; its inhabitants might have bounded out of bed with the elasticity of india-rubber balls, if curiosity would have acted as a brisk motive power. And long may it be so! How many people can rise to even an occasional contemplation of the infinite, and if they lose their interest in the finite, the very finite of the gossip of Quixstar, what is to become of them?—go mad possibly, or sink into idiocy; if they could only keep to what is lovely and of good report, but somehow average human nature is so prone to turn up the seamy side of things.

The name Quixstar is of obscure etymology. In old records the first syllable is spelt Cuick—a word from the Celtic, meaning either cuckoo or creek, and in Latin it has been written Cuickstarlineum; but the modern orthography is Quixstar, in pronunciation popularly often reduced to Quixstir or Quicksir, and even Quicker. The cuckoo still haunts the glens, where the river runs that on its journey from the distant hills comes wandering past Quixstar; it might have taken a more direct road to its destination, but time being no object, and trouble as little, it preferred the circuitous one.

The Eden, as the river—or more strictly speaking, rivulet—was called, had been renowned both in song and story before it reached Quixstar, but like the truly great it went on its way doing all the good it could, as if quite unconscious of its fame.

Across a foot-bridge from the town there stood a small building known as "The Cottage." One morning it was told throughout Quixstar that the Cottage had changed owners — had been sold to a Mr. Sinclair. Did any one know Mr. Sinclair? Who was he, what was he, where did he come from? Ere long, by putting little bits of information together, answers to these questions leaked out. He came from Ironburgh; he was a merchant; he was wealthy. This so far allayed the public hunger for a time. Then it was seen that the Cottage was undergoing a metamorphosis; from an humble one-storied building it was spreading out below, and rising above, to a size fitted, as advertisements say, to accommodate a genteel family.

The house nearest the Cottage, on the same side of the water, and only divided from it by the breadth of a road, was occupied by Mr. Gilbert, the schoolmaster of the parish. It was an old house comparatively, one end of it covered with ivy to the very top—altogether a leafy bower, with an old-fashioned garden sloping to the water's edge, but separated from it by a wall, also ivy-grown. It was a place very dear to Mrs. Gilbert; she had spent all her married life there. The school was on the other side of the water, not ten minutes' distant. Across the foot-bridge, past Peter Veitch's cottage, and round a corner, and you were at it, and in the middle of one side of the town. The foot-bridge spoken of was a kind of private property, only pretty generally used, but there was another bridge,—a handsome stone arch of recent erection replacing a very old structure. The road across this entered at the head of the town; above it was the romantic glen of the Eden; at the other end of the town stretched away on both sides of the river the woods of Sir Richard Cranstoun. In point of situation Quixstar was a fortunate little town.

An old family, sitting among old trees, or at least having a seat or seats in the middle of a fine array of leafy patriarchs, is to be thought of with reverence. Small people or simple people speak of such a family as if it were a fetish or Grand Llama, and if its members have the ability, like the men of Issachar, to read the signs of the times, and to read them aright, they are in their place as leaders of the people; if not, they are like the cocoon out of which the life has gone: the spirit of the founder may still be winging about the world, but they are only the empty shell. The Cranstouns were an old family, and whether they kept up the prestige of their ancestors or not, it is certain the trees did; they had not been planted yesterday, and it may give a slight clue to the head of the house to say that he would have heard of a general European war with small emotion compared with what he would have felt had it been proposed to him to cut down one of his majestic vegetable pets. And really it would have been a pity to cut any of them down, the creatures were so beautiful, and had gladdened the eyes of so many generations: standing below them, you felt as you do when reading a work of genius that has lasted some hundreds of years. You have your own enjoyment, and you think of the enjoyment of all the men and women who have cried and laughed over it, and it is too much—you hasten away to the commonplace; it is the expressed essence of life, and like other essences a small dose stimulates, a large one leaves you stupefied and baffled. In case hopes may be raised that this " old family " are to appear much in this story, it may be as well to say that is not likely;

and if they do, the reader will find them wonderfully like a new family, save and except probably some prejudices clinging to them, as a chicken sometimes carries about a bit of its shell, which will adhere and make it look funny, though it is not aware of the figure it cuts.

CHAPTER II.

PETER VEITCH, whose cottage has been mentioned, was a well-known inhabitant of Quixstar, although in humble plight. He was a gardener, not restricted to any particular spot, but having a fatherly eye on many of the Quixstar gardens. In spring he was a man of consequence, and like most people he could enjoy that. His services were in great demand. Not but that there were other gardeners in the place, who would undertake to do your work quicker, cheaper, and even better than Peter, and leave your little share of the earth's circumference looking beautifully tidy and ship-shape, till time revealed that only the surface had been scratched, the weeds refused decent burial, the manure omitted, and rubbish sown instead of seed. It was then that you humbled yourself before Peter Veitch, and that that just man showed the magnanimity of his nature by not crowing over you to your face—merely laughing in his sleeve. But Peter had his drawbacks: he liked and took his own way rather than yours, he worked diligently and conscientiously, and raised good crops, though he lacked the touch, the final distinctive touch which all great artists, in whatever line, give their work. You remember Apelles and his friend, who drew lines, instead of leaving cards with each other—well, Peter's eye was not so fastidious as it might have been, but you can't have anything perfect in this world.

"Peter," said Mrs. Gilbert, while standing in her garden, looking at the gardener busy at work, "do you know anything of the people who have bought the Cottage? It is said they are rich."

"Ay," said Peter, stopping with his foot in rest, and his body leaning on the top of his spade. "Oh ay, he's a man wi' a mint o' siller."

"A retired merchant?" said Mrs. Gilbert.

"He made it in the snuff and tobacco line in Ironburgh, they tell me. It maun be a better job than delving, I'm thinking."

"More lucrative, Peter, but not so honorable or pleasant, surely. You'll be expecting to be at work in the Cottage garden immediately?"

"Weel, like eneuch; but, odd, there's little pleasure working to thae retired bodies; they're extraordinary maggoty, and they aye think they ken a' thing."

"And, Peter—this new-comer, what's his name?"

"Sinclair—Adam Sinclair, Esquire."

"I daresay I heard that; well, I hope he'll be a good neighbor."

"It's a question—time'll tell, but I hae nae notion o' thae retired bodies wi' naething to do. Of course the like o' me working in a yard is here the day and away the morn, but I whiles pity their women-folk, they've a heap to pit up wi'."

"But, Peter, I understand this man is a bachelor, so his women-folk won't be afflicted."

"Ah, is he?" said Peter, with the sudden interest begotten by a new fact, "weel, he's no like to be the easier dune wi' for that, unless he's a sleepy-headed dreamy kind o' body, and that's no likely, as he's rich, and it takes a' folk's senses to keep siller in this world, forby to mak' it," and Peter began to use his spade again, for though a crack was one of his prime luxuries, he had a sound conscience.

Standing there in her own garden, Mrs. Gilbert was a noble-looking woman. Time, and maybe circumstances, were beginning to tell on her fair face; there was a look of care in it, and lines were where as yet lines need not have been, but it was a noble face, not a face that you could tire of. Mr. Gilbert has been heard to say that it was not his wife's beauty that attracted him,—that it was some time, indeed, before he knew that she was good-looking, which blindness might be satisfactory to him, as indicating that he was above being taken by such an empty thing as beauty; but made one regret that so very good a thing should have been thrown away. When you see a good, or beautiful, or noble thing, you feel it should be put to some noble use, although the better and nobler a human being is, the more willing will he be to do any kind of work that falls in his way. It might be a matter of speculation what Mrs. Gilbert would have been and done had she been a queen, or the wife of a great man, which Mr. Gilbert was not, or the directress of a religious community, though it probably never crossed her mind that she was not in her right place; but surely there must have been times when Mr. Gilbert could not help feeling as if he should put off his shoes, for the place where she stood was holy ground—at least one would think so, but you never can tell. It can't be a pleasant thing for a man to be overshadowed by his wife's superiority; if they can, people are apt to shirk what is not pleasant; it must need a small mind or a great one to sit down contentedly under it, and if the mind is great enough to feel contented in such circumstances, that proves equality at least, so that your premise is gone.

1*

Mrs. Gilbert's father had been a draper in a country town, to which Mr. Gilbert chanced to come as assistant teacher. They met, and the result was, that they married and settled in Quixstar, where Mr. Gilbert seemed to be in his right enough place; but Mrs. Gilbert reminded you of a beautiful flower in a small flower-pot, where it had not room to develop in luxuriance. The draper had another daughter, who at the same time went through the same process as her sister and the teacher, with a young man in an ironmonger's shop—Raeburn by name. They settled in Ironburgh, where, in the iron trade, Mr. Raeburn in not many years grew rich. The Gilberts had three children, a boy and two girls; the Raeburns had seven, all boys. Commonly the small income has the larger number of olive-branches attached to it; here, for once, to the non-parental eye, things seemed as they should be.

Mrs. Raeburn was a little pretty-faced woman, whose attempts at authority in her own family were generally swamped; indeed, to hear her speak you would at times have thought she regarded her children as her natural enemies, while she showered a weak fondness on them to which they did not always submit with a good grace —for they were fine manly boys, hasting to get out of her presence, and let the superfluous steam off in some way. Likely you are prepared to hear that Mr. Raeburn was an uneducated, vulgar, purse-proud man, whose house was crammed to the door with fine furniture, and its walls covered from floor to ceiling with pictures in gaudy frames—one who put on airs of patronage among his less prosperous connexions, and audibly wondered how they could exist on such incomes as they had. That was not the kind of man he was at all; but if he comes into this story now and then we shall see for ourselves what he was. The brothers-in-law were as complete contrasts as their wives. If you could have changed Mrs. Raeburn into Mrs. Gilbert, and Mrs. Gilbert into Mrs. Raeburn, you would have felt that you had made nearly a perfect arrangement. Mr. Gilbert would have been as happy, probably happier, with a pretty-faced, weakish woman; and Mr. Raeburn, though he loved his wife, and was in a measure blind to her failings, would have found life a different thing passed alongside such a woman as Mrs. Gilbert; and for Mrs. Gilbert, why, she would have been in the big flower-pot. We know that Jove gave men the sunshine and the rain into their own hands to make the best of them, and they were glad in a short time to beg him to take them back again; so perhaps you and I might not have made a much better thing of it supposing we had superintended the courtships of these four people; and as it is likely they themselves were well enough pleased with existing arrangements, we must try to be so too, although it seems impossible to prevent a kind of unconscious irritation in the presence of what we think unfitness, any more than a feeling of rest and enjoyment in the beauty of fitness.

It would appear that the people of this history belong to the middle class, possibly even to what is called the lower middle class, that unfortunate section of society around which it is so difficult to throw an interest. If they had happened to belong to the upper ten thousand, among whom there enters nothing that is mean or sordid, nor any finely-moulded falsehood, nor even a *soupçon* of naughtiness, except by way of piquant sauce to so exquisite a dish, then indeed the reader might find something to reward his trouble; or if they had been among picturesque poverty, having a ruffian boldly dashed in with ochre and lampblack;—but a retired tobacconist, a man who had prospered in the iron trade, and a country schoolmaster! But we need not read the book, or we may imitate Transatlantic ingenuity, which by means of any number of jackscrews raises a whole block of houses from a low situation to a high one, without the inhabitants being the least aware of what is doing. Put in the jackscrews of your imagination, change the accessories, and the people will do in high life; or dig a hole and sink them among dirt and squalor, and still you will find the same human nature; but the easiest plan is not to read any further.

The inevitable minister, too, bids fair to be inevitable, for you can hardly have a parish schoolmaster without a parish minister, and whom John Knox has joined together it would be presumption to put asunder. The minister of Quixstar was not a perfect man any more than the schoolmaster. Considerable excuses should be made for him, however; he was fifty years old, and during all that time he had been most atrociously healthy. We have all heard of the great blessing of a sound mind in a sound body, which it undeniably is; but I have known sound minds that one would not have grudged getting a trial of rickety lodgings now and then. If you have a spirit finely touched, and with insight, it will do in the very soundest body, but there are spirits which—to use an Irishism—only feel when their own personal flesh is pinched. Mr. Kennedy might have felt, for he was not without his share of affliction; his wife was a confirmed invalid, seldom or never seen or heard of—that is, people spoke about her as they will about anything, but she was set aside entirely from active life. It was said that her disease affected her mental faculties in some degree. Be that as it may; we leave the curtain that shut her in from the world reverently unlifted.

Though profoundly sorry for the poor woman, and awed by a sense of the mystery of suffering, it is not to be regretted that it is unnecessary to speak of the minister's wife; she might have been a good-natured woman, toiling at the business of being very agreeable to every one, or, if not very good-natured, to those only to whom it was necessary or expedient to be so; or a coarse-grained nature, whose style of sympathy made you shrink; or she might have been feeble, or commonplace, or intermeddling—any of these characters would have been easily drawn, but they would have been unpleasant, and if, as Peter Veitch would say, "A minister is an ill craw to shoot at," his wife is not a better mark; or she might have been a good woman, and the goodness of a good woman is an atmosphere which, when you can describe the incense sent up by the sweetbriar after a summer evening shower, you may hope to describe. This style of goodness belonged to Mrs. Gilbert, but how is it to be put on paper? Mr. Kennedy was kind and attentive to his wife, but not crushed by her affliction; on the contrary, he bore up under it well.

CHAPTER III.

A MAN without women-folk in some shape is, in Great Britain, at this moment, nearly an impossibility. Here and there in the southern hemisphere, no doubt, there are huts in which, if you were to enter, you would find a man —a man, too, who may have "moved in the best society"—paring potatoes for his dinner, or washing his clothes, or baking damper, with a face so overgrown with hair that his mother would not know him. In writing home he will tell he is seeing life, and how jolly it is, how free from conventionalism, and all that. Well, we will respect his privacy when the big salt drops fall on the long rough beard, and the word "banishment" rises to his lips as he yearns for the music of a woman's voice, and the deft ministrations of her hand. How often has he twisted up the end of that worsted thread and tried to get it through the eye of his darning-needle! He remembers his mother had no difficulty in threading a darning-needle—and he flings it down with a smile and a tear; but be sure he enjoys this life—no conventionality and no humbug!

Mr. Sinclair, living in the heart of Scotland, could not keep house in this style. His household goods arrived in charge of two women-servants and several upholsterer's men, and it was soon known that he himself would shortly appear. Like Mr. Kennedy, Mr. Sinclair was a man of fifty, possibly a year or two more. It is no use saying whether that is old or young; hale gentlemen of seventy will think he was barely in his prime, while the youth of twenty-one will consider that he was in extreme old age. He had been a wholesale tobacconist, and he, or at least his ancestors, had owned also a retail shop. There were people in Quixstar who had seen it, and the Highlander that stood over its door,—the finger and thumb of one hand holding a pinch within an inch of his nose, while the other extended the friendly box to an invisible acquaintance. These things were against Mr. Sinclair; still, he was reputed to be so rich that the gentility of Quixstar felt they could hardly overlook him if he were at all presentable. The next thing known was that letters came to the post-office addressed Adam Sinclair, Esq., Old Battle House, Quixstar. Where was Old Battle House? Had Mr. Sinclair rebaptized the Cottage, asked an amused public? Yes, he had done that, as he had a right to do. He said to himself, there might be fifty Quixstars, each having a hundred Cottages—the name was vague and indefinite, and did not sound well. Remains had been dug up which attested that at some remote period a battle had been fought in the neighborhood; he detested cottages, lodges, and villas; a man's house was his house, so he changed the name of the Cottage to Old Battle House —and it was ingenious, it must be allowed; if there had been a lady in the case one would have given her the credit of it. Very soon his figure was as well known on the roads as that of the minister or the rural policeman.

Mr. Sinclair was lonely, or presumed to be so; there is no doubt at least that he was alone in his own house, so far as companionship is concerned, but probably that did not distress him. It has been said that every human being has a history, and if that history could be faithfully told it would be profoundly interesting. But there are histories and histories, and to talk of their being faithfully told is to talk of being omniscient, and further, of being omnipotent. To know what is true, and to be able to tell it, even in the puny measure that men may know and tell, has been a power in all ages, a power which men have called genius, and which has been but charily distributed. Mr. Sinclair may have had a very interesting history, but it is not given to me to tell it; I don't know it; I know nothing of him before he came to Quixstar, and only the outsides of his life after he did come. His inner being may have been like Vesuvius—in a state of upheaval every now and then, but if it was it never boiled over. He was always like himself, very like himself, and in his own way appeared to enjoy life; in his own way, for he had a way of his own.

It is good merely to see a man enjoy life. The dreary people are supposed to be the people of finest fibre, and generally they are of curiously fine fibre as concerns their own feelings; but give me the cheery man, who, if he has sorrows—as who has not?—hides them and shows a brave face. There is real courage in that, and the very doing of it strengthens not only himself but his fellow-creatures.

Although he lived alone, Mr. Sinclair was not without relations, with whom he interchanged occasional visits and letters. Mrs. Thomas Sinclair, the widow of a brother, was the person who kept up the closest correspondence with him. She wrote frequent and very long letters, so long that he often did not read them further than to gather their general import, and when he answered them it was in the style of the people who advertise at the rate of eighteen words for a sixpence. If brevity is the soul of wit, Mr. Sinclair's letters to his sister-in-law were about the wittiest things that passed through the post-office. But as Mrs. Sinclair remarked, "It was quite Adam's way; old bachelors get so peculiar."

Peculiar or not, Mrs. Sinclair had conceived a bold idea—she determined to go with her children and take up her abode at Old Battle House, and she told her intention to all her acquaintance, except her brother-in-law, the person most interested, one would think.

"Mr. Sinclair," she explained to her friends, "is no doubt peculiar, but I think we'll be a great benefit to him. A house without a lady is always dull, and the children will make it quite a home for him, and if he were so inclined, he might in some sort supply a father's place to my poor children. I am told there is a good school in Quixstar, which would do for Tom; if he turns out a great man, it will be nice to say in his biography, 'This eminent man was first sent to school at the small picturesque town of Quixstar' (although, to be sure, he has been at school a good while already); 'the good old schoolmaster still survives to enjoy the celebrity of his pupil.' Indeed, if there was a primitive old woman in the place, I would like to send him to her for a little, if he were not so big; a great man beginning his career at a dame-school has such a very nice effect. I remember remarking this to his papa, who was struck with the idea, and thought it good. There are the girls, to be sure; but I am told girls attend the school at Quixstar as well as boys—girls of the humbler order probably, but I'll see; I could even take them in my own hand for a time if I found it necessary; and do you know," she proceeded in a slightly more confidential tone, "I consider it altogether in the light of a duty to go to

Quixstar? Mr. Sinclair has I doubt been rather unfortunate in his feminine acquaintance; at least his ideas of women are low; he always speaks as if a respectable servant who knew her work, and did it, was the highest type of woman; now you can easily imagine that when he is a little older, a designing woman of that class might have little difficulty in getting round him; indeed, he is quite the style of man to wind up by marrying his cook or housekeeper, and if I can prevent that I'll not think I have made a sacrifice in vain."

It seems a pity sometimes that people should not be aware of all the kind things that are said and thought of them; and it is a pity, but let us be thankful that we don't hear the other class of remarks. Imagine Mr. Sinclair hearing one woman overhauling him to another in this fashion! It is to be feared his opinion of the sex would not have been greatly raised.

Mrs. Sinclair wrote to her brother-in-law, offering a visit, and he, ignorant of the benevolence of her intentions, told her by all means to come. Thus matters stood till circumstances precipitated Mrs. Sinclair's arrival.

CHAPTER IV.

MAGDALEN FAIRGREVE, or Maddy, as she was generally called, was what is known as a "faithful servant." She had been a faithful servant to Mrs. Sinclair ever since that lady's marriage, and something more—there was a kind of Mrs. Morley and Mrs. Freeman relationship between them. Many times the lady had thought of dismissing her faithful servant, if she could have been sure of getting another who would look as well to her interests, which she was very far from being; besides, an old attached servant was a respectable thing in a house, and when Tom was a great man she would tell anecdotes of his childish days, and figure in the biography alongside of the schoolmaster. At this date Maddy was not old, although she had been so long in Mrs. Sinclair's service. Notwithstanding a strong will, and a tough, not very fine, nature, her feelings towards her mistress and the children were genuine and unselfish, and that is more than could be said of her mistress's feelings to her.

With the weakness which thinks to gain strength from mystery, Mrs. Sinclair had said nothing of the proposed removal to her attached servant, but the air of the house told Maddy something was astir; she soon found out what, and resolved to go to Quixstar herself, and come back mistress of the situation—the more, as she had an old friend there.

A branch railway runs right into Quixstar now, but at that time it thought itself well off to be within some miles of a station. Maddy was an entire stranger in Quixstar, and she had never chanced even to see Mr. Sinclair, as, being trustworthy, she was generally left at home when her family paid visits. She left the train, and walked leisurely on till she came to the village, looking ridiculously quiet and pretty and picturesque, lying in the haugh below the summer afternoon sunshine. She met some "urchins just let loose from school," and, pointing to Old Battle House, the first building that caught her eye, she asked what house that was.

"Spleuchan Ha'," said one of them without an instant's hesitation.

"Spleuchan Ha', bairn! nobody ever ca'ed a place that," said Maddy.

"That's what it's ca'ed hereabout, ony way."

"But it's a nickname—who lives in't?"

"Mr. Sinclair."

"And what's the right name o't?"

"Spleuchan Ha', I'm telling ye, and if ye dinna like to believe me, ye can chap at the door and speer."

"Callant, I wonder where ye learn so muckle impudence in a place like this?"

"We're no in impudence yet, mem; but maybe the maister'll put us into it soon," and he looked in Maddy's face with a sleepish simplicity, but with a tell-tale glitter in his eye.

"Ye little birkie," said she, "ye'll either mak' a spoon or spoil a horn some day, or I'm mista'en—what's your name?"

"John Graham," said he, winking to the troop that tarried for him.

"Rin away then, and there's a penny to ye, an' see

if ye can keep a civil tongue in your head." The boy looked abashed at this returning of good for evil, said "Thank ye," and was off, skimming the ground, to tell his luck to the rest.

Maddy looked after him, and said to herself, "A bit fine sharp laddie—he'll just be about ages wi' our Tommy;" for in this familiar way did she name the incipient subject of the biography, although her mistress had been at pains to teach her a very different style of address.

After a little inquiry, Maddy knocked at the door of Peter Veitch's cottage. Mrs. Veitch, who opened it, looked at her for a moment, then exclaimed, "Maddy Fairgrieve! wha wad hae thought to see you here?"

"I expected ye wadna ken me, Jess."

"Ken ye! I wad hae kent ye if I had met ye on the tap o' Arthur's Seat."

"Weel, I wadna been so surprised at ye kennin' me there; it's a place that's no unco thick o' folk on ordinar' occasions."

Soon after Peter senior came in, and Miss Fairgrieve explained that she was thinking of coming to reside in Quixstar.

"No possible!" cried Mrs. Veitch; "are ye gaun to be married, Maddy?"

"Na, na, no sae fast," said Maddy.

"Fast!" said Peter, "I dinna think there wad be ony fastness in't; ye've ta'en time eneuch to think about it, ony way."

"She's very right, Peter," said his wife.

"Then if she's right," said Peter, "ye was wrang, Jess."

"Weel, I'll no say but I was."

"Ay," said Peter, "women's hearts are aye in the

road o' their heads, and I'll no say it's an ill arrangement."

"A first-rate arrangement for your wife there, that has the use o' the head on your shouthers, but what comes o' the like o' me?"

"Ye may say that, Maddy," said Mrs. Veitch.

At this juncture the door opened, and a pair of wild, bright eyes peered in. "Come away, laddie," said Mrs. Veitch to her youngest born, "and get your parritch, they'll be clean cauld.—Ye'll no ken this ane, Maddy?"

"Ay, I ken him.—Come away, Johnnie."

"Johnnie!" said Peter senior, "we dinna ca' him Johnnie, he's my name-son."

"He tell't me that his name was John Graham," said Maddy.

"Peter," said his father sternly, "did ye tell a lee?"

"No; onybody wad hae kenned I was jokin', and I was vext after—she gied me a penny."

"Sic nonsense, Maddy," to his visitor; then to his son, "A lee's nae joke, and I'll gie ye a lickin' that'll help ye to mind that."

"Hout, Peter," said Mrs. Veitch, "let the laddie be, and he'll just gang to his bed wantin' his supper."

"I'm awfu' hungry, mother," said the urchin; "I'll tak' the lickin'."

"Weel, get yer parritch, and I'll wait," said his father.

"Na; I'll hae my licks first, and that'll be ae gude job ower," said the youngster, repeating a pet phrase of his father's. Now, who was ever impervious to the delicate flattery of hearing either his wit or his wisdom quoted, especially by a favorite son?

"Weel, I'll let ye off for this time," said his father; "but mind, Peter, if ever I hear o' ye tellin' a lee again, ye'll hae reason no' to forget it—it's an awfu' thing to tell lees."

Young Hopeful sat down, and drawing his bicker to him, began shovelling porridge and milk into his mouth with great alacrity and neatness. He finished his supper in silence, then coaxed the cat to him, and began rubbing its fur the wrong way for purposes of experiment, till his mother told him "to gie ower tormenting the puir beast."

Then Maddy told how she had been a servant with Mrs. Sinclair ever since that lady was married, how Mr. Sinclair of Old Battle House was her mistress's brother-in-law, and how Mrs. Sinclair and family were coming to live there, and that she had come to see what sort of place it was, and what sort of man Mr. Sinclair was, before she made up her mind to accompany them.

"The mistress," said Maddy, "is often no' to my mind, and I've whiles thought o' leavin', but the house wad gang to ruin if I was not there to look after it, and I like the bairns; but fancy, after the way I've toiled for them a', me hearing her tell them that they were not to learn my coarse, vulgar way o' speaking; I hope they'll never be beside nobody that'll learn them nothing waur; however, if it's a pleasant place, and Mr. Sinclair onything o' a canny man, I can manage *her*."

"As for the place," said Peter, "there's no a faut till't? as for the man, he's ane o' the folk that think they ken a' thing, but a decent enough body, as far as I see."

"Ye ken, Maddy," said Mrs. Veitch, "Peter's nettled at him interfering wi' him in the garden."

"Weel," said Peter, "I dinna doot he kens the business he was bred to, but he thinks he kens my business too, and he comes out wi' a book and reads a wheen havers about how this thing should be done and the other thing should be done, as if I hadna wrocht in a garden since I was the height o' that table."

"But Peter," said his wife, "there's sic a thing as progress; the warld doesna stand still, and we're no' ower auld to learn."

"How wad ye like to be tell't that ye didna ken what was the best kind o' peas to saw at this season?" asked Peter.

"Hout, man, there's aye something to put up wi'; I'm sure it's just as easy to saw ae kind o' peas as anither," said Mrs. Veitch.

"May be," said Peter sententiously.

"Weel," said Maddy, "I canna say but that I think a man has a right to direct about his garden; I wadna mind that, if he didna interfere in the house—that's a thing I canna thole, and, to do them justice, men dinna often try't. I never fell in wi' a man o' that kind but once."

"I daursay, Maddy," said Mrs. Veitch, "the like o' you, gaun frae place to place, 'll see mony a queer thing."

"I havena been in mony places, but, as ye say, there's aye something to put up wi'. The queerest place I ever was in was just afore I went to Mrs. Sinclair. The gentleman kent everything that came into the house, and the price o' everything, and how lang it lasted, and how lang it should hae lasted; na, he gied out the very soap for the washin's, and he howkit the taties for the denner, and I didna object to him doing that if he liket, but he took out an auld pitcher lid, and every worm that turned up he flung into it, and then gied them to the hens. The first time we saw him do it, I thought the other servant and me wad hae gaen into fits."

"It beat a'!" said Peter.

"Ay, that's a lesson to ye, Peter," said his wife. "I tell't ye folk were never ower auld to learn."

"When I tell't Bell Sinclair," said Maddy, "she said she hoped the folk didna think o' the diet o' worms when they were at their breakfast, but I dinna see how they could help it."

"And was he a gentleman?" asked Mrs. Veitch.

"Oh ay! a gentleman by way o'. I often wondered the mistress could thole him, but she was an easy-gaun body, and it was as weel."

"Some men should hae been women," said Mrs. Veitch.

"I never saw the man I wad hae liket to hae been me," said Maddy energetically.

2

CHAPTER V.

NEXT day Mr. Sinclair unwittingly gave Maddy an opportunity of bringing her own personal powers of observation to bear upon him.

She set out to walk to the station, accompanied by Peter Veitch the younger, who had an errand of his mother's to execute, namely, to hand in a bundle to a house on the other side of the station. Peter set off at his usual active pace.

"Now," said Maddy, "whatever ye may be gaun to do, I'm no' gaun to rin a' the road; no' but I could do it if there was ony necessity. I wonder ye didna get yer mother to put your bundle in a bit brown paper, it wad have looked a hantle genteeler."

"Wad it?" asked Peter, eyeing the bright speckled bundle which he had slung over his shoulder on the end of a stick, "the napkin keeps a' thing firm."

"My man, if ye were a wee aulder ye'll no' carry a bundle in a spotted napkin, or I'm mista'en."

Now it was too bad of Maddy to wake up the boy to the sin and misery of carrying a speckled bundle. There are few pleasanter sights to be met on a country road than a rustic youth with a clean-cut well-shut mouth—only it is apt to be open—bright eyes, and a speckled bundle, but, like the capercailzie, he is dying out, and is only met with now in remote districts.

Peter kept faithfully alongside his companion, and gave her all the information about country matters he was master of, telling her to whom the various vehicles belonged that passed. "That gig," looking at one coming up behind them, "is Mr. Sinclair's; he's in't himsel'; he keeps a gude horse; that's Jock Murray drivin'." Suddenly the handsome, well-built dog-cart pulled up alongside, and Mr. Sinclair said, "My good woman, if you are going to the station, I can give you a drive." This was a way, not generally adopted in this country, if anywhere, Mr. Sinclair had of drawing the bonds between fellow-creatures closer—whether it was manly, gentlemanly, or tradesmanly, it was a peculiarity of Mr. Sinclair's.

"Thank you, sir; I'll be obliged," said Maddy's sharp brisk tones, "but there's this boy?"

"Very well, get in," said Mr. Sinclair curtly.

She got in, and Peter sprang in after her like a monkey, then Mr. Sinclair looked round and said, "All right," and they drove on. It was a brilliant era for Peter, only his pleasure was somewhat dashed by the secure and legitimate nature of it; if he had been hanging on behind without the owner's knowledge, then indeed his bliss would have been complete; as it was, he sat a little awed by his rare and elevated position.

"Isn't this fine, Peter?" said Miss Fairgrieve. He nodded assent.

At the same moment they reached a cottage on the roadside; a man came out of it completely equipped in the garb of Old Gaul, and playing the bagpipes full screech. Probably Mr. Sinclair's horse had never had an opportunity of hearing that instrument in all its majesty before, and not altogether unnaturally his first idea was to put as great a distance between it and himself as possible. He started off at a tearing gallop, literally flying like the wind. The driver's whip was jerked from his hand, and in trying to catch it he let the reins go. Mr. Sinclair leaned over to recover them, lost his balance, and was pitched into the road. Miss Fairgrieve gave a loud scream, but kept her seat. Peter moved forward, but she grasped him, and said, " For your life, bairn, sit still."

" I'm no gaun out—let me be," said Peter impatiently; and he wriggled himself out of her hands, and over into the front seat, where, sticking on by one hand, he used the other to hook up the reins with his stick. They were nearing a toll-bar, and the toll-man, hearing the rush of the runaway horse, darted out and shut the gates, but by the time they reached it Peter had managed to check the animal, and was sitting triumphantly beside the crestfallen driver, having saved horse, carriage, and toll-gate from a furious smash.

" Can ye turn the beast round ?" said Maddy. " For ony sake gang back, and let us see what's happened to Mr. Sinclair."

Peter not forgetting his own errand, pitched his nongenteel bundle to the toll-man, and bade him send it on, then coolly drove back, the original Jehu not having recovered his scattered senses.

They soon met a man whom Mr. Sinclair had sent to find out their fate, and he told them that Mr. Sinclair was lying where he had fallen, not able to move with a broken leg. " It's a mercy it's not his neck !" said Miss Fairgrieve promptly.

When they arrived on the spot Mr. Sinclair did not look the picture of patient resignation. A man and a woman from the cottage were standing by him. The woman turned and said to Maddy, " He's in for six weeks on the braid o' his back. Our John got his leg broken wi' a kick frac ane o' the horse, and it was six weeks or he daur steer."

"Weel," broke in Miss Fairgrieve's sharp tones, "is the gentleman to lie six weeks on the road? Ye'll no hae sic a thing as a mattress?"

She went with the woman to the house, and got out a narrow stiff mattress, to which Mr. Sinclair was cautiously lifted, then the men who had collected hoisted him and it together across the seat of the vehicle, the cushions of which served for a pillow, in which way it was thought he would get home as comfortably as circumstances would permit.

While this was being done Maddy asked Peter if there were a doctor in Quixstar.

"Doctor!" said Peter, "there's three, and ony ane o' them'll be ower glad to tak' off his leg."

"Whisht, laddie," said Maddy.

"Weel, it's true, and he'll never ken; they just put a pickle o' some stuff up his nose, and he'll never find it—as sure as death, the doctor's laddie tell't me."

"Callant, ye have a tongue that wad clip clouts," said Maddy, and a smile stole over Mr. Sinclair's face, in spite of the pain he was suffering.

Owing to this grievous accident Maddy missed the train, and by consequence had to stay another night with Mrs. Veitch, and she had much pleasure in recounting Peter's cleverness, his quickness of brain and hand on the occasion.

"He's a clever wee chap," said the gratified father.

"Oh, there's nae doubt he's clever," said Mrs. Veitch, "and ye'll be blawing him up about what he's done, then the next clever thing he does ye'll be threatening to thresh him for't!"

"Woman," said Peter, "do ye no' ken that there's some things that's richt, and some things that's wrang, and some things that it's a matter o' opinion whether they are richt or wrang; ye think it's wrang for Peter to run off to the dam-head to the dookin' wi' ane o' your scones in his pouch for a chitterin' piece, and swim about like a fish, but it's just what I used to do mysel', and callants'll be callants to the end o' time; but when he tells a lee, that's a different thing."

"Weel, weel, ye'll maybe be o' my way o' thinking when he's brought hame drowned some day. It's nae langer than yesterday that I saw a wheen laddies standing roond ane o' the big trees in the park, and lookin' up at it, and when I lookit there was our Peter whiskin' frae branch to branch like a squirrel at the very tap o't. I grew sick and dizzy, and cried to him to come down; he drappit frae branch to branch till he cam' to the last, then put his arms round the tree, and slid to the ground, laughing and telling me he had often been up a higher tree than that. I put it to you, Peter Veitch, whae's to haud the laddie in claes at that rate?"

"Ay," said Peter, "I maun hae a word wi' him about that."

"Weel," said Maddy, "he has common sense, and if he's neither drowned nor killed he's likely to turn weel out."

"Deed, I dinna ken, Maddy," said Mrs. Veitch, "it's a sair thought when bairns come up and hae to gang away frae ye. When they were a' young I whiles thought I was hard toiled, but after a' ye're never happier than when they're a' round the fireside, and ye can gie them a dad on the lug when ye like." And Mrs. Veitch sighed over this image of departed joys.

"But Peter's no gaun away yet," said his father

cheerily; "we'll gie him another twel'month o' the schulen, he'll be nane the waur o't."

"He's been lang eneugh at the schule if he's to be a trade," said the mother; "but if he wad think o' the ministry—"

"Ay," said Maddy, "mak' a minister o' him, he'll gie't to the folk het and hashy."

"I dinna see," said Mrs. Veitch, a little offended, "but he wad be as guid a minister as the lave."

"Better—far better," said Maddy.

"If he were to think o't himsel' I wad be well pleased," said the gardener; "but we canna force the callant."

"We can only hope he'll be weel guided," said his mother.

Maddy reached home next day without further adventure than ensconcing herself in the smoking compartment of a railway carriage. A guard looked in, and asked her what she was doing there.

"Doing?" she said.

"Ay, doing; d'ye want to tak' a bit smoke to yoursel'?"

"Me smoke!" said the indignant Maddy, "but it's no me that's stupid, it's you—putting a notice over the door it wad need a magnifying-glass to read," and she changed her seat for one the guard showed her to, kindly telling her to sit with her back to the horses.

CHAPTER VI.

WHEN Mrs. Sinclair heard of her brother-in-law's accident she set off immediately for Quixstar to make herself of use. She was fond of being of use—an excellent quality if people can make themselves of use as the sun shines or the dew falls, but rather different when it is done as the paddle-wheels of a steamboat do it.

Mr. Sinclair was slightly dismayed when he saw her; however, he said and thought it was kind of her to come; and when a man is weak and suffering he feels kindness more perhaps, and if there are few people left in the world that call him by his Christian name, why, even if he is not of a sentimental vein, he is touched by hearing the old sound, and Mrs. Sinclair called him "Adam," and did not stay long with him, for all which he was grateful.

By and by people began to call, among others Mrs. Gilbert, and when she was gone Mrs. Sinclair hastened to let her brother know what a good neighbor he had.

"She is such an intelligent woman, Mrs. Gilbert," she said. "I may say intellectual—positively intellectual, and she takes such an interest in education, which is, to be sure, natural from her position; but she entered so warmly into my ideas about the dear children; and do you know her own girls attend their papa's school? and if they do, I think mine may. There are different opinions respecting the propriety of boys and girls attending the same school, but if it is injurious to either, why, I say, are boys and girls born in the same family? That being the case, it would seem they were intended to act and react beneficially on each other—does it not, Adam? What a pity such a woman as Mrs, Gilbert has no boys!"

"She has boys—one at least, if not two."

"And never mentioned them! Most extraordinary! Are you sure?"

"Quite sure."

"I would expect them to turn out something—great men always have intellectual mothers. I sometimes say to Tom, 'Tom, my boy, although your mamma does not pretend to intellect, still she is not quite a dunce either.'"

"And what does Tom say?" asked the invalid.

"Nothing, most likely. Tom does not speak much, he thinks a great deal more than he says."

"Perhaps he takes that from his mother?"

"Do you suppose I think a great deal, Adam?" said the lady with a pleasant smile. "You see," she said, as a sort of apology, "in my position I am forced to think—by the bye, what would you like for dinner to-morrow? cook wants to get away for a day, and I suspect the other girl is no cook; as for Maddy, she knows less of cooking than I do, although she considers herself so invaluable; but if there's anything particular you would like, I'll get cook to make it before she goes."

"I'll take anything."

"Would you not just say what you would like?"

"Oh, anything; it does not matter."

"We'll manage amongst us then. But Adam, do you think I should send the girls to Mr. Gilbert's school?"

2*

"Is it worth while? How long are you going to stay here?" asked the host with blunt innocence.

"I was thinking, if you don't tire of us, all summer at least, and it's a pity to lose so much time."

"Certainly send them, if you like."

Mr. Kennedy called, and to him also Mrs. Sinclair explained her position. "Did he think she should send her children to Mr. Gilbert's school?"

"Ah, he's a very worthy man, Gilbert—has his weaknesses, no doubt, as we all have, but a worthy man, and, I believe, a good teacher. You don't object to your children mixing with the multitude?"

"That's just the thing, Mr. Kennedy, my one objection—do you think that insuperable?"

"Well, it's for you to decide."

"Mr. Gilbert's own girls attend it, and there is nothing rude or unmannerly about them."

"No; well, as I said, it's for you to decide."

"Ah, yes! it's a heavy responsibility the care of fatherless children; in any case, it is a very heavy responsibility—so much so, that one would sink under it if they did not so sweetly repay all one's toil."

"Yes," said Mr. Kennedy shortly.

Unlike most manses, there were no children in the manse at Quixstar, a fact Mrs. Sinclair was well aware of, but she would have dilated to a lame man on the pleasure of dancing, with no notion that he might not enjoy the topic. However, in knowing Mrs. Sinclair you had this consolation, that there existed at least one person about whom you might dismiss all anxiety. She carried the conviction to your mind that she had passed and would pass through the world with great comfort to herself, and it is a luxury to have one such acquaintance. She also asked the advice of the doctor who attended Mr. Sinclair, but he was a man of few words, and averse to having his time frittered away, neither had he studied the art or science—which you will—of making himself agreeable, so that he did not throw much light on the subject. When he went home he said to his wife or sister—I forget at this moment in what relationship the lady who kept his house stood to him, but it does not matter; he said—

"Females are the most curious beings. If you ask them a question they start off at a tangent into the most utterly irrelevant matter, and there's no bringing them up,—you must just wait helpless until they stop. That Mrs. Sinclair may be called the 'speaking lady.'"

Accordingly between the doctor and his wife or sister, she was thereafter known as the "speaking lady." This doctor was a very quiet, apparently unobservant man. Men or women who visibly take notes may be trusted to carry nothing of much value away; it is the people who don't seem to notice that take into their minds and memories things great and small, as a whirlpool sucks in ships and feathers, or as a bivalve grows fat by lying with its shell open.

"Well, I have done it," said Mrs. Sinclair to her brother-in-law, "and I do think it is an admirable arrangement."

"What have you done?" asked Mr. Sinclair.

"I have sent the children to Mr. Gilbert's school. But here comes your dinner," and she pushed a small table up to Mr. Sinclair's sofa, on which the servant set the tray she carried.

"What's this?" said Mr. Sinclair, as he put a spoon into a basin of some kind of soup; "why, it's swimming with fat, and smells of onions—see, take it away, I can't eat that."

"If you would only taste it, you would find it very nice; cook's away to-day, and you said you would take anything."

"Anything in reason! you don't suppose a man tied to a sofa has the appetite of a ploughman," and he thought, "Three women in a house, and they send up a sickening mess like that! I wonder if any one of them has common sense."

Mrs. Sinclair rang the bell and had the obnoxious dish removed and something less offensive substituted, and, happily ignorant of the flagrant mistake she had made, she pursued her theme—

"Indeed, I feel I have done a wise thing—for Tom, at least; of course, there's the risk of low companions—that boy Peter Veitch, and such like."

"I hope they'll never rub against anything worse than Peter," said Mr. Sinclair.

"I have no reason to believe otherwise than that the Veitches are decent people, but that boy is very forward," Mrs. Sinclair said.

"He is clever," answered Mr. Sinclair.

"It is certainly not a style of cleverness I envy for Tom, far less for the girls, but we'll see how they get on."

Mr. Sinclair had not a passion for children, by any means; no doubt he had hitherto kept a friendly eye on his brother's children, and meant to continue to do so, but they appeared to him very ordinary specimens—in all respects ordinary. He did not think the less of them for that; he thought that ordinary people passed through life with more comfort to themselves than extraordinary people, and did perhaps as much good on their way. What Mr. Sinclair's own estimate of himself was is not known, nor is it known whether there had ever been a crisis of any kind in his life; but either from experience or observation he had gathered this opinion concerning the blessedness of ordinary people. One thing is certain: he had gone into a business very distasteful to him, to please his father; he never learned to like it, but he had not the strength of character necessary to take circumstances by the horns, still less to bend them to his will —that power would have marked him as extraordinary —and he had remained in it till he came to Quixstar. I lean to the opinion that there was no mystery in Mr. Sinclair's life, no striking story—that he was what he was by a natural and gradual process. Mr. Kennedy, who, when Mr. Sinclair had got the length of the sofa, was admitted to his room, was not impressed with his intellect, but Mr. Kennedy was not a man apt to make discoveries of this kind; rather he was deeply impressed with the ignorance and stupidity of most people. At first Mr. Sinclair considered the minister's visits a bore, but probably there are few persons who, consciously or uncon sciously, are not pleased with attention, and there was what his parishioners called a "youthiness" about Mr. Kennedy—he seemed.to shake health from his hair as a comet is said to do pestilence—that made him not out of place in Mr. Sinclair's chamber, where there was neither sickness of body or mind, but merely a broken leg "going on favorably." His cheery "Ha! how do you find yourself to-day?" his detail of where he had been, of what he had been doing, and of all the news of the district, amused Mr. Sinclair. These two men liked to hear the murmur of their *bourg*, and why shouldn't they? If it was not the great wave that echoes round the world, it was part of it, and their part of it, and it would have been a pity had they not been interested in it; but you will understand that in common with most people they disliked gossip, and when they got into a stream of it, they had the satisfaction of feeling themselves martyrs while listening, of looking down on the medium, and of hearing the news without any trouble or loss of dignity in asking questions.

"I am really glad you are getting on so well," said Mr. Kennedy. "You have much to be thankful for, sir."

"I suppose I have," said Mr. Sinclair in no very thankful tone.

"Yes, a great deal. You don't find your nights wearisome? It is the longest day just now; I notice all invalids count immensely on that. Curious; it never matters to me whether it is light or dark when I am in bed; and in winter I often tell my sick friends that they are well off to keep snug, and not be obliged to tramp about as I do."

"Perhaps, like me, you have not been much accustomed to illness?" said Mr. Sinclair.

"I never was laid up but once, long ago, with a sprained ankle. It was a terrible business, I mind—a terrible business. Well, is there anything I can do for you? Perhaps I may have a book that might suit you; let me think—something light and entertaining. Yes, I have some volumes of anecdotes on religious and benevolent subjects that would be the very thing; I'll send one. Oh, trouble—it's no trouble."

When he went home, he sent the volume, thinking, "That will just about fit him; he is a pretty intelligent man. I hope he is not as pig-headed as tradesmen who have made a little money often are, and that he won't work mischief in the parish."

When the book was laid on Mr. Sinclair's table he laughed, and did not feel as if he would grow in stature under Mr. Kennedy's teaching.

CHAPTER VII.

ALTHOUGH thus kindly dealt by, Mr. Sinclair was not the less thankful when, with the help of a stick, he could walk through his garden. At the foot of it he had a favorite resting-place, where he often stopped and looked at and listened to the water flowing on. On one particular day he stood a long time watching a group quite unconscious of his presence. Owing to a three days' incessant rain, such as our climate delights in, there had been a recent flood, during which the Eden had been coming past with great gliding business-like strides, brown and drumlie, the foam getting no time to play itself. On, on it went; but now it had leisure to sail round the stones, that were coming to sight again after the flood, to sweep into the mimic bays, to hover about and sparkle when the sun's rays caught it, and then to venture forth on its further voyage.

On the broad wooden bridge were the schoolmaster's children and the Sinclairs, intently occupied floating sticks and straws and corks down the stream, and watching their onward course, each as interested in the progress of his or her particular craft as if something of moment depended on it. Mr. Sinclair's reflections, as he looked at them, were most likely afternoony in their complexion. Perhaps he gave a sigh to the memory of his own boyhood—not that there were any very delicious remembrances mixed up with it, only that then he had life before him, now it, or what might be supposed to be the best part of it, was behind him. He remembered when he and his brother were very young, taking Tom into a room which was seldom used, and cutting out all his beautiful curls—why, he could not recall, whether from jealousy, or envy, or what; but he never forgot how his mother punished him, for Tom was her favorite openly and avowedly. Tom was gone; he had not done much good in his life, but neither had he done much positive evil; and *there* were his representatives, in whom he ought to have felt an overwhelming interest, but did not. "They'll get through the world like other people, I suppose, if their foolish mother does not spoil them," he thought.

Mrs. Sinclair was at an upper window of the house, and she also was watching the children. She saw the girls, but Tom she did not see.

"I wonder what he is about?" she thought; trying some kind of experiment likely. "I think it was Mungo Park that dropped pebbles into the water to ascertain its depth. I wonder if Tom will be famous as an explorer; he might benefit mankind, but it would be dangerous.—Maddy," she said, catching sight of that individual, "I don't see Master Thomas. I am afraid he is lying on the damp grass; run down to the water-side with that mat," pointing to a deerskin on the floor, "and say that I would prefer that he should not lie, but if he will lie, let him lie on the skin. Boys are so thoughtless, and he'll be sure to catch cold."

Maddy obeyed; she darted through the garden door opening to the river, and discovered Tom on the under branch of a tree, hidden by the leaves, eating peas, with which he had filled his pockets, throwing the empty shells into the water, aiming them first at any head within reach. She gave her message with less ceremony and more point than she got it.

Yet a third person was watching these children. Mrs. Gilbert had been sitting in her parlor window during the afternoon sewing, and in her work-basket lay a copy of Cowper. Cowper in these days is voted old-fashioned and slow; but to get away from all the chatter and smatter and tremendous intelligence of the hour; to fall in with a woman who does not know everything; who sews and reads Cowper, is very refreshing. Passing Mrs. Gilbert's window, and seeing her thus employed, you would have felt inclined to turn and pass back again, merely to get more thoroughly the soothing influence of the picture. On this afternoon she had put down her sewing, and gone out into the soft glory of the summer day. There was still the clear shining after the rain; the earth was very black, and every green thing was greener; globules of the purest liquid stood trembling and sparkling on the curly-leaved vegetables, one or two snails had ventured out and were munching a salad —they drew in their horns as Mrs. Gilbert passed, their way possibly of lifting their hats. Mrs. Gilbert was not without a sense of all these things; but her world was her children—they were her passion. She stood looking at them, but it was not with the silly good-natured pride with which Mrs. Sinclair surveyed hers, nor with the dry, dutiful criticism which Mr. Sinclair brought to bear upon his nieces and nephew. She trembled for John, her first-born and only son. She had once found him out in a lie; he had once borrowed money, only a shilling or two, from an aunt of his father's that lived near them. She had brought John to a sense of his sin, and there had been no repetition of it; but it had cost her tears and anguish, and when she was in a melancholy mood, as sometimes happened, she thought, " What if he should go astray?" There he was, however, by the water's edge, looking innocent enough, but his mother could not get rid of her anxiety. His sisters, too—what was to be their fate? Somehow Mrs. Gilbert never thought of matrimony as novel-writers do, as the end of care and the beginning of lasting bliss; she always found herself planning to make them independent of it. But how to do that? Besides, they promised to be good-looking, and it vexed her: good looks are so apt to attract weak or wicked men. You will say she was unreasonable. She was, very; deep love is apt to be unreasonable. But such moods were passing; her brow smoothed, and she felt as if she had nothing to wish for.

Had she anything to wish for? I'll tell you, though I feel quite as reluctant to reveal Mr. Gilbert's weakness, as I would have done to write of any little tender story of disappointment that might be hidden away in Mr. Sinclair's life, if I had known it. Mr. Sinclair ought to be thankful that if there is such a thing, I don't know about it; people can't tell what they don't know, and that is about the only security for silence. But I knew Mr. Gilbert well, and liked him; it is so easy to like people with whom you are not in hourly contact, and whose shortcomings don't run right against the grain of your own shortcomings. Mr. Gilbert was vain and self-conscious to a degree, but only to a degree. Oh, what a wicked thing it was of the fairy who presided at his birth to scrimp the dose! If her hand had only been bigger, or if she had filled it twice, he would have gone through the world triumphantly. As it was, his own opinion of himself was not sufficient to him unless it was indorsed by other people, and he was an unappreciated man on the lookout for slights. If you are on the lookout for anything, you are pretty sure to fall in with it. If Mr. Gilbert had grasped the nettles on his way firmly he would have got on, but he shrank from them, and was constantly being stung.

Mr. and Mrs. Gilbert called this weakness a more than usually fine sensibility, a delicate organization, and Mrs. Gilbert soothed and coaxed and propped and supported it behind the scenes, and loved her husband not the less but the more all the while that it was the worry of her life. A manly vice—if there be a manly vice, perhaps riding steeple-chases, for instance, which is a vice because it risks life for no good end, and is not without manliness because it does risk it—would have been less irritating, one would think. David might well speak of the love of women; but he used a poet's license when he said his and Jonathan's surpassed it—the thing was impossible.

Mrs. Gilbert was thankful to see that her son had not inherited this delicate organization of his father. Public opinion had little purchase on him as yet, perhaps too little, but he had good abilities; and though she knew that dulness is often safe, she could not help, as she gazed at them, feeling proud of her clever boy and pretty girls.

She had reached this pleasant point in her cogitations when Peter Veitch came up, and seeing Tom Sinclair lolling on the deerskin, he said—

"Where's your parasol, Robinson? Arle me for Friday; see, there's the print o' my feet."

An urchin passing at the moment cried, "Mind the auld man's watching ye!"

"What auld man?" asked Peter. "Ou 're no' doing ony mischief."

Mr. Sinclair, hearing what was said, was looking

about for the old man who was watching, when he saw the boy point to himself, and say, " There, at the fit o' his garden." Mrs. Gilbert, from the spot on which she was standing, had both seen and heard, and she could not avoid smiling, as there was no necessity she should. Mr. Sinclair smiled too, and turned and went up his garden, with food for meditation probably. Mrs. Gilbert had in two separate instances about this time let a man know indirectly that she did not think him so young as he had been, and the words were not out of her mouth when she saw she had not given pleasure; yet she had done it innocently, under the idea that a squeamishness about growing old was most strictly a feminine weakness; but she made a note of it, and determined she would not offend again.

Tom Sinclair and his sisters Bell and Effie were to stay the rest of the day with the Gilberts; and when Mrs. Gilbert called them in, Peter Veitch was left alone to ponder and slowly come alive to the fact that between these his school-fellows and himself there yawned a great social gulf. But this glimpse of human institutions did not weigh on his spirits. He was disappearing like an arrow to throw himself into some other pursuit, when Mrs. Gilbert, who had a fondness for the boy, asked him to come too.

"You had better run home and tell your mother where you are to be, and come back," she said.

"No, no," said he, "she never expects me till she sees me. I wasna gaun hame the noo at ony rate."

Peter was not by any means the creature of habit—quite the reverse; he ate when he was hungry, and would have slept when he was sleepy without reference to the rising or setting of the sun, had his father's indulgence gone the length of allowing him, which it did not.

But his food was a simple affair; his portion was merely set aside to stand till he came for it, so that his erratic ways did not throw the household machinery into confusion. Indeed, he preferred that his porridge should stand three or four hours only covered with a towel, for then they had got a thick "brat" on the top, which he considered a peculiar delicacy; so that, except during school hours, he was singularly free to follow out his numerous engagements.

When Peter was ushered into the unwonted splendor of the schoolmaster's sitting-room he could not quite imitate the stoicism of the North American Indians, who, however dumfoundered on seeing the triumphs of civilization, neither uttered a sound nor moved a muscle. He looked sheepish. He found the company already round the table. Mr. Gilbert shook hands with him very kindly and said—

"I hear you have been sailing a fleet this afternoon. Well, we'll see how fleet you can all be in disposing of the good things, and how fleet you can be in learning your lessons.—What part of speech is fleet, Mary, my dear?" looking at his youngest daughter.

"A noun."

"So far right. Always a noun?"

"Sometimes a prison," said James Raeburn. (James Raeburn was one of Mrs. Gilbert's nephews, who had been sent to Quixstar for his health and education.)

Mr. Gilbert's face darkened; he was jealous that his nephew sometimes tried to amuse himself at his expense. Mrs. Gilbert hastened to say—

"Yes, James; quite right.—Are your father and mother well, Peter?"

"Yes, ma'am."

"Is your father busy just now? He must give us a day or two soon."

"Yes, ma'am."

Peter answered in monosyllables; he was slightly overawed, rather an unusual circumstance with him. But he was in the presence of "the maister," and as a guest on terms of comparative equality, and therefore was experiencing a novel sensation,—besides, the scene was imposing. No doubt, if Lady Cranstoun had walked into the room, with its low roof and papered walls, she might have thought of a bandbox; and its little windows hung with netted curtains—Mrs. Gilbert's own work—might have suggested a doll's house or travelling caravan; and it is likely that the table arrangements would not have struck her as being all that elegance and luxury might have called for; but you see she was at one part of the social scale, and Peter at another; and to him everything looked grand. Probably if he had been let loose either in the schoolhouse or Cranstoun Hall, in no long time familiarity would have bred not contempt but indifference, as it always does with respect to everything that is merely external. I daresay Lady Cranstoun often yawned in the midst of her luxurious appointments, and fell into a nap more apoplectic than comfortable, where the doors were all clad in cloth, and could neither bang nor slam, as the doors of humble people love to do.

Mr. and Mrs. Gilbert went out to enjoy an evening walk together, and Peter got over his bashfulness, and was persuaded by Tom Sinclair to play at what Tom called draughts, and Peter the dambrod—a game suited to the taste of Tom, slow and not involving active exertion, but which Peter would play fast, for he saw through the moves, and made up his mind what he was to do in an instant, whereas his opponent hummed and hawed and looked very wise and deliberate before he stirred a step. James Raeburn was writing exercises for next day; and the four girls were in one of the windows talking as girls talk, the chatter being as natural and, if you are in a proper mood, as pleasant to hear as the song of birds.

John Gilbert was standing at the table, and the attention of the others was arrested by his clearing his throat ostentatiously, and then he began to read from a paper he held in his hand, throwing in remarks of his own as he went on. He read—

"' Clara and Julia de Lacy were the daughters of a gentleman '—I should rather think so. 'Mr. de Lacy had an agreeable person' "—

Effie Sinclair started up and cried—" Give me that paper, John Gilbert! it's mine. Where did you find it?"

" Prove your property; where did you lose it?"— ' An agreeable person,'" he went on, "' superior abilities, and an engaging address.'—Bravo."

" It's a shame!" cried Effie. " Give it to me! give it, I say!"

Taking no notice, he continued, "' Clara and Julia were tripping across the velvet sward of the charming park that surrounded the mansion of Mr. de Lacy. Clara looked at Julia and smiled; she was about to make an arch remark.'—What a pity she did not make it!"

The tears were in Effie's eyes as she tried to snatch the paper from him. He mounted a chair and resumed—

"'An arch remark, when a woman was seen approaching, startling the timid deer as they browsed peacefully under the shade of oak and cedar'"—

" Will none of you help to take that from him?" cried Effie.

Peter rose from his game. " Gie the lassie her paper," he said.

" Give her that," said John, taking his handkerchief

out; "give her that to weep in. It's clean, Effie; I have not used it.—'Shade of oak and cedar. The woman was decently but poorly clad; and when she came near, she courtesied and requested charity.'"

"You have no business to read that!" Effie cried. "What a shame!"

"Gie her the paper," Peter repeated. "Do ye want a het lug?" and he doubled his fist near John's head. "Gie her't at ance, and be dune wi't."

"'My good woman, said Clara,'" John pursued in a kind of solemn chant; "'my good woman, on principle I never give indiscriminate charity.'—Goodness, Effie! what kind of charity is that?" asked John.

Effie disappeared, rushed to Jane Gilbert's room, flung herself on the bed, and gave way to a passion of tears,—she knew quite well what should be done on such an occasion; and then she paced the floor of the apartment to fill up the measure of what is expected of a heroine. Her sister and Jane and Mary Gilbert entreated for admittance in vain. "Peter Veitch," they said, "had rescued her paper—here it was. Would she not let them in?"

"There's no use minding what John does; he likes mischief,—all boys do," his sister says.

"Effie, either speak or open the door at once," Bell Sinclair says, "or we'll think something has happened to you. Oh, Effie, speak."

Thus adjured, Effie unlocked the door and admitted her friends.

"Now Effie," her sister said, "if you had had the sense to take no notice of John, he would soon have stopped reading; he only did it to tease you."

"It was very rude," sobbed Effie, "and you all laughed."

"We could not help it," said Bell; "he did it so cleverly."

CHAPTER VIII.

MRS. SINCLAIR sat up late that night composing a letter to Mr. Gilbert. She liked to compose a letter, and the occasion was a good one. She said—

"DEAR SIR—When I came to reside at Quixstar with my dear fatherless children, the subject of their education cost me much anxious thought—it could not be otherwise. From what I had heard of you previous to my arrival, and after that step was taken, I said, 'Here now is a man to whom I can, D.V., commit those dear children.' My anxiety was lessened, my burden was lessened so far as you were concerned, my only remaining dubiety was, 'Can I allow my children to mix with the children of the humbler classes of the community?' I made up my mind to run that risk for a time, believing that the advantages counterbalanced the disadvantages. I made up my mind to allow my children to run that risk *during school hours*, with the full resolution to preserve them as much as in me lay from such contact when not absolutely necessary. In accepting your hospitality for them this evening I could by no possibility foresee that they would be exposed to mixed company, nor that they would be subjected to such rudeness as has shaken the nerves of my darling, sensitive Effie. I don't object to the boy Veitch's character; I fully believe that he is honest and truthful; but he is not the style of boy I wish my children to associate with, although his behavior appears, from what I can gather, to contrast favorably with that of—I am forced to say it —of your own son. The error was in leaving them without superintendence. My object in writing is to give my opinion, so that the same thing may not occur again, which I think better than to withdraw my children from your care at once, without assigning a reason. —I am, very sincerely yours, E. SINCLAIR."

When Mrs. Sinclair had finished this letter she read it over and admired it—she was in the habit of admiring her own work, as also had been the late Mr. Sinclair; she had liked to hear him say, " Yes, my dear, that's just the thing—very good indeed," and she thought she could not do better than give his brother the same opportunity. " There is nothing a man likes better," she thought, " than to talk things over with an intelligent woman. I am not clever nor intellectual, far less strongminded, but I may claim to be intelligent without much presumption."

Next morning the first thing she did on going down stairs was to glance over the newspaper, as was her habit, and when Mr. Sinclair arrived she gave him the benefit of her newly acquired information. Now a man, or at least such a man as Mr. Sinclair, to whom his newspaper is a part of his day, does not like to have the tidbits torn out and thrust before him raw and mangled, any more than he would like to sit down to an ill-got-up beef-steak half an hour before dinner; but Mrs. Sinclair would have lived with her brother a thousand years and not have discovered this, so she continued the practice, secure that she gave him much pleasure. After the news, she handed him her letter to read, asking his opinion of it. When he had read it, she said, " Well ?" She had watched his face, but gathered nothing from it.

"I would not send that," he said.

"Not send it! What would you do with it?"

"I would put it in the fire."

"For what reason?"

"What's the use of making an ado about nothing?"

"Do you call the influences that surround my children in their most plastic years nothing?"

"No, I don't; but that boy Veitch is as good as them any day; you can't expect boys to behave themselves from morning to night like good children in a story-book."

"If my children are to learn to speak like the boy Veitch, how are they to get on in life?"

"If they have anything worth saying they'll manage to say it. It would be well if Tom had as much energy in all his body as Veitch has in his little finger."

"Tom's energy is latent yet; poor boy, he is not over strong."

The children coming in to breakfast, the lady, as was meet, had the last word.

Mr. Sinclair was not the sort of uncle he might have been. He was not the wicked uncle of the old times, but neither was he the genial uncle of the period. All the notice he took of his nieces and nephew on this occasion, for instance, was to look up from his newspaper, push the bread toward Tom, and say, "Eat, child, eat, or you'll die of inanition."

Now if Mr. Sinclair did not notice what Tom was about, he was blind; and if he did notice, he was satirical, and satire is a weapon to be kept for occasion.

Bell laughed, and Effie whispered, "What is inanition?"

Said Bell, "I suppose it is a disease people take who don't eat enough; we need not be frightened about Tom;

he's like Sancho Panza, he always eats as if he might not see food in a hurry again."

"Child," said Mr. Sinclair, once more looking up from his paper, "what do you know about Sancho Panza?"

"That he was fond of eating," said Bell promptly.

"Tom, my boy," said his mother, "a little more ham? Never be ashamed of a good appetite, rather be thankful for it."

Tom was not in the least ashamed of it, and took more ham.

When they were leaving the room, Mr. Sinclair said quite suddenly, "As the weather is fine, I'll take you to see the glen to-day."

This had an uncle-ish sound, if it had not been such a bare statement, and been felt to be a command, like an invitation from royalty, so that there was nothing for it but to comply.

"I am afraid," said Mrs. Sinclair, "I have an engagement that will prevent me accompanying you."

"The children can go without you, I suppose?" said Mr. Sinclair curtly.

"Oh, certainly, they can go without me, but—"

"Very well, they'll go."

The children had their own plans for the Saturday holiday, and would much rather have declined the expedition in such company, which was exactly what Mr. Sinclair would have done too if it had been a matter of taste with him, but it was a matter of duty; he wanted, if possible, to look further into the natures of his brother's children, and he thought that he was making a good opportunity for that purpose.

Some miles above Quixstar the glen of the Eden was worth going a good way to see. There was a ruin of an old castle perched on the brink of a precipice, and there was a modern house on a less painful elevation, the proprietor of which did not allow the public to drive through his grounds; but on certain days, in consideration of a silver piece paid at the gate, people were at liberty to walk through them. Mr. Sinclair and his young friends alighted at the gate, and leaving the dusty road entered fairy-land. But fairy-lands in the form of emerald turf and flowerbeds of all shapes and every bright contrasting hue, kept in such order that you would think some invisible being with a penknife was continually on the watch to lop any pushing blade of grass or rash bud or blossom that overstepped bounds, are not in these days confined to the grounds of landowners; advancing taste has brought them even to the poor man's door. Old Battle House was equal in this respect to Eden Castle; but when the visitors went on a little they stopped beside a low stone fence, and those who dared looked over it down a wall of living rock that descended and descended sheer down so far that the water below looked like a thread, and a horse in the valley like an ant. It made one shudder. It was a wild, rocky, mountain-looking feature set among the lazy gentle scenery round it. They must have been people with clear heads and strong minds that lived in that old castle. No doubt it was founded on a rock, only a modern lady looking out of one of its windows overhanging that frightful precipice would have felt her nerves tingle to her finger-ends; but in those days, likely, people ignored nerves altogether. The Eden came lingeringly through the glen, as if loath to leave it, and gave nature ample time to set off the exceeding beauty and richness of her green robe with its silver sheen. As far as you could follow its windings, the glen was thickly wooded; away in the distance the top of a hill appeared, filling up the background, and giving the finishing touch to the picture. The trees could not be very ancient, few of them looked so, but the hill had stood there as sentry for ages.

During their drive Mr. Sinclair had given the children a brief statement concerning the historical memories of the place, and when he brought them to the edge of the precipice, and told them it was thought that possibly Shakspeare* had stood on that spot and looked at that same scene, he expected their faces to kindle and their tongues to burst into notes of admiration.

Effie ran back frightened and in dismay. Bell and Tom looked about with as much expression in their faces as a pair of sheep, and said nothing. This shows that these young people were not quite of to-day. Children of to-day are equal to any emergency, even to patronizing and drawing out an elderly relative; but at this time they still had a sense of awe and reverence, and were apt on occasion to be bashful. Besides, these children felt anything but at home with their uncle, and older people than children must feel at home and secure of their ground before they shine in any degree.

There they stood, and there Mr. Sinclair stood watching them, but no chink appeared through which he could get a peep into their minds, and he came to the conclusion that, as mind did not break out, there must be a very small modicum of it in possession. However, if Shakspeare had lurked in Quixstar, neither Mr. Sinclair nor Mr. Kennedy was the man to find him out any more than Sir Thomas Lucy. It takes something of Shakspeare to discover Shakspeare.

"Come," he said, "we'll walk round, and see how it looks from below."

* A mistake of Mr. Sinclair's, surely.

" Will it be a long time till we have dinner?" said Tom.

"Two hours. You're not hungry, are you?" said Mr. Sinclair.

"Mamma gave me some sandwiches," said Bell, "but I forgot, and left them at the gate."

"Very like a girl," said Tom. "Run back, Effie, and bring them; you'll do it in a minute."

Effie ran. These girls were taught indirectly, if not directly, to think their brother a superior being, and he was nothing loath to avail himself of his superiority. He started with capital vantage-ground, if he could only keep it. Effie was good-natured, and obeyed. Bell, with prophetic stirrings of the present movement, was more apt to stand out for her rights. Tom consumed what of the provender he wanted, then gave his sisters the diminished parcel to carry. Mr. Sinclair, observing the action, wheeled round, and said, " Carry that yourself, Tom," whereupon Tom, not expecting to need more till he got home, left it behind him to save himself trouble. Comparatively few human beings need to be carefully trained to selfishness.

They took the path that led down into the glen, then turned and came below the precipice. Mr. Sinclair thought that if looking over it had failed, looking up at it might be a success; but still the oracles were dumb—at least when he was within hearing, or, when they spoke, it was not of battlemented crags. " There's a lady sketching," said Effie; "it's Miss Raeburn." Turning round, Mr. Sinclair saw Miss Raeburn, and being slightly acquainted he went up and spoke to her, and looked at her work. Of course it was the ruin on the top of the rock.

" Do you like that kind of work, Miss Raeburn?"

"I like it, and I don't like it. I like if I may but touch the hem of Art's garment, but I am always kept in the valley of humiliation."

It is diverting to watch an interview between a romanticish lady and a straight-forward business man. If Miss Raeburn had heard another person address Mr. Sinclair in this strain she would have laughed. "You see," she said, "it is intended for the old castle, but it is like the leaning tower of Pisa."

"You have not got the moon in yet; I notice ruins always have a moon in the right-hand corner."

Miss Raeburn looked to see if Mr. Sinclair had the hardihood to laugh at her work to her face, but he seemed serious enough, and she said, "No; it is not a moonlight scene."

A man, Dixon by name—a jobbing gardener from Quixstar—happened to be mowing a patch of ferns not far off. He came up with a plant in his hand, and said, "See, Miss Raeburn, is this what ye was wantin'?" Then, looking at Mr. Sinclair, he said, "A heap o' folk mak' an unco wark about brackens noo-a-days; for my part, I never use them for onything but to bed the sow."

"That is a charming association," said Miss Raeburn, "but I'll keep this.—Thank you, Dixon, I am a little fernytickled."

"They are pretty.—How grand that rock looks from here!" said Mr. Sinclair. "Well, good-bye, I won't interrupt you further," and he went on in pursuit of his juvenile party, who were playing at hide-and-seek among the trees, and he thought, "It's a pity Miss Raeburn should spend her time on what she'll never make anything of; but it's often the way with women: they have no notion of the value of time, or of the folly of trying things beyond their power."

"Here, Tom," he cried, "bring your sisters. We must be going home now."

Thus ended Mr. Sinclair's first planned attempt to watch the young idea shooting, and although it had resolutely refused to shoot, he felt that he had done his duty.

Who was Miss Raeburn? Briefly, she was a sister of that Mr. Raeburn who had married Mrs. Gilbert's sister, and she lived in the aristocratic part of Quixstar.

CHAPTER IX.

THE oftener Mrs. Sinclair read over her letter to the schoolmaster she was the more convinced of the propriety of sending it. In business matters Mr. Sinclair might be a competent enough adviser, but on an occasion of this kind on her must rest the responsibility; and she sent it.

When Mr. Gilbert got it he was so far gratified. It was written in a copperplateish hand, on thick cream paper, and bestowed in an envelope to match —paper and envelope being stamped with Mrs. Sinclair's monogram, the letters E. and S. felicitously twisted together. The material clothing of a letter never passed unnoticed by Mr. Gilbert. Sometimes he got notes from the parents of his scholars written on a half sheet of paper which had evidently been torn from its other half after a journey by post, and once even an envelope had been sent with a name printed on it, and marked out, and his (Mr. Gilbert's) name substituted. Think of it—an envelope that had been enclosed in a circular all ready to be despatched to a gentleman who wished to push the business of tuning pianos!

One man would have read such missives and thought no more about them, another would have noticed and smiled, but this was a small style of iron that entered Mr. Gilbert's soul. Very likely the people who do these things intend no disrespect: they are merely thrifty souls who will let nothing be lost; but Mr. Gilbert argued that if they had been writing to Sir Richard Cranstoun, or even Mr. Kennedy, they would have been more choice in their stationery; and he was wroth, and the comfort of his day was gone, and not only the comfort of *his* day, but that of his wife's also —not that such a thing could ruffle her, but she was vexed through her husband. However, taking the letter altogether, there was not wanting something soothing to Mr. Gilbert. He gave it to his wife to read. It was what she expected; the intimacy had been too sudden and close to last. Mrs. Sinclair had walked into their house and out of it at all hours; she had praised Mrs. Gilbert and her arrangements, and Mr. Gilbert and his—everything was perfection, and she was all butter and honey; but Mrs. Gilbert had been long enough in the world to know that this was not likely to go on; so had Mr. Gilbert, but he did not know it. There are people who are as ready to believe what they wish to believe this week as they were last week, although last week's belief has proved an utter absurdity; and people too with powers both of mind and observation will go on in this way to the end of their days, a new disappointment only leading to a new belief.

Mrs. Gilbert did not say, " I told you so,"—she had not told him so, she knew better; nor did she say, " Just what I expected,"—there are cases in which both wives and husbands have to be careful of what they say to each other. But Mr. Gilbert said, " That's what's come of having the boy Veitch the other night. I thought at the time it was not very prudent. It seems she had heard of me before she came here." Now Mrs. Sinclair had related this circumstance nearly every time she had seen either the schoolmaster or his wife. "It's a pity," Mr. Gilbert continued, "for she seemed a woman of sense."

"It appears to me," said Mrs. Gilbert, "that there is rather a want of sense in expecting to dictate to us who we are to have in our house, and who we are not; and if she judged by her own feelings, she might know that we are quite as anxious about our children as she can be about hers."

"That's all true," Mr. Gilbert said, "but you miss the point; you are apt to be not very logical. Her letter may be senseless and impertinent; but there are ranks in society, and I thought at the time it was injudicious to have the boy Veitch."

"I like Peter Veitch."

"There now—that's no reason."

"I was not giving it as a reason; I was only stating it as a fact. But do you notice what she says about John? That's a much more serious affair. I should be sorry if he has been rude."

"He'll have to apologize; what else can we do? And after all, she will likely withdraw her children from the school."

"Very well; she must just withdraw them."

"But it's discouraging," said Mr. Gilbert. "It's not merely the loss of three pupils, although that's something. A man condemned to toil in a place like this needs encouragement."

"And first and last you have got a good deal. I like the place; I don't know where I would be happier."

"Is that true now? Would you not like to see your husband in a better position?"

"I am not ambitious," she said. "I suppose men have more of that than women. My only ambition is that our children do well."

"They would be none the less likely to do well if their father did better. If a man could only get out of this hole into a place where there was some scope!"

"By 'do well' I did not mean worldly success, although that is very good when it comes.—Well, will you write to Mrs. Sinclair, or shall I? Perhaps it would be better for you to do it—more respectful?"

Mrs. Gilbert got this delicate piece of business to do, and did it so well that the cloud which had gathered so ominously dispersed; the signal was "Lower drum," and there was fair weather.

Thus was Peter Veitch tabooed by Mrs. Sinclair, but, being happily unconscious of it, neither his health nor spirits were affected: he pursued his pleasure and business with unabated energy. It was sometimes his business, when there was a pressure of work, to help his father for the two hours between leaving school in the afternoon and six o'clock, when the labors of the day stopped. If Mrs. Sinclair saw him at work in the garden at Old Battle House she considered him in his proper place, and approved of him, and even if she happened to be passing would stop to notice him.

One evening he was working in front of the windows of Mr. Sinclair's sitting-room, when the steeple-clock struck the hour of liberation. A little before, Mr. Sinclair had thrown open one of the windows, and then Peter had noticed him go out at the garden gate. The room was empty. He went forward to the window and looked in, then he laid his hand on the sill and swung himself up like a monkey, went in, and stood in the middle of the floor, looking curiously all round. He stretched himself on a sofa, and the cushion sank below his weight—he had never known such a luxurious sensation. He rose and went to an easy-chair which was basking vacantly by the side of the fire. It was getting dark of an autumn afternoon, and the warmth and glow of dim light had a soothing and eerie effect in the gloaming. He sank into the chair, and leaned his head on the back of it. He knew he should not be there; but he also knew he was doing no harm—he was merely trying what kind of a thing it would be to be a gentleman, and he was fond of experiments of all kinds. His eye fell on the handle of the bell, and without hesitation he rang it so vigorously that he heard it sounding in the distance, and lay back in his chair again to see what would happen.

Miss Fairgrieve started when she heard Mr. Sinclair's bell ring with such violence. She generally knew everything, and she knew that the only persons in the house at that moment were herself and Bell, who was in the dining-room. Her shrewdness notwithstanding, she was superstitious. She knew a thief would not ring a bell, consequently it must be a ghost. She went to the dining-room and said to Bell—

"Did you hear your uncle's bell ring?"

"To be sure I did."

"What could ring it?" said Maddy, who, brave in the face of mortal, felt stricken by the mystery.

"Uncle, likely," said Bell.

"But he's not in. There's not a living soul in the house but you and me. What do you think did it?"

"The easiest way to find out would be to go and see."

Maddy did not move. Bell laughed.

"Capital!" she cried; "you are frightened, Maddy! Come, and I'll take care of you."

Another imperious ring was heard.

"It's some one in a hurry, certainly," said Bell.

"Maybe it's the Evil One!" said Maddy.

When they opened the door a commanding voice said—

"Light the gas there, will you? What's the meaning of this dawdling?"

"Bless me! it's a human being after a'," said Maddy, as, her courage suddenly restored, she went boldly in, followed by Bell. But Peter was hidden in the shadow, as he lay back in his luxurious chair.

Bell seized the poker and stirred up a flame, which revealed the boy lying lazily with his eyes half shut, and a smile lurking about the corners of his mouth.

"It's you, ye little impudent monkey!" said Maddy, in angry vexation at having revealed her vulnerable point.

"Maddy expected to see horns and hoofs," said Bell.

"What business have ye to fricht folk that gate?" asked Maddy.

"I didna think onybody would be frichted," Peter said, lolling in the chair. "Eh, it wad be fine to be a man in authority!"

"A man in authority, ye little mischief! What puts the like o' that in your head?"

"Why shouldn't it be in his head, Maddy?" said Bell. "There's nothing to hinder him being a man in authority if he likes."

Peter was looking round on the book-cases.

"Has your uncle—has Mr. Sinclair, read a' thae books?" he asked.

"Read them!" Maddy answered; "no' the half o' them, nor the quarter, I'll wager. He'll hae ane out for weeks and weeks, aye the same ane, and he'll be writing wi' a pencil on bits o' paper—writing ye can neither mak' heads nor tails o'."

"Uncle is fond of mathematics," said Bell. "It's the differential calculus he's working at."

"It's no different; it's aye the same thing," said Maddy. "I'm sure if I had fiddled as lang at onything, I wad hae made something o't. But men are slow—most awfu' slow."

"But they are sure, Maddy, and know the reasons of things. That's what makes them superior, they say."

"Superior!" said Maddy, "is there ony superiority in taking a roundabout road when ye can get a short cut?"

"Well, but they say a bee can take a short cut."

"Weel, men should think shame if a bee can beat them for common sense."

"It must be grand," said Peter, "to ken a' that's in thae books."

"If ye could mak' ony use o't," said Maddy. "But I had a cousin; his faither was a rich man, an' he thought edication was everything, an' he gied the laddie his fill o' edication—just his fill, and he had naething to do but tak' it in. And what did he ever mak' o't? Naething. He's just a minister in some wee bit country place. Ye never hear tell o' him—ye never see *his* name in the papers."

Maddy, you see, had no idea of passive genius—the dumb ones of heaven.

"But he'll ken a heap," said Peter. "It wad be fine to be Mr. Sinclair, and sit in this chair and read thae books whenever ye liket."

"Maybe he thinks it wad be fine to be you," said Maddy.

"Maybe!" said Peter ironically.

"Weel," said Maddy, "how would ye like if ye couldna see a thing without spectacles?"

" I dinna ken. I often hear my faither say they're a great blessing."

" Oh, nae doubt they're better than being clean blind. But how wad ye like, if ye had had a watch wi' a yellow face and yellow hands a' your days, to have to tak' to ane wi' a white face and black hands ?"

" What hardship wad that be ?" asked Peter, not perceiving the point.

It might have been thought that this recent slight change in Mr. Sinclair's arrangements would have passed unnoticed ; but what escapes sharp feminine eyes ?

" Uncle's sight must be failing—it must be a curious thing to wear spectacles," Bell said meditatively; " surely people so old as that would never think of marrying ; mamma is always afraid of uncle marrying ; she says he is sure to marry a servant."

" A servant ! " cried Maddy, " he shouldna fling himsel' away on a servant; a servant can do her ain turn—she's independent; he should marry ane o' the kind o' beings that are fit for naething in this world, and yet maun live—that's the kind o' thing he should marry."

" There he is," said Bell ; " I hear him coming in.

Peter jumped up and darted through the window like a bird, Maddy began to replenish the fire, and Bell busied herself closing the shutters, while the object of their remarks walked into his room marvellously unconscious of the charming line of usefulness that had been chalked out for him.

CHAPTER X.

How, with his peculiar touchy nature, did Mr. Gilbert get on in his school? Not well, you think, for boys and girls have a speciality for finding out raw spots—they don't see, nor analyze, nor synthesize, but they discover, simply, as all discoveries are made, and then they feel the importance of their discovery, and put it to good use one way or another.

But nature had been kind to Mr. Gilbert in externally fitting him up ready-made for his profession. He was of a fair average height, he had dark eyes, over which eyebrows were set in tufts of stiff coarse hair, his face was a rather long oval, his under lip was thick and hanging, his hair left his forehead standing very prominently out, while it stuck up hard and straight round his head like a dark coronet; looked at from the back it resembled a good-sized bird's nest, a white bald place in the centre suggesting a biggish egg lying in it. That mouth, with the pendulous lip and the fierce eyebrows and hair, did much good work in Mr. Gilbert's school-room. And Mr. Gilbert had common sense, and not an inferior mind, for there is no end to the contrasting qualities that will meet in one person; and his common sense had told him long ago that he might as well give up his business at once as betray his weakness to the young crew under his command. And he did not betray it; he might flare up into a passion not unfrequently, but he did not tell them it was because he suspected some of them of laughing at him—all such confidences he reserved for the ear of his wife; and although it would be hard to say that a man was never to appear before his wife except in full dress, still Mr. Gilbert, being able to control his weakness in some circumstances, he should have concealed it from his wife; it is pleasant to be looked up to, and he might have doubted how long his wife would have looked up to him if he was always telling her that he was generally undervalued; besides, if Mrs. Gilbert had been a very ordinary woman, people would have come to the knowledge of her husband's weakness through her—there is no way you can more correctly get the missing bits that you are wanting when you estimate a man than through his wife. But Mrs. Gilbert was a strong-minded woman. That phrase is understood to be a synonym for a disagreeable woman. It is an entire mistake. Think of a great gift of God having come to be a byword in the mouth of fools! But it is a strong will that the superficial confound with a strong mind, and a strong will joined to a weak mind is nuisance enough in man or woman—most people between the cradle and the grave will find use for all the strength of mind they can lay their hands on, and let those who have it be devoutly thankful. Mrs. Gilbert, however, would have used her arm for a bar before she would have admitted the public to look at her husband in undress. An ordinary man might have passed for a great king with such a consort beside him on the throne, for Mrs. Gilbert had in her the royal qualities of pride and ambition, but as the wife of a country schoolmaster they were pretty well battened down under the hatches. With the optimist, let us believe it was all for the best.

The special Mordecai that sat at Mr. Gilbert's gate

at this time was James Raeburn, and he was quite as innocent of evil intention as the historical Jew. The boy had been delicate, and returning health and strength brought an exuberance of animal spirits which effervesced in a way often offensive to Mr. Gilbert, who thought he presumed on the wealthy position of his father, and on his—Mr. Gilbert's—comparatively humble circumstances, the truth being that James thought neither of the one nor the other, nor was he in the least aware of being the thorn in his uncle's side that he was. Mrs. Gilbert was glad when the time for her nephew's departure drew near, notwithstanding that she loved the boy. He was to go home after the examination of the school, which wound up the scholastic year in Quixstar.

Mr. Gilbert was a good teacher—not first-rate, but good. To the making of the highest order of teacher enthusiasm is necessary, and no man always thinking of himself can be enthusiastic; but he can like children—they minister to egotism—they are ignorant and he is wise—they are subject and he is despot. In any case being a despot is not an easy business; but what must it be to have your reputation at the mercy of some scores of thoughtless beings, whose love for learning is questionable, and whose love for play is beyond a doubt—they are flint hard to strike fire from.

The examination was approaching, and Mr. Gilbert and his assistant had for some time been drilling the school specially with a view to that great event. Scotch parents are known to be very much alive to the advantages of education, and interested in the progress of their children, and happy was the boy who could go home at the end of the day, and, to anxious questions as to his place in the class, say dux. Who was to be the dux at the coming examination was the murmur of a large section of the *bourg* at this time. There were five boys at the head of the school contending for the place of honor, which only one of them could get; they were all reputed clever. Mrs. Sinclair was persuaded that unless there was gross injustice Tom would be dux, he in reality being nowhere in the race—and having a knowledge of this, he made light of the distinction. Human wisdom is apt pretty often to be at fault, especially in relation to future events; none of the clever boys carried the day; there was a plodding boy in the school, and he was the tortoise that beat the hares. The hares took the defeat easily and with good humor—down to Sandy Fairley, certainly not a hare, but the booby, happily not keenly alive to his position, as how could he, having kept it for some years, till in the effort to drive a measure of knowledge into his head the palms of his hands had hardened under the tawse? Never mind—he is now the respectable and thriving head of a numerous household. One wonders if his school days are wrapt in the enchanted haze that in middle life is apt to gather round that time, or if burnt leather and tingling fingers—the actual elements— are as real as ever; not likely, he'll be dull indeed if he has not contrived to gloss up things some way.

The great day came, and in the course of twelve hours was swept as ruthlessly into the past as all the days, great and small, that had gone before it, but not without leaving memories. Little Mrs. Raeburn, for instance; she had travelled from Ironburgh to be present on the occasion, and she has never forgotten the face and figure of her son James as he sat between Peter Veitch and his cousin. She was surprised he was not dux, so Peter Veitch's father and mother were surprised he was not dux; as for Mrs. Gilbert, she believed that her son got less than justice from his father, fearful lest he should be accused of partiality, but this rivalry generated no bad feeling among the boys, nor, indeed, among their parents, except that Mrs. Sinclair, being signally disappointed that Mr. Gilbert had failed to bring out Tom's brilliant parts, made up her mind to a change of arrangements for next year. Nevertheless, she lent her countenance to the event of the hour, and Mr. Gilbert, being ignorant of her secret intentions, was spared that annoyance till after.

On the morning of the examination day every urchin connected with the school washed his face in soapier water, and got into his Sunday clothes with much greater zest than on Sundays. Peter Veitch was happily ignorant of the mysteries of the toilet. The last suit of clothes he had got had been made by a tailor, who had not learned his business in Bond Street, under the solemn warning of Mrs. Veitch that if they were not big enough to serve some years of Sundays, she would entirely withdraw her patronage. Peter, not having as yet wakened up to the consciousness of personal appearance, slipped into the roomy garments without the least misgiving. It did occur to him, however, when looking at the square inch of mirror that hung by the side of the window in the apartment that served as dining-room and kitchen, that his hair was not in such order as was desirable, so he went into a closet his mother called the milk-house, put his palms on the top of a dish of milk on which the thick rich cream lay like velvet, raised them gloved with cream, which he rubbed vigorously into his hair, and going back to his looking-glass combed it down, and that not quite succeeding, he seized an old worn clothes-brush and brushed it smooth; he had never seen a hair-brush, but there and then he invented the idea of that toilet indispensable, only to find, like many people who strike out a bright idea, that it is not by any means new. Is the happiness of having the free use of the wisdom of our ancestors not more than counterbalanced by the mortification of finding that we can hardly have an original idea?

The schoolroom looked fresh, so did the scholars, and so also did the master, as he stood smiling and bowing to groups entering at one door, and keeping an eye of severe and anxious aspect on the hives swarming out and in of the other. He was equal to the occasion, and he enjoyed being the man of the hour. The examiners occupied seats in front of the young host—reverend gentlemen they were, connected with the district: Mr. Kennedy, with his "youthy" out-of-doors air, and his quick sense of the surface of men and things, and inability for seeing further; and a little man with sharp eyes and nose, who looked very decisive; and a tall, shambling man, dreamy and good-natured; and a stout, short man with a sloping face, and a way of holding up his head "like a hen drinking water," as Peter Veitch irreverently whispered to the boy next him. These were all; as yet the Government Inspector was not. Behind the clergy were the laity; a goodly number of what were technically known as parents and guardians. Mrs. Gilbert was there, and Mrs. and Miss Raeburn, and old Mrs. Gilbert, the schoolmaster's aunt, and Peter Veitch, senior, who had left his work for an hour or two, and put on his Sunday coat, the neck of which was so stiff and deep it might have served a horse for a collar; the buttons on the back having stuck fast in one place, while the buttons on the backs of other people had been travelling up and down continually, as the caprice of fashion ordered. Mrs. Veitch, too, was there, anxiously wondering if Peter's class would be over before it was time to milk the cows. Mrs. and Miss Smith also lent their countenance on this day. They were members of a clever household in the aristocratic part of Quixstar. Mr. Smith had been bankrupt oftener than once, but the family held up its head, ignored circumstances, and abated nothing of its dignity in speech or action, nor, so far as could be judged, in thought, and lived in style—at least in style for Quixstar. How it was done simpler people did not know; but it was done, and well done; even Mrs. Sinclair, though perfectly aware that Mr. Smith was not worth a penny, felt rather overawed by the general bearing of the Smiths. Their cleverness did not consist in book-knowledge, although if you did not meet them often, you would not have thought them deficient in that; what there was of it was most skilfully displayed, like the goods in a shop window which has a mirror at each side and one behind, giving to comparative barrenness an air of great plenty. Some of the numerous boys of this family were at Mr. Gilbert's school. They were too spirited, their mamma knew, to be nailed for any length of time to a book; so that she was not surprised that their position in the school was not the highest, still it seemed like the irony of circumstances that when honor of any kind was going, it should fall to the lot of John Johnston, the butcher's son, who was dux of the school, rather than to one of her boys. The butcher and his wife were present to enjoy their son's elevation, proud and happy, with a prophetic feeling in their hearts that their son had got his foot on the first round of the ladder that leads to success in life.

The business of the day went on; classes were gone over; copy-books lying open on desks were examined, and such true observations as "Youth is the season for improvement," "Education is an excellent and lasting patrimony," were found well and correctly set forth; and the scholars had all acquitted themselves creditably, when more than one reverend gentleman suggested to the master that they had seen quite enough to convince them of the thorough efficiency of the school. Mr. Gilbert's face beamed; matter-of-course words were not matter of course to him; if he was easily offended he was as easily pleased. No doubt he had just cause of pleasure in having done his work well, but a compliment was very dear to him (to whom is it disagreeable?), and he would have gone on to the end of his programme, but at length it was conveyed to him that people were feeling the dinner hour nearer than it had been, and he drew the proceedings to a close, and declared the day's work done. Then Mr. Kennedy rose and said—

"My dear young friends, in these beautiful copy-books lying behind us, I find written, ' Youth is the season for improvement;' now, I was once a little boy ('Ye're no very big yet,' whispered Peter Veitch to his neighbor), and when I was a boy, that was my spring-time, you know, and this is your spring-time, when you must sow knowledge, industry, integrity, perseverance, and a great many things, if you mean, as I daresay you all do, to go creditably through life according to your respective stations. From what I have seen to-day, my dear young friends, you bid fair to do that. I cannot, sir (turning to Mr. Gilbert), compliment you too highly on the thorough teaching and admirable order maintained in this school. If there is one profession I would be inclined to rate more highly than another, it is that of training the young mind of our community. May you, sir, be long spared to your arduous but grateful duties."

Mr. Gilbert again looked very gratified, while Mrs.

Gilbert felt annoyed ; which was the wisest you can judge —Mr. Gilbert who swallowed easily anything in the shape of a compliment, or Mrs. Gilbert, who could only brook that article when it was served up with equal parts of sincerity and delicacy. If people cultivate fastidiousness about anything, it is apt to grow upon them to such a pitch as makes this world a very uncomfortable place to live in. The tall dreamy-looking man next rose and said—

" Mr. Kennedy has told you that he was once a little boy. I would like to put another remarkable fact alongside that, and it is this : I was once a little boy too (a laugh) ; not so long ago but that I can remember sitting where you are—I'll not say which end of the form I was nearest (a laugh). There used always to be one gentleman at our examinations, a big portly man, with a gurly-burly voice, who looked pretty closely into things. Once when we were being examined in arithmetic we were set to extract the square root of something. I knew nothing about it. I might as well have been set to extract the root of one of these big trees. When this gentleman looked at my slate he gave an awful frown, and said, ' Boy, that's wrong. Do that again.' I could not put it right, but, happily for me, we were just what we all are at present, a little tired and a little hungry, and I got off. Mr. Kennedy has told you what good qualities you must cultivate to get on. I hope you'll cultivate them all ; but there is a short sentence about getting on, which I shall tell you. It won't impress you much now, but when you leave school, as I understand some of you are about to do, and begin to look back to it, when you disperse to all quarters of the globe, as you likely will, and call up before you, as distinctly as you see it to-day, this school, the notched forms, the inked and cut desks, the faces of your school-fellows and your teacher, your playground and your games, perhaps you will remember me as I remember the gentleman I spoke of, then you will recall this short summing up of success in life, 'Contentment with godliness is great gain.' Boys, I can wish you nothing better than that that sentence may be the bird of peace to you in after life, bringing calm when you are beaten with storms."

Whereupon Mr. Kennedy started up and said—

"I hope you will all cultivate contentment with the places you are in. You have done well to-day, which shows that Mr. Gilbert does well every day. You will have five weeks of vacation; give three cheers, and we shall dismiss."

Immediately there was a noise as if the building were coming down, which lulled and swelled for some seconds.

Mr. Kennedy turned round to Mrs. Gilbert and said—

"You must feel very proud to-day, Mrs. Gilbert. I really envy your husband. There's nothing I would like better than to teach. It's noble work."

"I had no idea you were so enthusiastic, Mr. Kennedy," she said. "I should think you would have little difficulty in getting a school if you would prefer teaching."

Mrs. Gilbert knew that Mr. Kennedy regarded her husband as a kind of henchman, and she did not like it.

Mr. Kennedy turned to Mrs. Raeburn, "What a pity," he said, "that Mr. Raeburn was not here to be delighted with his son's appearance; a fine boy—a very fine boy—one of seven, I understand?"

"Mr. Raeburn would have been here, but business prevented him," said Mrs. Raeburn. "I expect him to-day yet."

"Oh, indeed, and you're going to take your boy back; all the better, I am sure, from having been under the care of Mr. and Mrs Gilbert."

"Oh, very much better indeed, and his papa and I are very grateful," etc., etc.

CHAPTER XI.

THE dinner at Mrs. Gilbert's was not likely served *à la Russe*, more probably *à la rustic;* it was strictly a family party, and before they sat down, Mr. Raeburn arrived to make it complete.

A family party is not unnaturally supposed to be a very blessed thing, as it ought to be, but by a sarcastic twist in human affairs sometimes it is not. Job was a patient man, he was also a wise one when he offered up sacrifices after a family party in case they had sinned in their hearts. Mahomet too must have had a family party in his eye—he had reason to dread them—when describing Paradise he said, " Ye shall sit opposite one another, and all grudges shall be taken out of your hearts." Six people, exclusive of the young generation, were round the schoolmaster's table, wearing the appearance of good-fellowship, but the grudges had not been taken out of all their hearts. Mr. Gilbert was persuaded, and had made known his conviction to Mrs. Gilbert, that if Mr. Raeburn had intended or wished to be present at the examination he might have been so. " Business was the excuse, and he might have business, but nothing so desperately pressing that it could not have been delayed for a few hours, or managed without him, but of course he did not think it worth while. I believe," he wound up indignantly, " he does not know the value of education, except so far as it can help him to make money." In reality, Mr. Raeburn had been very anxious to come, and had said so, but Mr. Gilbert knew better.

Miss Raeburn sat opposite her sister-in-law, and lost herself in astonishment as to what could have been the attraction for her brother—neither looks, nor mind, nor even money, and a man so superior in every way; for Miss Raeburn, like many sisters, had the amiable weakness of believing that her brother was no every-day prize for any woman, and there sat his wife, ordinary among the ordinary.

Newspaper matter is generally safe in most companies, and Miss Raeburn threw the topics of the day on the carpet with considerable success, and in time the feast came to a close not more ignominiously than many of a more ambitious kind have done.

Mr. Raeburn went home with his sister, and sat for an hour with her. "Do you like to live here alone?" he asked.

"Yes, I like it, or probably I wouldn't do it. I am a good deal given to do what I like."

"Yes, I know; but do you not feel dull at times?"

"To be sure, if a kitten lives it must grow into a cat, but I often feel inclined to run round after my tail even yet. Do you never feel dull?"

"I have not much time to be dull."

"But you should take time, or make it; it must be dreadful never to feel dull."

"You're always like yourself, Joan. What I was going to say was, wouldn't you think of coming to live with us?"

"You have never had any reason to think that I have been disappointed in love?" she said.

"No; I hope you haven't."

"I never have, and I don't think it's likely I shall be now; too late, I doubt, too late."

"Don't speak nonsense. I was asking if you could think of coming to live with us?"

"And you don't see the sequence of ideas? Well, it takes a disappointment of the kind I have mentioned to turn out in perfection the kind of article you want: a meek, wise, clever, handy idiot, with no more apparent will or wish of her own than harlequin has bones. No; I am not good enough yet."

"What do you do from morning to night?"

"I enjoy myself."

"I'm glad to hear it. I thought you would not know what to do."

"Not a bit; besides, I can enjoy myself remarkably well doing nothing."

"You would enjoy yourself much better with us."

"Thank you. No; I'm not good enough."

"You used to be fond of company. I wonder you like to live here alone."

"Better hang loose than an ill tether."

"Oh, as for tethers, unless they are something desperate altogether, one gets accustomed to them. You come to like anything that's your own, if it be but a dictionary or an umbrella."

"Do you remember, Jamie, when you went first from home, how I used to describe my bonnets in my letters, and you criticised them? Those were innocent days. You have no time for that now."

"Describe your bonnets, and I'll do so still."

"Not you! The world is too much with you. Besides, I hardly know now what like my bonnets are myself."

"You're wrong, Joan. I may be with the world a

good deal, but the world is not with me. I get plenty, but I don't spend much—at least that people see. Probably they say that my mind is narrow, not able to expand with circumstances, but I can't in conscience bring up my boys in luxurious tastes and habits."

"You are right."

"I try to do my best. I thought maybe you would have helped me."

"If I could; but it would not do. It's no use speaking."

"So I suppose. You are really happy here—you are sure?"

"Quite sure."

"Well, I'll have to go now, or the schoolmaster's face will grow dark."

"Yes, go by all means, although I would like to have you longer; but better go than give offence."

He went, and Miss Raeburn fell to musing. "It would not do," she thought. "I wonder he does not see it would not do. Jane would grow jealous, and I would lose my temper, and live in a state of chronic irritation, and despise myself for doing so, and I have so much enjoyment here; life has such a keen relish, although you don't get people to believe that. 'A dictionary or an umbrella!' and it has come to that. Poor Jamie, I'm vexed for him. I wonder his pride let him confess it." Thus Miss Raeburn; and she was sorry, no doubt of it. Still there is a certain satisfaction in hearing a person allow that his wisdom may have been at fault, and if it had been a less serious matter Miss Raeburn would have felt this, but as it was she only pitied her brother. She might have spared herself the trouble. Mr. Raeburn had made the dictionary and umbrella remark not thinking of his own case at all. He was well enough pleased with his wife. A man brushing about the world, and having a large business to manage, has something else to do than recall phrases and attach weight to them they were never intended to bear; but some women are apt to do this. They sit and think; they do a good deal of their work and think—for it needs little attention; and while a man has the tear and wear of big wheels grinding big things with movement and sound, a woman has the tear and wear of small wheels revolving quietly, and grinding—well, grinding sometimes things not worth turning over twice; and this was what Miss Raeburn did with her brother's remark. But there is something in it. Having selected your dictionary and chosen your umbrella, you are apt to stand by them.

When Mr. Raeburn and his wife were alone that night she said, " Do you know that Mr. Gilbert is offended because you did not come in time for the examination?"

" Yes, I know; I have explained the reason to him, and if he will still be offended I can't help it."

" It's a pity, though. You see a man of your wealth and influence is so much counted on—"

" I know that perfectly, and Gilbert thinks I look down on him. I look down on no good man. I am not so idiotic as not to value wealth, but I know I have won it when many a better man has not; and as for position, every man is born to a position that will tax all his powers to fill. I have no patience with Gilbert's small touchiness. It would be nothing to me to give him four times what he charges for James's year here, but I daren't do it; he would think I was insulting him. Whether I should think more or less of him for that I'm not sure. It's not often you can kill a dog with a bone."

4*

"Well, it's a pity," sighed Mrs. Raeburn.

"Yes, I have been trying to get help for you, but have failed."

"How? what help?"

"I asked Joan to come and live with us."

"And she won't? I daresay not. I know nobody so well off. I often envy her; she has neither care nor toil. I am always tired and anxious when the servants quarrel, and the boys are unruly. I feel as if I could fling everything at my feet, and run away."

Mr. Raeburn exerted himself to comfort and cheer his wife, showing that she was more to him than a dictionary or umbrella; and it was well, for the fibres of both their natures were to be strained as they had not been yet, and also, in sailor phrase, spliced more closely than they had been hitherto.

CHAPTER XII.

NEXT morning Bell Sinclair was in the garden, standing at her uncle's favorite point of view, looking over the wall to the water as it murmured away down below the bridge. She saw Peter Veitch coming along, and when he was near she called, "Peter." He glanced up. "What did you put on your hair yesterday that made it look so funny and streaky?"

"Cream.—Do you ken what's happened?" he said, in a very subdued way, compared with his usual brisk tones.

"No. What has happened? nothing bad?"

"Jamie Raeburn—" and Peter stopped, his voice failing him as he realized the fact, "Jamie Raeburn—"

"You have not been doing any ill, you and he?" she asked, "have you?"

"No. He is drooned. I saw him taken out o' ane o' the holes up the water no' half an hour syne." Both were dumb for a second after such awful news.

"Was nothing done—were they doing nothing—to bring life back? People are often—"

"He had been ower lang in, Bell. If I had been there I could have saved him, I think. I could hae gotten him out quick; but there was naebody there but wee laddies."

Bell heard the breakfast-bell ring. "I'll have to go in, Peter."

He nodded, and with all their deeper thoughts of this, the first tragedy that had come close home to them, unsaid, they parted.

"Who was that you were speaking to over the wall, Bell?" asked Mrs. Sinclair.

"Peter Veitch. Oh, mamma—"

"Peter Veitch! How often have I told you to hold no unnecessary intercourse with people of his class? Did you address him first, or did he address you?"

"I spoke to him, and he told me that Jamie Raeburn was drowned this morning when he was bathing."

"Jamie Raeburn! How did it happen?" asked Tom, with his mouth full.

"Indeed! a very sad thing," said Mrs. Sinclair, "however it happened. It is a painful dispensation to his parents. Let it be a lesson to you, Tom, to be careful. I don't know that I should allow you to bathe. It will cast quite a gloom over the locality."

"The water is so low just now, I would not have thought it dangerous," said Mr. Sinclair.

"It was in a deep pool," said Bell.

Mr. Sinclair glanced at Tom; he was eating more seriously than usual. He was generally serious at meals. Mr. Sinclair's nieces were not eating, and tears were gleaming in their eyes. He looked at his watch; it was half-past eight.

How was the news received at the schoolmaster's house? Mrs. Gilbert had been up early; she generally was. The great objection to women attempting the practice of medicine is stated to be their want of strength and nerve, but so far as an outside spectator may judge, the ordinary work of a doctor seems a joke compared to what many women undergo—not in straining to ape a class above them, but merely trying to make the most of a narrow income in their own sphere. Keeping up appearances may sometimes be a farce, but letting them down is apt to be a tragedy. Mrs. Gilbert, like many other good women, kept them up. She looked well to the ways of her household. Usually she had a servant recommended as being one to whom she might intrust untold gold, but that was the only thing she could be trusted with untold, and as it was not an article lying about in every corner the advantage was the less. The eye and hand of her mistress must be constantly about her, or there was a chance world immediately. Nor in this was Mrs. Gilbert to be pitied. Work, active handwork, even what is called menial, is no hardship, and if not overdone is the best tonic for body and mind. A doctor may say that he is worked to death. Mrs. Raeburn said she was always tired, but Mrs. Gilbert never said to any one, and could not say to her husband, that she was wearied, although that was a frequent thing, for he would at once have made out that she was reproaching him, and that she was contrasting her own lot with her sister's. Many a woman has been silent in similar circumstances, but it is a dangerous thing teaching man, woman, child, or nation to hold its tongue. A death-like torpor or an explosion is likely to be the result. Silence is not always golden, it is sometimes wretchedly leaden.

Mrs. Gilbert was up early, and she saw and spoke to James as he went out. All she said was, " Good-morning, Jamie ; is John not going with you ? "

" No; he is lazy this morning," and, whistling carelessly, James shut the door with a bang, which Mrs. Gilbert thought would rouse her inmates, and she felt annoyed, but speedily forgot her annoyance, having all kinds of small details to attend to.

The family were assembled, with the exception of James, and breakfast was on the table. Mrs. Gilbert proposed waiting a little for him, but his father said, "No; James knew the hour, would Mrs. Gilbert just go on." Mr. Gilbert said, "Certainly, go on," and they all sat and ate and chatted, Mr. Gilbert and Mr. Raeburn, hitting on some topics about which they agreed, and still James did not come. "There he is!" said his mother, as footsteps approached the door, but it was only the untold-gold maiden, to say that a person wanted to speak to Mr. Gilbert. Mr. Gilbert rose and went out to meet the messenger of evil tidings. "Impossible," he said, "drowned! impossible." "It's true tho', sir," said the man; "the doctor has been working with him for an hour, but it's no use; he thinks he had struck his head on a stone, and had been stunned."

"Tell your mistress to come here," Mr. Gilbert said to his servant, who was listening with a whitened face. Many times he had been stung by the boy's thoughtless sallies, but this was awful—drowned! It was soon all known—nothing could alter it, neither his mother's tears nor his father's hidden grief. He was the first of these school-fellows to end his career. In time he became, even in the hearts of his father and mother, a kind of tender dream; by others he was forgotten, or remembered as a fact—merely a thing that had been. Out of Mrs. Gilbert's great grief for her sister and brother crept a feeling of thankfulness that her own son was spared to her—her only son, her first-born; the Raeburns had six left, but if John had been taken, on whom she and his father built so much, how could they have borne it? It was a saying among the heathen, "whom the gods love die young," and it is certain that death, the death of a child, is not the heaviest sorrow given to man to carry. The Gilbert children were awe-struck; it was a fearful shadow that had come in at their door. Mrs. Sinclair went to call and offer her sympathy to Mrs. Raeburn, but that lady declined to see any one, and Mrs. Gilbert was commissioned to tell her that she, Mrs. Sinclair, knew her every feeling, having come through it all twice—she had had two lovely children torn from her by death, but from the first she considered they were provided for far better than she could provide for them; and a great deal more she said which Mrs. Gilbert did not think necessary to transmit to the bereaved mother. Mrs. Sinclair asked the children to Old Battle House for the day—"for," she said, "it would be unbecoming for them to amuse themselves here, and they can't sit still all day and weep." She took them with her, and John and Tom employed themselves quietly in the stable-yard sawing wood for some purpose of their own, while the girls went into the garden, where Mr. Sinclair chanced to overhear them laughing. He took out his watch and said to himself, "Tears at half-past eight, laughter at half-past three —shallow from beginning to end; they are all alike."

It did not strike Mr. Sinclair as a happy thing that children should have short memories for their griefs, and be easily diverted from them for a time. If he had been crying and laughing in the course of a short time it might have been feather-headed enough, but that children should do so is the happy arrangement of a higher power. It is to be feared his nature had met some sort of wrench, that he had been deceived,—whether in love or friendship cannot be known; but such a deception creates a frightful recoil; it makes faith and love shrink to the furthest corner, never perhaps to come fairly and frankly out again. However, it might only be Mr. Sinclair's ignorance of children, and his want of observation;

at any rate, if there was such an episode in his life it was well Mrs. Sinclair had no inkling of it, for inevitably she would have raked it up—there are people who will trail ghoul-like fingers through such a spot from maliciousness, or to gratify a low curiosity; she would have lugged in the topic to offer sympathy, or merely as a thing to talk of, and unconsciously would have earned life-long dislike, or something very much stronger; she would not have been long at Old Battle House.

When Mr. and Mrs. Raeburn left, Miss Raeburn went with them. Her sympathies were moved by the circumstances, and although, unlike Mrs. Sinclair, she had no propensity for going about to make herself of use, she organized her brother's household; things fell into shape before her with no appearance of effort. The fact that Miss Raeburn had nothing but herself to superintend was a waste of power; but waste is a law of the world, and she did not feel it so herself; she had made her choice deliberately, and held to it. Meagre, you will say, her nature must have been, wanting in something possibly, but yet you know, though a vessel may be small, if it is full what is there to desire?

CHAPTER XIII.

OLD Mrs. Gilbert, the schoolmaster's aunt, was at once feeble-minded and simple-minded—a character it is remarkably easy to put in a ridiculous light. She enjoyed much the kind of religious meetings where the pasture seems not only bare, but sickly, and the literature on her tables was of the same order; but she was so kindly and humble and industrious, that you felt, though you could assimilate next to nothing out of her mental pabulum, it must have had some life-giving power, or she could not have thriven on it as she did. Now, she liked the Gilbert girls well enough, but she was foolishly fond of John, so fond of him that she bribed him to go with her and another old lady to a weekly prayer-meeting. John walked along the street with them, and sat out the hour demurely. It was a queer old church in which this meeting was held, with galleries in unexpected places, in which, if you sat in an ordinary position, your back was to the speaker. This did not distress John. He arranged himself as comfortably as circumstances would permit, and circumstances permitted a good deal of comfort in a quiet way, for the pews were so deep and the lights so sparse that he was entirely sheltered from observation, and could amuse himself measuring with his eye the great brown beams over his head, or spelling out the half-obliterated texts of Scripture that had been painted long ago on the front of the galleries. When more familiar with the situation he wrote his school-exercises for the next day, Mrs. Gilbert supposing he was taking notes of what the minister was saying, which gave her a glow of happiness, especially as she always found him able to respond intelligently to any remarks she made after. Mrs. Gilbert did not mention to any one that she gave John a shilling an hour for his company on these occasions, nor did he mention it, for he had the idea that if his father and mother knew of this source of income it would be stopped at once; and he was right. It was Mrs. Gilbert's custom to have her young friends to spend an evening with her once a week, and on the week after the breaking up of the school, and the sudden and melancholy death of James Raeburn, she asked the Sinclairs also, proposing to improve that distressing event to them all. Now a person whose life is on the lees, and who has seen death so often that in talking the very word seems to have shed part of its awful meaning—at least such a person as Mrs. Gilbert—has no idea what effect a subject like this has on the minds of children. Much better surely to prepare them for life than for death; they were not likely to forget the naked fact which had been put before their eyes with such startling power. Her intention was good no doubt, but it was overruled by nature's law—you cannot put an old head on young shoulders. The awe-stricken faces of the group disappeared instantly as they burst into the garden, where they found their school-fellow, Peter Veitch, at work.

"Peter ought to have his tea with us," Bell remarked.

"I wonder to hear you," said her sister. "What would mamma say? He is not at all in our sphere."

"No," said John Gilbert. "Peter is not fit to eat with

Clara and Julia de Lacy, the daughters of a gentleman." He stopped, for he had begun to peel a turnip with his teeth, which he had drawn from the earth and washed in the burn. The others followed his example; the turnips were delicious, eaten while sitting on the top of the garden dike. When Peter's hour of release came the boys had a game, the girls looking on from the top of the dike; then they all adjourned to a forest of gooseberries, and came pretty close up with happiness. Being hurt by fruit or raw vegetables was a thing unknown, nor did they take cold, and as yet cod-liver oil was not; the cod might enjoy his liver in the cool retreats about Newfoundland—for that virtue could go out of it was still among things not generally known.

But the dark shadow came back in the night. John and Tom were hardier spirits, and they buried their heads in the bedclothes, and put themselves rapidly to sleep with the multiplication-table; but the girls wept bitterly. Bell could not sleep; her imagination got the upper hand, and terror took possession of her, till, do as she would, she could not suppress a loud scream, which brought Maddy to her side immediately.

" What is it? what is it?" she asked.

" Oh, I could not help it, Maddy! I thought I saw James Raeburn in his coffin, and he moved! I'm certain he moved!"

" Wheesht, wheesht, bairn!" said Maddy soothingly, stifling her own eeriness at such a statement; ye've been dreaming."

" But do you think it possible, Maddy? Oh, it would be horrible!"

" It's no' possible. Try no' to think about it, and fa' asleep."

" But I can't sleep! Oh what a fearful life an undertaker's is, to feel so often as I have felt since James died! Money can't pay them!"

Maddy could not help smiling. "They get used to it, ye ken; they get used to it," she said.

"Used to it! I would never get used to it. I would be in a perpetual state of grief or terror."

"Have ye heard about Peter Veitch?" asked Maddy, with the instinct all nurses have of diverting, turning the thoughts to something else as the speediest consolation.

"No," said Bell eagerly. "I saw him to-night, but I heard nothing particular."

"Guess what business he wants to be?"

"He is very clever. I can't guess; I never heard him say what he thought of doing."

"What would you think of a sailor?"

"It is dangerous; he might be drowned."

"No fear! he's just a bit cork. But I'se warrant his mother will be clean against it. I'm sure folk that hae bairns havena their sorrows to seek."

"I don't think Peter will ever be a sorrow to his father or mother."

"If he persists in gaun to the sea, his mother'll greet her een out about it."

"He'll not go if his mother does not let him," Bell said in a drowsy tone, sleep having come suddenly on her.

Maddy waited a little, and all being quiet, she, in the language of Effie's models of composition, retired once more to her couch to seek repose.

CHAPTER XIV.

PETER VEITCH was a youth of affairs, and erratic in his habits, if he could be said to have habits. His mother sometimes remarked "that often she did not see him the whole blessed day," but of late he had hung a good deal about the house, watching his mother performing her small household duties, while he employed himself with the model of a ship he was making.

"Mother," he said suddenly one day, "I think I could keep a house myself, and make the meat too."

"I dinna see there's onything to hinder ye, if ye like to tak' patience and pay attention. I've kenned men that lived their lanes; but it's no common, and I hope it's no in your lot."

"But I may be cast on a desert island, mother."

"Weel, when that happens, it'll be as weel that ye dinna ken about housekeeping, as ye'll no likely get a' the bits o' things that's needed lying ready to your hand; and what ye dinna ken about ye'll no miss sae muckle.—Laddie, hae ye nae notion o' what ye wad like to be ? Wad ye no care for being a gardener, like your faither?"

"I'm no gaun to be a gardener, mother."

"Then what wad ye like to be?" and a light flashed in her face. "Wad ye be a minister? It wad cost a heap, but we wad manage it."

"If I wanted to be a minister, or a doctor either, I

would manage it, but I'm no gaun to be onything o' the kind."

"Then what are ye thinking o'? Ye'll hae to mak' up your mind or lang."

"I've made up my mind lang syne, but I never tell'd ye for fear o' vexin' ye."

"Vexin' me, bairn! Ye'll no vex me if ye learn an honest trade and behave yoursel'."

"Mother, I want to be a sailor."

Mrs. Veitch looked at her son, and her face grew white. "Laddie, ye'll no say that again unless ye want to be the death o' me," she said. "Ye dinna ken what ye're speaking about. A sailor! that comes o' readin' that Crusoe book. If I had kenned, it hadna come within the door."

"It's no the book's fau't, mother; readin' it didna mak' me want to be a sailor. It was because I wanted to be a sailor that I read it."

"Ye'll never gang to the sea wi' my consent, Peter. Ye dinna ken what a hard, coarse life it is; beside the constant awful risk."

"Mother, I've set my heart on't. What wad ye do for your tea and sugar if naebody gaed to the sea?"

"I'm no saying that naebody should gang to the sea; I'm only sayin' that ye shouldna gang. I'll never get a wink o' sleep if it's a high wind. The life o' a common sailor—"

"But I'm no gaun to be a common sailor."

"Laddie, what can ye be?"

"I can be an uncommon sailor."

"Ye maun aye hae your joke, Peter. But it's a hard life a sailor's—very hard, and puir pay."

"Gardeners dinna often mak' siller either, mother."

"But it's a pleasant job—what the Almighty set the

first man to do afore there was sic a thing as sin and misery in the warld."

"Ay, but Adam didna gang out o' ae gentleman's place into anither, making a' things right and tasting naething. If him and his wife had hunkered for days among strawberries, and packed them a' up for the market, without putting ane in their mouths, I wadna blamed them for eatin' an apple when they had the chance."

"Peter, that's a daurin' way o' speakin', and if ye gang awa' to the sea ye'll just break lowse frae a' that's guid."

"I'm nae mair likely to do that on the sea than on the land."

"Weel, weel; ye'll see what your faither'll say."

"He said I wad see what my mother wad say."

Mrs. Veitch said no more; she could not say more just then, and Peter also wisely let the subject drop. But perhaps Mrs. Veitch was herself to blame for her son's strong seagoing propensity. It has been stated as a softer touch relieving the rude recklessness of the race, that the thrifty wives of the Norsemen, when they handed a towel to their husbands, warned them not to plunge boldly into the middle of it, but to go round the sides, and come to the middle in due time, making the towel serve a certain fixed period, and serve it well. Judged by such traits as this, Mrs. Veitch's veins must have run Norse blood wholly; so how could the boy help seeking towards the sea? Besides, the name Veitch is the modern form of the grand old Norman De Vesci, which brings in his father guilty also. No wonder that the instinct of the old sea-rovers broke out in Peter, thus hemmed in; he had hardly a choice.

One morning Mrs. Sinclair having tossed up the newspaper topics as usual, said to her brother-in-law—

"I hear that boy Veitch wants to go to sea, and his parents are in great distress about it. Could you not prevent it? Take him as groom or something? I've spoken to Mr. Kennedy about it, and he says, 'Let the boy go; if he tires he'll come back, and if not, why —the navy must be manned,' but it is his parents I feel for. I have a deep sympathy with parents."

"I don't want a groom," said Mr. Sinclair.

"And Peter would not be a groom. I think he means to rise in the world," Bell said.

"Poor stupid thing! What does he expect to rise to?" asked Mrs. Sinclair.

"To be Admiral of the Fleet, probably," said Mr. Sinclair.

"There's nothing too absurd," Mrs. Sinclair said. "If people would only, as Mr. Kennedy says, know how much happier they would be by resting contented in the positions in which they find themselves!"

"Is Mr. Kennedy unhappy because he is out of his original position?" asked Mr. Sinclair.

"What was his original position?"

"His origin was not lofty."

"Maddy says he once worked at the same bench as her father," said Bell.

"Indeed!" and Mr. Kennedy fell in Mrs. Sinclair's esteem from that hour. It is to be hoped he never had a greater fall.

Mr. Sinclair meeting Peter Veitch in the garden shortly after, said to him—

"I hear your son wants to go to sea, Peter?"

Leaning on the handle of his rake, Peter gave a sigh and said—

"Ay, sir; it's ower true."

"Well, Peter, when a boy's head is filled with that

idea, he is not likely to do much good at anything else. Better let him have his full swing at once."

" Ay, sir."

" But do you not think so ?"

" There's just ae thing that hinders me seeing the thing in sic a distinct light."

" What is that ?"

" Just this : that I happen to be the laddie's faither."

" True, Peter; but when a boy's inclination for any line of life is so decided, it is a cruel thing to thwart him —a cruel thing;" probably Mr. Sinclair was thinking of his own experience—" And you are not the first father that's had to give in in such a case."

" Na; I'm no the first, and I'll no be the last. If looking at other folk's trials is ony consolation, it's o' a kind that may be gathered by the bushel."

" What I mean to say, Peter, is this. If you make up your mind to let the boy go, I know a captain of a vessel, a respectable man, on whom you might depend for doing well by him, and I'll fit him out. I'm in his debt, and would like to serve him," and he walked away, leaving Peter to chew the cud.

" He means weel," Peter thought ; " but he kens naething aboot it. It's a queer thing that a wilfu' laddie bent on breaking his mother's heart, should get a gentleman to step forward to help him to do it—very queer."

But Peter did not wish to break his mother's heart, and his mother felt that, whatever she might say. He had that dash of tenderness in his nature—a bit of woman—which no good man is without, but it hardly made him falter in his determination, and it could not change it. Coming in one afternoon with a headache, he laid himself up in the old-fashioned chair by the side of the fire, and leaning his head in the corner where its stiff upright back and elbow met, he shut his eyes and listened to his mother's footsteps. Boys are not usually sentimental, but Peter was soothed unconsciously, and when his mother stopped in one of her many journeys between the table and the fire,—for she was ironing, and was often changing her irons—and looking at him, said, " Puir thing, he has fa'en asleep," and went and brought a shawl, which she laid softly over him, she did a thing he never forgot. The fireplace was a wide open one, the primitive grate—only some iron bars fixed between stones, which stones, even those behind the fire, were all white—the smoke curling up warily and softly, while the kettle stood among the white scenery like a big snail, black and shining. The screen on which Mrs. Veitch hung the clothes as she finished them was standing between the window and the fire, and shaded Peter's face from the light; the cat was sharpening its claws on the foot of it—a favorite employment of pussy's. Mrs. Veitch gave it a push and said, " Gae way, beast," then glanced at her son to see if the noise had roused him, but his eyes were still shut. He was not sleeping though. Many times when he was up among the rigging in cold and fog, and his ship dancing like an egg-shell on a wild sea, this " cottage interior " came up before him. The drowsy afternoon, the subdued hum of the town, his mother's footfall and pussy's scratching, made themselves heard amid the mad roar of winds and waters. For he carried his point, and went to sea; and his departure was not by any means an event in the place. His father went with him to the station, saw him into the train, shook his hand, and said—

" See and behave yersel', Peter ; and mind, never tell a lee."

" I'll try, faither."

And the boy was launched. The father watched the train till it disappeared in the distance, then walked home slowly, and with a heavy heart. The son could not sit still; he leaned back, and he looked out of the window, and he whistled; he was in a state of boundless elation: he had gained his end; he was abroad in the world on his own resources; body and mind were effervescing with young life, and he did not know fear. It is to be doubted that for a time he did not think so often as he should have done of the old folks at home. His mother had gone with him to the end of the house, and said—

"Fare ye weel, Peter, and tak' care o' yoursel', and dinna forget to write when ye have a chance."

"Yes, I'll write—I'll no forget," that was all, and Mrs. Veitch turned back into her house, and sat down and uncurled and smoothed out her apron-strings, her face set and vacant, till the kettle began to boil and make its lid dance, diverting her thoughts to her little household cares. When her husband came in he drew his chair close to her, and laid his hand on hers, and they looked each other in the face, with an expression something like that of a child that does not know whether to laugh or cry, and won't do either. The wrench was a grievous one, but there was hope in it.

"Weel, he is fairly off," said Peter; "but he'll be back again some day."

"Ay, if he's no drooned, and doesna dee o' hardship."

This pair had other children, but these had left the house, and were jogging on in a decent honest way; they caused no anxiety; Peter was their youngest, the light of the house, and they had a craving, hungry sense of loss, wakeful nights and empty days, but what could they do, except what most people have to do some time or other—tighten the hunger-belt and move on? When people sit and brood over their sorrows, necessity or conscience is the policeman who taps them on the shoulder, and says, " Move on, move on; you are doing yourself no good, and you are hindering the business of life;" and they move on, and the healing process is begun. Nature never makes a rent but she immediately sets about trying to repair it. She can't fill the gap and put things as they were, but she will smooth and beautify it, she will blow seeds into it that will grow and fructify; and woe betide the man who will persist in pulling them up and exposing the unsightliness!

When Miss Raeburn came back from setting her brother's house in order, she was not long of calling for Mrs. Veitch. " And Peter is away," she said. " I wish I had seen him before he left. I'm fond of Peter."

Instead of condoling with Mrs. Veitch on the waywardness of boys in general, and of her son in particular, Miss Raeburn took Peter's departure as a matter of course.

" I don't wonder at his choice. If I had been a boy I think I would have gone to sea too."

" Maybe; but I hope when Peter's had a trial o' the sea he'll come back, and content himsel' at hame."

" But you mustn't hope that. You must think that he'll stick to his business, and be a credit to it and you. If a sailor is not extra bad he is likely to be extra good; and Peter will hold by the right."

" Weel, I hope so. He was a clever laddie, and there was nae ill in him. The minister ca'ed ae day, an' he said the navy maun be manned, as if our bit callant was gaun to mak' ony difference to the manning o' the navy, puir thing! And Mr. Sinclair, he would help him too, and get him a ship wi' a gude captain."

"Indeed. I am glad to hear Mr. Sinclair took an interest in him. I hardly know Mr. Sinclair; he seemed to me a dry kind of stick, but he mustn't be that altogether."

"He was kind eneuch to Peter; but," she said bitterly, "it's easy for folk that hae nae bairns o' their ain to say the navy maun be manned."

"It makes a difference, no doubt," said Miss Raeburn soothingly; "but there's no fear of Peter. You'll be proud of Peter yet, Mrs. Veitch."

"I've been far ower proud o' him already, and that's the reason he's been sent away; and maybe I'll get used to it; but oh, the day's lang, and the house is dull."

CHAPTER XV.

MRS. SINCLAIR was determined to have a tutor for her children, in consequence of the place Tom held in his class at the examination. Such a position was only possible to him either by palpable neglect or partiality on Mr. Gilbert's part. She had not yet mentioned her plan to her brother-in-law, as she was not sure how he might receive a proposal to add another inmate to his household. She was not even sure that she herself had a firm root in Old Battle House, till, to her surprise, Mr. Sinclair said one day, "How long do you mean to stay here? I've been thinking that if you care for this place you may as well remain as go back to Eastburgh."

This proposal looked as if it were an impromptu, but like Sheridan's brilliant things it had been carefully thought over in bed, and was at least pointed, if not polished. Mr. Sinclair had considered that these were his brother's children, and that it might be his duty to keep an eye on them. Mrs. Sinclair, it is true, was not his ideal of womanhood, but she was kindly and good-natured, and his sister-in-law, so he took this step.

"My dear Adam," said the lady, "you could have said nothing that could give me more pleasure. We'll stay; we could be better nowhere. The house is comfortable, the climate good, the scenery fine, and the society not inferior; and you'll help me to do my duty to those dear children. This arrangement quite relieves my anxieties."

"Well, I'm very glad to hear it."

"And do you know, I've been thinking—Mr. Gilbert, to be sure, is a good man, and for Mrs. Gilbert, I have nothing against her—"

"I should think not," said Mr. Sinclair, wondering what was coming.

"No, nothing; but my family, I find, are of too sensitive natures for an ordinary country school, and I have been considering the propriety of engaging a tutor."

"Nonsense!" said Mr. Sinclair on the spur of the moment; "I mean that Gilbert is a very fair teacher, and you'll do more harm than good by making another change."

"Do you really think so? because I have set on foot inquiries for a tutor already. I should be sorry if withdrawing my countenance from Mr. Gilbert should hurt him—"

"Oh, I have no doubt he'll be able to stand it. The question is, Will you not injure your children?"

"I hope not—I fondly hope not—if I get a proper person. Mr. Kennedy has spoken to a friend of his in Eastburgh, a man of experience, and he is to bring his judgment to bear in the choice of one."

"Then possibly there is one engaged already?"

"It is possible, but not likely."

"If he is not engaged, I would stop the thing at once;" and he walked away thinking, "She is a foolish woman. It would take a microscope to discover Tom's sensitive nature;"—while Mrs. Sinclair thought, "He has no sympathy; still, I would give way in anything less important, but where my children are concerned I am adamant."

Adamant may be, and no doubt is a very good and necessary thing in its place, still you would have said that if children could be spoiled Mrs. Sinclair was the woman to do it; but though treatment is much, the material to be treated is more.

When Mr. Gilbert resumed his duties he found his highest class decimated. James Raeburn was gone, Peter Veitch was away, Tom Smith was at an academy in Eastburgh, and John Johnston, the dux of the school, had entered a lawyer's office in that city, while—unkindest cut of all—Tom Sinclair was reserved for private teaching. Mr. Gilbert's son kept the top of the class, but it was a small honor to be at the top of a row of mediocrities. The schoolmaster's eyebrows looked bushier, and the pendulous under-lip hung heavier, and his feelings betrayed themselves to the scholars in—to them—flashes of unaccountable anger, and he went back to his house feeling himself an injured man. "To think," he said to himself, "that Raeburn should be making thousands a year while I drudge on here for a paltry pittance, and even the opportunity of drudging seems fast disappearing!"

"Well," said Mrs. Gilbert cheerily, as he came in, "the children tell me the school has not gathered fully yet."

"Gathered—no! and the question is, Will it ever gather?"

"It has always gathered yet, and there seems no reason why it should not gather this year as usual."

"Do you know that Mrs. Sinclair has not sent back her children?"

"Yes; but the loss is hers, not ours. That she should fail to appreciate your abilities does not surprise me."

"Oh, her judgment goes for nothing, true enough; but you can't make the general public comprehend that, and it is a slur on my reputation."

"Which your reputation can stand triumphantly."

"Well, well, Mary, I can only hope that your son may be more successful in life than his father has been."

Mrs. Gilbert declared herself perfectly satisfied with her husband's measure of success, which was true, although, as he was not satisfied with it, many times she wished it had been greater.

Mrs. Sinclair secured her tutor, and the evening before he was expected she took an opportunity of saying a word to her children on the subject. They were in the dining-room, and Mr. Sinclair was standing in one of the windows with his hands in his pockets looking out.

"Now, my dears," she said, "you know we begin a new era to-morrow. Mr. Doubleday comes—"

"What a name for Tom!" cried Bell. "I could stand a doubleday now and then, but poor Tom! Perhaps, though, it may sometimes be read a doubleholiday."

Mrs. Sinclair would have enjoyed her daughter's pun more if it had not been at her son's expense.

"Well, I want to speak to you for a little," she said. "What do you think is my chief earthly wish?" pausing for an answer.

"That papa were alive," said Effie.

"That Tom may be a great man," said Bell.

Tom's coming greatness at this moment wrapped itself in silence.

"Tom, my boy," his mother asked, "have you nothing to say?"

"No," was Tom's answer.

"Effie, my dear, to wish that your papa were alive is to wish what is impossible; to wish that Tom may may be a great man is to wish what is possible enough; but my chief wish for you all three is your welfare. In getting a tutor I have consulted that before everything. The young man who is coming is poor, of course, but you must not think less of him for that; and as he can have seen nothing of society, his manners may be awkward, but I don't desire you to copy them. He is a good scholar, and all I want you to do is to attend faithfully to your lessons, and treat your teacher as your equal."

"As their superior, you mean?" said Mr. Sinclair from his window.

"Yes, children, remember he is your superior in age, and he knows more than you."

"And it is possible he may turn out a great man some day," said Mr. Sinclair.

"If he does, Tom," said Mrs. Sinclair, using the spur gently, "he has begun in very disadvantageous circumstances compared with you."

"I don't want to be a great man," said Tom.

"You won't be disappointed, I suspect," thought Mr. Sinclair.

"Tom, my son," said his mother, "that very speech shows greatness. You can't help it."

"If I can be great without helping it, I'm willing," said Tom.

"Goodness, Tom!" said Bell, "are you to be the Great Sinclair? Mamma, are there any dormant peerages in our line?"

"Really I don't know, Bell."

"I know," said Mr. Sinclair.

"And are there any?"

"Yes; they are all dormant together."

"Tom, you must waken them," said Bell.

"Be quiet, Bell," said Tom. "I tell you I don't want to be great."

"But if you can't help it—Thomas Sinclair, Earl of Quixstar."

"That will do, Bell," said her mother; " don't tease."

Next day, when the tutor's chariot wheels were heard approaching, Bell and Effie ensconced themselves in the windows behind the curtains to get a glimpse of the coming man. Tom, true to his great philosophizing nature, was lying on the sofa, the current of his existence no way ruffled.

Mrs. Sinclair entered with Mr. Doubleday, and introduced him to his future pupils. He was not tall, and he was thin; a downy film was on his chin and upper lip, although he looked old enough to have grown a heavier crop; the corners of his mouth were turned up a little on his cheeks, which gave it a crescent shape, the effect of which was peculiar, and he had no forehead to speak of, or if he had, it was hidden by the hair growing far down on it, and then standing sheer up like the scrubby verdure on the side of a steep hill. Nor was this exterior lighted up as it ought to have been by the soul within; on the contrary, his face might have been that of a sheep, for all you could read in it. Perhaps the soul found it difficult to get up an effective illumination through the small, dim, short-sighted eyes that served it for windows.

"All the tutors I have read of," thought Bell, "had young ladies falling in love with them; it will be a very long time before any one falls in love with our tutor. I never saw such a comical mouth; it is like the pictures I have seen of elves."

Nor had Mr. Doubleday "an elegant manner and an engaging address." Even Mrs. Sinclair's mind misgave her, notwithstanding he had been so highly recommended. Hitherto she had striven to keep her children unspotted from the vulgar, and here, by her own arrangement, was a man sent into her house apparently to defeat her efforts, and it was vexatious, but being her own arrangement she could not immediately quarrel with it. If Mr. Doubleday were merely awkward, she trusted to her own influence to mould his manners, and she set herself to do it—to put him at his ease, as she thought; the truth being that Mr. Doubleday could have stood before kings perfectly at his ease, not from an excess of assurance, but of simplicity. He was a curious being. After he had been some time in the house, Maddy pronounced, as her verdict on him, " that it was surprising what he had, and what he hadna,"—an oracular utterance, which might be applied to most people. So far as appeared on the surface, what he had was an aptitude to teach, and a child-like unworldliness; what he had not was a capacity for putting his best foot foremost; consequently you will not expect to hear that he was ever Prime Minister or commanded the Channel Fleet, or in any shape often or ever saw his name in the newspapers, Maddy Fairgrieve's greatometer. . He felt annoyed, as an unreasoning animal may do by a fly creeping on some part of its body which it can reach neither with tongue nor tail, at Mrs. Sinclair's efforts to mould his manners, and he generally withdrew to his own room, guided by the same kind of instinct as leads the animal to take refuge in the water.

By diligent and continuous hammering, as the months slipped by Mr. Doubleday began to elicit sparks from Tom's latent intellect, and even to make him take pleasure in his lessons; with the girls he had no difficulty—they were not stupid by any means, and they were easily managed. Besides, their mamma kept dropping in his ear that she did not wish them made learned women;

he was to lend his efforts to make them generally intelligent, that they might be able to converse well and agreeably. It was hard to ask Mr. Doubleday to put the roof on a building for which he was not to lay any secure foundation, and judging from his own powers in this line he was not very likely to do it; but Mrs. Sinclair trusted a good deal to herself on the point. The likelihood was that her children would inherit a conversational gift—at least they were not likely to be infected with it by Mr. Doubleday. He was rather a silent person; he did not get very intimate with any one; nobody ever heard him say a word of his prospects, his retrospects, his parents or relations, if he had any; even the place of his birth was unknown. Mrs. Sinclair had put him into the prophet's chamber—the minor prophets' chamber, a small room which overlooked the stable-yard, but he was not sensitive to affronts—not that there was anything creeping or abject about him, but he did not notice them; it never occurred to him that he was not in the best room of the house; it was as natural for him never to think of himself as it was for Mr. Gilbert to be always thinking of himself.

There was one thing about the tutor that worried Mrs. Sinclair most particularly, and that was his dress. She said to her brother-in-law, " I'm sure it is strange where annoyances come from—there's Mr. Doubleday, he's a good teacher, and if he is no acquisition in the house he gives no trouble, but he dresses like a scarecrow."

" Does he? I have not noticed it."

" Like a scarecrow; and he went to the shoemaker's, it seems, with an old shoe in each pocket to get them mended, and the servants are laughing at him; and I don't wonder. It is a pity he has so little common sense."

"If Sir Richard Cranstoun had taken his shoes to the shoemaker you would only have thought him eccentric."

"Yes, if Sir Richard had done it, which is impossible. And, thinking he might be short of money, I paid him a quarter's salary in advance, and spoke to him about dressing better."

"You spoke to him about it! I could not have done that."

"I thought it a duty."

"You don't know what the lad may have to do with his money."

"I know that his first duty is to make himself look respectable. Why, people will say I don't pay him sufficiently."

"But if you do, you don't need to care what people say."

"But I care, and if I see it necessary I'll speak to Mr. Doubleday again. If people are not respectable they will not get respect."

"Well, they can want it; that kind of it may not be the breath of his nostrils; he won't perish."

"If people are to be in this world they must mind appearances."

"I don't see the *must*."

"But I see it very distinctly.—There's my friend Miss Raeburn coming in; I am very glad.—Now, Miss Raeburn," she said, after the usual salutations were over, "What do you think of Mr. Doubleday when you see him? do you not feel inclined to pity him?"

"I feel inclined to pity a great many people—not him particularly. I think he enjoys life. I watched him a good while one day. He and I were walking the same road; he did not notice me; he was kicking a small stone before him; sometimes he spoke to himself, sometimes smiled, and always kept sight of the stone—following it and giving it a kick farther on."

"Do you think he can be crazy?" asked Mrs. Sinclair anxiously.

"Not a bit. I think his mind was away in some vague happy reverie, and kicking the stone was a kind of unconscious effervescence of his mood. No, I don't think he is to be pitied."

"But he wears shabby clothes, I am told," said Mr. Sinclair.

"Oh, but that does not disturb him, and they are in keeping; Mr. Doubleday dressed up would not be Mr. Doubleday. No, no, the old clothes don't interfere with his enjoyment."

"But they interfere with mine," said Mrs. Sinclair; "it's all very well for you, who are not responsible, and for Mr. Sinclair, who does not see; but I both see and feel, and if he is to be here he must dress better; I can't have him going about like a beggar. How would you like, Miss Raeburn, a member of your household going about an object of pity? How would you like to be pitied yourself, for instance?"

"I don't in the least doubt that I am pitied, but as I pity a lot of people, I can't in reason object to being pitied, and it does me no harm."

"It ought to do you good," said Mr. Sinclair.

"Perhaps it does," rejoined Miss Raeburn.

"And what do you think you are pitied for?" asked Mrs. Sinclair; "for being a single woman? I assure you I have known single women who were highly respected and most useful in their circle, and when they conduct themselves well, people don't laugh at them."

"But I don't object to being laughed at, Mrs. Sinclair," said Miss Raeburn. "If I could in any way add to the enjoyment of my fellow-creatures I would feel that I had not lived in vain; besides, it's a diversion I often indulge in myself, laughing at people—mostly in my sleeve, it is true, and really I can't help it."

"Now, Mrs. Sinclair," said her brother-in-law, "see the advantage of being strong-minded. Miss Raeburn can stand either pity or laughter."

"Well, I am not strong-minded, very far from it, and it is well for you, Miss Raeburn, that you are; but, excepting always my great bereavement, there is nothing any one can pity me for, and far less that they could laugh at."

"It is a mercy," said Miss Raeburn, "that those that need the armor have it, and that those who haven't it don't need it."

CHAPTER XVI.

It was generally thought and said that Mr. Sinclair had been a very active business man, but there is reason to doubt that. A genuine business man in ordinary health does not at fifty retire to lead a sort of demi-idle, demi-student life in a country place. He had been the head of a large and flourishing business, but, like Queen Elizabeth, his merit had probably consisted more in knowing when he had good servants and letting them do the work, than in doing it himself; and when he abdicated, he likely followed the bent of his taste. But though he liked retirement and his own sitting-room very well, it is not necessary to suppose that he could not enjoy the company of such a lady as Miss Raeburn, or the contrast between her and his sister-in-law—quite the contrary; he had even a romantic vein in him, which cropped to the surface occasionally, and might have been worked with advantage if there had been any one to work it.

"Well, Mr. Doubleday," he said, as the tutor entered, followed shortly by his young friends; "have you got the labors of the day over?"

"Yes, sir," he said, taking out a fat overgrown silver watch and looking at it; "it's past six o'clock."

"I'm sure it is," said Mr. Sinclair.

"Labors of the day!" Mrs. Sinclair said.

"I trust you and the dear children consider them pleasures."

"I don't know. I try to make it labor both to them and to myself."

"Do I understand you aright?" asked Mrs. Sinclair.

"I don't know, ma'am."

"You said you tried to make the children's lessons labor to them?"

"Yes."

Mrs. Sinclair was dumb.

"And do you find they like it?" asked Mr. Sinclair.

"I find they don't like it," said Mr. Doubleday; "hard work is part of the curse."

"Mr. Doubleday!" cried Mrs. Sinclair.

"But," said Mr. Doubleday, "there is goodness in it. Hard work is good for a fallen race. Few people learn anything that is worth learning easily."

"But my children are clever, and learn easily. They need not work hard."

"The girls are quick, the boy is dull," said the tutor.

"Really, Mr. Doubleday, I never heard any one say that before. You must be taking a wrong method with Tom. Although I am the boy's mother, I can't help seeing his abilities; they may not be quite on the surface—"

"No, ma'am; not quite on the surface, but I don't despair of making something of him, although it will be uphill work for a time."

Now this might be—and taking fallen human nature into account, like Mr. Doubleday, probably it was—fun to Miss Raeburn and Mr. Sinclair, but it was death to Mrs. Sinclair; so much so, that she lost sight of the shabby clothes in the tremendous and peculiar enormity of hearing Tom stigmatized as dull. But think of Mr. Doubleday with his personal appearance, his unfortunate dress, and his atrocious truthfulness—only the possession of the intellect of an archangel could enable him to force a path in this world. And Mrs. Sinclair, although she was perpetually blundering—good-naturedly, it is true—on the weak points of others, became instantly alive when she herself was operated on in any vital part, in which she is not by any means singular.

"Well, but, Mr. Doubleday," said Miss Raeburn, "Tom will waken up; boys generally do waken up after a while."

"He may want a little rousing," said his mother; "but you never made a greater mistake, Mr. Doubleday, than when you called him dull."

"He does not get time to be roused," said Mr. Sinclair, who saw the tutor's dismissal casting its shadow before, and wished to prevent it. "He is never long enough with any one teacher to get into a system. I don't wonder he is dull."

"Oh, Adam! how can you be so cruel, when you must have seen how I have striven to do the best I can for these fatherless children, and know what sleepless nights I have, thinking of Tom's future."

"His present is of more consequence meantime," said Mr. Sinclair.

"That's unfeeling enough," thought Miss Raeburn, but she did not know that Mrs. Sinclair's pathos came in so often as to have lost a good deal of its effect.

"So far as I have seen," said Mr. Doubleday, "he has no particular bent in any direction, but he is not likely to do much harm in the world. I have known boys who were positively vicious."

Poor Mr. Doubleday! He did not know that truth, or what may be supposed to be truth, had better sometimes be left at the bottom of its well.

Aught of evil that had gathered was dispersed however by the entrance of the children, and after tea Mr. Doubleday went to his own room, not to chew the cud of offended dignity, as the genus tutor is apt to do, but to get on with the process of making himself a dungeon of knowledge.

"That man certainly has a crack," said Mrs. Sinclair, when the door closed after his exit.

"Cracked or not," said Mr. Sinclair, "I would advise you not to think of another change."

"He has not been brought up at a court, that's one thing easily seen," remarked Miss Raeburn.

"I doubt I have been unfortunate," Mrs. Sinclair said; "but I can hardly think of dismissing him immediately."

"Don't mamma," said Bell; "we all like him. Only this forenoon there was a button hanging off his coat, and I said I would sew it on; you should have seen how grateful he was; I was ashamed it was such a trifle. When I do a thing of that kind for Tom, I am glad to get off without a scolding for not doing it right."

"Clever," said Mrs. Sinclair after Mr. Doubleday's young friends had left the room. "Mr. Doubleday says the girls are clever; I hope they are not too clever; clever women are often disagreeable—men don't like them."

"Don't they?" said Miss Raeburn.

"No, they don't; you must have heard that surely, Miss Raeburn?"

"I was not aware; you see my experience is not wide, and not being clever myself I can't say."

"Perhaps you would give us your opinion, Adam?" said Mrs. Sinclair.

"Well, when I have been persecuted by dulness, I have thought the opposite quality might be a good change, but, like Miss Raeburn, my experience is not wide."

" Far too narrow, and, I doubt, not very fortunate, or you would think more of women than you do. Do you know, Miss Raeburn, Adam thinks women quite inferior to men; but I have hopes of converting him yet."

" You won't," said Miss Raeburn. " Mr. Sinclair, like me, has been brought up in that faith, and it goes with his grain; it goes against mine, and yet I have not been able to shake it off; it's a superstition I hardly expect to be able to shed before I die, although reason and observation are all against it."

" Perhaps, if I have been unfortunate in my feminine acquaintance, you may have been in your masculine, Miss Raeburn?" said Mr. Sinclair.

" Well, I have never come across any of the dozen representative men of the age, still I cling to the superstition, because it is a rest even to think of a lesser providence from whom you can get a certain sound when you are in perplexity, even though you find the oracle—not dumb, far from it—but fallible, wonderfully fallible."

" Do you take advice often, Miss Raeburn?" asked Mr. Sinclair.

" That's my weakness, Mr. Sinclair. I always take advice when I think it good, and I often ask it, for I like to give pleasure. You can't please a man more than by asking his advice, except by taking it."

" How does he feel when you don't take it?"

" Like a man, I hope."

" He would need all his manhood to bear him up. I hope you'll not try me so cruelly, Miss Raeburn."

" When I ask you for advice, Mr. Sinclair, all you have you to say is, that you won't give it."

"Would that not be rude?"

"Well, you can say, 'I'm not a bit more capable of advising you than you are of advising yourself, Miss Raeburn.'"

"But if I did not think that?"

"Then you must either be rude, or give it and take the consequences; a little affliction might be good for you."

"I'm sure of it," cried Mrs. Sinclair, who caught the last words. "If, for instance, Adam, you had married and lost your wife, you would have been so improved—you have no idea. My husband used to say that; he used to say to me, 'If I had not had you, my dear, I might have grown as curt and dry as Adam.'"

Miss Raeburn could not help laughing. "Quite true, Miss Raeburn, I assure you," said Mrs. Sinclair.

"Am I curt and dry?" asked Mr. Sinclair.

"There now," said Mrs. Sinclair; "that's how people get into peculiar habits and ways, and don't know it, if they have no one to tell them; that's where a wife would have been so useful to you."

"But you said I was to lose her?"

"But you would not have lost her influence. I'm always thinking what would have pleased Mr. Sinclair, and then I can sympathize not only with all women who have husbands, but with all who have lost them."

"You can give pity also to those who never had them?" said Miss Raeburn.

"Quite so," said Mrs. Sinclair, "experience widens one's sympathies in a way you would not believe."

"In a way one would not believe—that's true, I am sure," thought Mr. Sinclair.

"Adam stayed longer with us to-night than he usually does, Miss Raeburn," said Mrs. Sinclair, when her visitor was about departing. " I think he enjoys your company; don't be long in coming back. I am sure if he were to marry a suitable elderly lady I would be too happy. Now that we are here he does not need to do it for the sake of comfort—he could not be more comfortable; but, do you know, I used to be haunted by the notion that he would marry a servant some day. Now don't be long in coming back."

" Thank you; no, I won't; but you must bring Mr. Sinclair to see me; he can't enjoy my company more than I do his and yours," and they shook hands, Miss Raeburn thinking, " Well, she is a good-natured goose after all, and he can't be ill-natured, or he would not have asked her to stay."

CHAPTER XVII.

It was true that Mr. Sinclair did not generally linger long in the family sitting-room, but occasionally, especially if it chanced to be a wet day, he remained a considerable time, walking up and down, a sort of peripatetic philosopher, varying his march by stopping to look out from the windows or to speak. Luckily there was no individual with finely strung nerves to be annoyed by the incessant motion and vibration, but neither was there any one to think that there was music in his footstep; it was merely "my uncle," or "my brother-in-law," who had a habit of walking in-doors.

One wet day Bell was sitting at the table working busily, her very heart in her work, which was some sort of millinery. As her uncle passed and repassed she noticed him look at her, and without thinking, but with a wish for sympathy, she held up a spray of artificial flowers to him and said, "Isn't that pretty?" He glanced first at the flowers, then at her, and said, "Poor thing!" and resumed his walk and the thread of his meditations. Bell went on arranging the flowers in her hat or bonnet, or whatever it was, while the three parts of pity and one of contempt that had made up her uncle's look and tone as he said "Poor thing!" entered her very soul and killed her happiness outright. However Miss Raeburn might enjoy it, Bell, in common with her mother, did not like to be pitied. She thought, "Uncle thinks me silly, but I'm not, and I won't be pitied; I'll get Mr. Doubleday to teach me mathematics and other things, and I'll work. Uncle thinks I care for nothing but my bonnet, but he'll see that I'm not altogether silly."

A whole course of lectures on the higher education could not have roused or quickened a mind so much as these two words of Mr. Sinclair's, "Poor thing!" But no thanks to him. A man who can't enjoy seeing a girl in her teens touching up her dress, and doing it with buoyancy and spirit for the mere unconscious happiness of seeing a very bright thing—herself—look brighter, you are sure not only misses that pleasure, but he misses many others that lie about for the picking up, and he is to be pitied, only that what people don't know of they don't miss; still, one can't help hoping that whether he knew it or not, Mr. Sinclair enjoyed his walk more with Bell and her finery beside him than if the room had been empty. Bell went on with her work; she was born a milliner, and she worked the more quickly for the sting she had got. Mr. Sinclair saw it, and he thought, "She is quite pleased with that trumpery; her soul is in it;" and again he pitied her, but being her nature—feminine nature—there was no help for it. But it was not her nature, only a very small part of it, appropriate to the short season it was meant to last, and the fleeting character of it might have drawn out his sympathy. From being a pleasure, dress will become a duty, a bore, a drag, and finally a burden, to be gladly laid down when the mortal shall put on immortality.

Yet Miss Raeburn thought a good deal might have been made of Mr. Sinclair had he been taken in time, as Mrs. Sinclair had suggested, and his sympathies gradually and naturally developed; and she was right, probably; if Bell had been his own daughter, for instance, he might have understood her better—for love, like death, carries a torch into hidden places.

Effie was not more fortunate in gaining her uncle's approbation than her sister. Not that she placed her delight in ribbons and flowers—far from it; but she read continually, and her reading was of a kind as pitiable in Mr. Sinclair's eyes as Bell's millinery. Did he expect that she was to take to the masterpieces of literature as a duck to the water? It would have been melancholy if she had, but there was no fear of it; she read endless tales, and she did more—she wrote tales, which she read only to her sister. Bell thought she copied them, but she said they were her own, which they were, so far as a talent for imitation and a good memory would permit.

As for Tom, his uncle did not expect much from him. If he kept quietly along the well-trodden middle way he would verify his relative's highest hopes.

A mother with great expectations, an uncle with very moderate expectations, and a tutor who never formed expectations of any kind, were probably complementary to each other, and made circumstances more advantageous to these young people than they on the surface appeared.

Bell did not find her sister as enthusiastic for more and deeper studies as herself, but she drew Effie into her plans, and got her mother's consent likewise. "If you really want to study these things, my child," said Mrs. Sinclair, "you may. You know I am apt to be too indulgent; not that it will cost me anything, for Mr. Doubleday's salary is the same whatever he teaches, but I daresay," and she brightened good-naturedly as the idea occurred to her, "as he'll have more trouble, I'll give him more money, and take the opportunity of speaking to him about his dress again,—he really needs a word even yet." And Mrs. Sinclair gave him this word with immense tact, as she thought, really with blundering good-nature. But Mr. Doubleday's feelings lay deep; she had not the power to reach them; and it was a mercy,—the poor man had crooks enough in his lot without a set of nerves on the surface for any stray fingers to play on, like telegraph-wires, by which a false agonizing message may be sent either from thoughtlessness or wickedness at any time.

"I'm afraid, Mr. Doubleday, we'll give you a good deal of trouble," said Bell, when they began the new curriculum.

"Yes," said Mr. Doubleday.

"I hope you'll not grudge it very much?"

"No; I wanted to do this at first, but your mother objected, and Mr. Sinclair said it would be of no use."

"It won't do us any harm, will it, Mr. Doubleday?" asked Bell.

"Harm! the getting of knowledge is ecstasy, pure ecstasy. Many a time I wish I could throw off my body as I do the clothes your mother bothers me about—that I might burst into infinity and know even as I am known."

The girls looked at him. "You mean," said Effie, "that you wish to die?"

"No, not till it is God's will. But never suppose it is no use learning; the more you learn, you will feel better and humbler and happier—at least I have found it so."

"But are people who know a great deal not proud of it?" asked Effie.

"The more people know, the better they see how ignorant they are.—Come, we must begin; it is a slow process, but I'll do my best not to tire you."

"Conic Sections," said Bell; "what are Conic Sections?"

"You know the figure of a cone—a fir-top?" said Mr. Doubleday.

"Yes, oh yes!"

'Well,"—and he proceeded to explain the mystery. Bell followed him closely. "I understand that," she said, "that's very plain; and that's the first lesson in mathematics, is it?"

"The first!" said Mr. Doubleday, smiling, "no, not the first."

"But you think I'll be able to learn mathematics, do you?"

"If you take trouble."

Bell felt when she had mastered her lesson a satisfaction which perhaps came within a hundred miles of Mr. Doubleday's pure ecstasy, and gave her some glimmering of the possibility of it. Mr. Sinclair had unwittingly shifted her mental soil a little, and behold, what farmers know as an unsown crop appeared— alongside millinery came up mathematics. A pupil who could and did sew on his buttons, and made an effort to sympathize with his thirst for knowledge, and put her lips to the same chalice to sip as she was capable, was a dangerous proximity, or would have been for an ordinary tutor, but Mr. Doubleday was not susceptible.

CHAPTER XVIII.

MRS. SINCLAIR was correct in her opinion that people would think she had got in Mr. Doubleday a bargain. The Smiths, the clever family that has been mentioned, said there was an unmistakable sensation of Smike about him, which was an exaggeration, but clever people are always under a temptation to exaggerate.

The Smiths' house bore some general resemblance to Old Battle House, and Mr. Doubleday being occasionally rather absent-minded, one day walked straight in, and sat down in a room where two Misses Smith were at work in one of the windows. The Misses Smith knew their man, and saw the mistake instantly, but they said nothing, and Mr. Doubleday meditated for half an hour or so, and then asked, " What time is dinner to be to-day ? " " It won't be for two hours yet," Miss Smith answered. " Oh," said he, " there's company," and he rose with the view of summoning his pupils to the schoolroom. Looking from a window as he passed, he suddenly became aware that he saw a hedge where no hedge should be, then he glanced round the room and said, " I haven't—have I come into the wrong house ?—I beg pardon, ladies," and with a very red face he made a hurried exit. This was the bones of the story, but the Misses Smith could not resist dressing it up in very funny flesh and blood—the last instance of absence of mind, and having happened in their own experience it was the more effective.

These young ladies, as a matter of course, never spoke of Mr. Doubleday under any other name than "Smike." Bestowing nicknames was a favorite branch of the family cleverness, and it is certain a happy nickname can hardly be the produce of dull brains; but they were only in the second class of merit, they took names made to their hands, but they affixed them cleverly, as when they called the chief butcher of the place —the father of the boy who was dux at the examination—a man of very bland and smooth manners, who could persuade you that fat was lean, " Old Bloody Politeful,"—also happily borrowed from a work of fiction.

On another occasion Mr. Doubleday made the same blunder, but this time he did not fall among thorns. He sauntered into the schoolmaster's dwelling; it was not at all like Old Battle House, but it was near it, and he innocently turned in at the one gate instead of the other, and was kindly received by Mrs. Gilbert, and made aware of his mistake. " But don't go, Mr. Doubleday," she said; " we'll be very glad to make your acquaintance—sit down."

Mr. Gilbert came in, and flung himself wearily into a chair; he had been acquainted with Mr. Doubleday for some time, and was not on ceremony.

" Well, Mr. Doubleday," he said, " if I had my days to begin again, I would not be a schoolmaster."

" Do you not like teaching? To me there is no pleasure like communicating knowledge, except acquiring it; I like to see a child's eye kindle."

" And how many of them kindle?" asked Mr. Gilbert. " But it's not the teaching I object to, it's the perpetual worry; you're every one's drudge. Just this forenoon Kennedy came in with his advice and interference; he might have been better employed on a Saturday. To-morrow he'll give us a collection of commonplaces, read in a drawling tone. Can't the man speak in the pulpit as he does elsewhere? how would he like if I were to call on him on Monday and give him my candid opinion of his performance?"

"If you thought it would benefit him, you should do it," said Mr. Doubleday.

"Whether it would benefit him or not, it would make the place too hot for me," said Mr. Gilbert.

"Not if Mr. Kennedy is of the right spirit. But you could leave the place."

"I would need to know where I was going first; a man who has given hostages to fortune in the shape of a wife and family must think what he is about."

"True so far," said Mr. Doubleday. "I thought Kennedy a good-natured man."

"So he is, when he gets everything his own way."

"This," said Mrs. Gilbert, as John entered, "is our only son," and she said, with not a little pride—he was growing a tall fine-looking lad—" And our family problem just now is what to do with him."

"We'll not make him a schoolmaster,—that's one thing clear at least," said his father.

"He might be anything," said Mr. Doubleday simply, and with undisguised admiration at John's goodly exterior.

"It's not so easy being anything, sir," said John, sitting down as if he were going to stay and listen deferentially to his elders; but he soon disappeared.

The two teachers talked about the details of their profession, and when Mr. Doubleday left both Mr. and Mrs. Gilbert went with him to the gate of Old Battle House. It was a still December night, with a heavenful of big burnished stars shining out of it. None of

these three were in love with nature; they liked her,—
Mr. Doubleday as far as his short-sightedness let him
see her beauties, Mrs. Gilbert with as much love as she
could spare from her children, and Mr. Gilbert liked her
in his garden among thriving vegetables and trim flowerbeds. It was as much as you could expect. The dozen
representative men of the age that Miss Raeburn spoke
of may love and pursue a dozen objects passionately
and successfully, but ordinary people are restricted to
narrower limits.

"How beautiful!" said Mrs. Gilbert.

"Grand," said Mr. Doubleday.

"Very fine," said Mr. Gilbert.

When you show your carte to any one, you know
at once, if you have eyes in your head, whether it is
being looked at with the gaze of love, or friendly interest, or mere curiosity, or indifference; so nature knows
her lovers right well too, and rewards them accordingly.
To what seems a very poor life she will give a depth
and height of enjoyment, and now and then a steeping
in bliss which other people have no idea of, and even
these three persons with their mild and, considering the
occasion, commonplace remarks, were unconsciously led
out of the grooves in which they daily ran more or less
smoothly, as they stood in the deep silence, into which
there entered in subdued and reverent mood the murmur of the river. Only two persons in Quixstar were
having a very close interview with the stars that night,
one a Mr. Singleton, brother to Lady Cranstoun, who
was at this time living, or rather dying, at Cranstoun
Hall; he had got himself seated at a window, and the
lights in his room put out, and he gazed and gazed till
death and the grave he was so near were shut from his
sight, and he lost himself in life and immortality; and

Miss Raeburn, who with a shawl round her shoulders and another on her head, was out on a balcony on the roof of her house. Miss Raeburn never told her love of nature, and unless you had been very intimate with her you would not have guessed it; but here she was, worshipping the heavenly bodies with all her might. Her servant came up to say that Mr. Kennedy had called. "My stars!" cried Miss Raeburn, looking up, "has he—well, ask him to come here."

Mr. Kennedy ascended; he had often been on the balcony on a summer's day, but not before on a winter night.

"Are you not afraid to risk your valuable health, Miss Raeburn?" he asked.

"You don't see, coming out from the light; but I am glad for the occasion," she said, "and on a night such as this I like to shake hands with David."

"David who?" asked Mr. Kennedy.

"David Jesse, perhaps—I'm not sure of his surname. I hope I am not irreverent, the King and Psalmist I mean."

"Ah!" said Mr. Kennedy; "the stars were finer in Palestine than here, I believe."

"These are quite fine enough for me," said she.

"Speaking of stars puts me in mind,—I was calling on Peter Veitch's wife as I came along; when she was at the door with me she looked up and said, 'There's the stars, puir things; I wonder if they are shining on oor Peter?' Curious notion of the woman to pity the stars."

"Ah, when Mrs. Veitch thinks of Peter she is touched with compassion for all creation."

"They've had a letter from the boy—better than his class usually write; it does not come hoping they are well, as it leaves him at present."

"Mr. Kennedy, that must be a happy form of expression, or it would not have recommended itself to such a mass of our fellow-creatures, or survived so long. I wonder who used it first. It is something to have sent a sentence rolling so far and wide. But I hope Peter's letter did not leave him ill, at least?"

"Oh, no; he's well enough; his mother will be too glad to let you see it; poor body, she believes every one as interested in Peter as she is?"

"It is a fine faith, don't you think?"

"Well, it pleases her, but it is apt to bore other people."

"That's not the way it affects me. Just the last day I was in Eastburgh, a young man I had only seen once or twice before, came up to me, and grasping my hand very firmly, said, 'Miss Raeburn, you have heard of my sister's death?' He never doubted my sympathy, and his faith roused my feelings nearly as much as his sorrow. As I walked on after he had emptied out all his grief, I thought, 'In time you'll learn to hide your sorrows. You won't believe that the feelings of every chance acquaintance beat in unison with yours;' but some people, Mr. Kennedy, keep that faith to the last, and it is the genius of the heart—it is more, it is the kernel of Christ's religion."

"You are enthusiastic, Miss Raeburn, but if you go about the world believing every one as interested in your affairs as you are, the chance is that you are a bore or a fool, or both."

"Then the fools have the best of it, Mr. Kennedy; for it is a glorious faith."

"In a delusion. You must take people as they are in this world, Miss Raeburn."

"Oh, try to make them better, and genuine sympathy will do much towards that."

" Give the mass of people plenty to eat and drink—that's the genuine sympathy they care for; and in this parish they are pretty well seen to."

" Yes; I often feel thankful for that, that nobody round us need be in actual want."

" No; our charities are well organized. Lady Cranstoun's soup-kitchen does a great deal of good, especially at this season."

CHAPTER XIX.

Hearing of Peter's letter, Maddy Fairgrieve called on her friend Mrs. Veitch to ask the particulars.

"There's no muckle in't," Mrs. Veitch said, producing it from between the leaves of a Bible: "see, ye can read it if ye like."

Maddy glanced over it. "He was sick for a day or two, but is all right, and likes his business," was her summing up of its contents; "that's a' gude news."

"I dinna ken," said his mother; "if he hadna liket it he wad hae come hame again."

"Peter'll no hen though, or I'm mista'en. I was in asking for Nanny o' the Nose (this was an old woman who had come to Quixstar from a neighboring hamlet, called Friar's Nose, a name which probably echoed a popular witticism some two or three hundred years old), as I cam past. I heard she hadna been weel."

"What's wrang wi' Nanny, puir body?"

"She tell't me a' about it. She had gotten some o' Cranstoun's kail (the vulgar name for the article dispensed from her Ladyship's soup-kitchen); gude kail she said, but ye ken there's a gey twa three things boiled up among them, and she saw something sooming about in them that fairly upset her, and she hasna gotten the better o't yet. She says puir folk shouldna be nice, but she couldna help it."

"I ken the feeling," said Mrs. Veitch; "and sometimes ye're easier scomfished than others."

"That's true," said Maddy; "but I've kent folk that naething wad upset; no puir folk either. They were born without the sense o' scunner, and really it's an advantage, especially if ye're a puir body."

"Weel, I dinna ken," said Peter, who had been listening; "if folk hae a sense o' scunner, even if they hae naething else, they'll try to fecht up to something better. I was in Dixon's house the nicht wi' a message I had for him. His wife was making the parritch, and I saw a thing I never saw before—but women hae a talent for invention, there's nae disputing that: she laid seven messes o' parritch on the table. They hadna a dish in the house, except a jug without a handle the milk was in. The bairns were cried in, and stood round the table like a wheen swine round a trough. If they had a sense o' scunner, surely they couldna come to that."

"I never heard the like o' that," said Maddy; "how are the folk sae ill off?"

"They're no' ill off," said Peter; "there's six-and-thirty shillings gangs into the house every week that Dixon and his son like to work."

"I pity the woman," said Mrs. Veitch.

"Ye needna fash," said her husband; "the woman matches the men. She has visits frae three sets o' benevolent leddies, wi' as muckle gumption as that table; and she tells lees by the yard, and a' liker truth than the very truth itsel', and gets frae them a'. If shame and her were even acquént they've parted company for mony a day."

"I wad hae thae folk threshed," said Maddy, with righteous indignation; "ye can only mak' the like o' them feel through their skins."

"Weel, I canna say I approve o' flogging," said Peter Veitch; " but I wad not grudge it on them, if it wad mak' them ony better."

"It could hardly mak' them ony waur," said his wife; " think o' the like o' them lickin' up charity, and mony a gude body ill, ill off, and saying naething and getting as little. Eh! the warld's ill divided."

"Ay, gudewife; ye've gotten a nut to crack there that's broken stronger teeth than yours trying't, and it's no crackit yet, nor ever will be as lang as we're here."

"I saw Mr. Doubleday passing the day," said Mrs. Veitch, "as if he was bound for a journey. The bairns maun get the play on Saturday, Maddy?"

"Ay, except a wee while in the morning. He'll be away to Eastburgh posting a letter to his sweetheart," said Maddy.

"His sweetheart! preserve me, has he a sweetheart?"

"What for no?" said Peter.

"Weel, I dinna ken. Some way a body doesna think o' the like o' him ha'eing a sweetheart. Ye wad think it wad never come into his head."

"Sweetheart or no," said Maddy, "he gets letters often aneuch, but he never sends ony away frae this post-office, so I jalouse he taks the answers to Eastburgh. There's mair in him than ye wad think, and he's awful saving."

"He'll be ettling at furnishing a house by and by," said Mrs. Veitch.

"May be," said Maddy; "he wad be the better o' somebody to look after him; and if he has a sweetheart she'll be able to do that, for I'se warrant she did the courting, and it wadna be done in hints. It wad need to be as broad as it was lang before he wad ken what she was after."

"Hae ye been trying't, Maddy," asked Peter, "that ye're sae weel up to it?"

"What wad ye say, Peter? I dinna think but I wad be better at it than a gey wheen men I've seen try it. They are great gowks whiles. But I'm putting off my time. Gude-nicht wi' ye."

"Ye'll get the stars to see ye yont," said Mrs. Veitch to her visitor at the door.

"Ay," said Maddy; "they're looking as if they had a' been new rubbed up wi' soap and whitening."

Maddy's notion, from a housemaid's view, corroborated Shakspeare's. She thought the heavens inlaid with patines of bright gold, susceptible of extra lustre.

CHAPTER XX.

THE pen, like some creeping things, likes a rough surface to travel over, and this one is beginning to be of the opinion of a gentleman who alighted one midsummer for a fortnight in Quixstar. He thought life at Quixstar dreadfully slow. He was a London *littérateur* in want of rest, and he came to this locality seeking it, and did not find it. Poor creature, his taste was so vitiated by the whirl and rapidity of life in the great city, that instead of resting he grew restive, and from sheer force of habit and want of anything to do, he sat down and made " a paper" of Quixstar for the periodical with which he was connected. And it must be acknowledged he hit its points cleverly, viewed from his elevation. He stepped from an omnibus on to the chief street of the place, and there was great calm. Grass growing round the paving-stones gave the street the appearance of a fairies' burying-ground. You thought there was no population till an empty barrel being rolled along brought man, woman and child to every door and window. The shop-doors were mostly kept shut. He timidly opened one, not sure but that to force an entrance might be a particular insult, and was served with a princely appearance of antediluvian leisure. He found that only two magazines were known in Quixstar, and nobody read both. His own periodical was unheard of. (He thought this melancholy. Rather he should have exclaimed, " Oh, sensible people! Oh, blessed place!")

The early dinner parties and small evening parties got his good-natured quizzical notice. The enjoyments of Quixstar were mild; its quarrels a storm in a tea-cup. "Dulness, dulness," he said, "is the genius that broods over the place, but the people seem contented—amen. The minnow in a pool is contented, for it knows not of the whale amid the roar of Polar seas." Mr. Spencer, so he was named, depicted bits of Quixstar with his pencil as well as his pen. He put on canvas the bridge, and Peter Veitch's cottage beside it, with a cow standing near the door in a meditative mood. Peter watched the progress of the work. He liked to look at or hear of anything beyond his ken, and the artist entertained him with the glories and wonders of London.

"I warrant, sir," said Peter, "ye think London the ax'tree o' creation."

"You should pay it a visit, Mr. Veitch, and judge for yourself."

"Na, na; we hae nae time here for jauntin'," said Peter.

"Time!" said the artist; "I think time is the most plentiful commodity you have."

"It's no' a commodity," said Peter; "ye canna sell't."

"Can't you? If I give you work for a day, don't I buy your time?"

"You buy my labor, no' my time. If time could be sell'd, Mr. Singleton at the Ha' wadna be deein' at twenty-three, and Peter Reid living off the parish at ninety-seven."

"That wouldn't be selling time, it would be selling life."

"And what's life so far as this warld is concerned but time?" asked Peter.

"True, but few would sell it."

"I'm no sae sure o' that," said Peter. "Ye'll no say what folk'll do for siller, and it wad be a trade in high wages and light wark."

"Faust and the devil," said the sketcher.

"We have folk here that dinna believe in the devil," Peter remarked in answer to the name mentioned with which he was familiar; the first he had never heard.

"Ah, they think he is an allegory, do they?"

"Weel, allegory or no, the mischief has been done; sure aneuch it's nae allegory."

"What queer fish is that?" asked the painter as Mr. Doubleday passed, apparently unconscious of him and his occupation.

"Queer?" said Peter. "Ay, he does look whiles as if he had been eaten and spued again."

"Eaten and what?"

"Ye read your Bible, nae doubt, sir?" said Peter.

"Well—yes I do."

"And wi' the understanding, ye'll find spue in the Bible, and it means—"

"I see, I see; but who is the fellow?"

"He is the tutor at Old Battle House, an innocent, but a dungeon they say."

"Innocence and a dungeon," thought the southern, mystified by Peter's very provincial notes; "well, they have gone together before now. Where is Old Battle House?"

"The first big house on your left hand after ye cross the brig there. Ye should mak' a picture o' it. It would be grander than my auld biggin'."

"But not so suited to my purpose."

"Ye should ken best. But do ye no' think that the cow there," pointing to the sketch, "has a bit touch o' foun'er in her fore-legs?"

"Touch of what?"

"O' founder. She's a wee shaky in the fore-legs, is she no'?"

"You mean she is not standing correctly. I don't see that."

"Then it's a' richt, for ye're the best judge, nae doubt, or should be."

The artist was fully persuaded he was, and when he left Quixstar he was also fully persuaded he left behind him a benighted people—a people who, given an orange, would fail to suck it: they had life, and they made nothing of it. But, his opinion notwithstanding, wherever there are human beings hearts will beat and brains seethe, and as for a daily round, a jog-trot, where is the life that does not in time settle into that? who is there who does not feel himself bricked in by circumstances? Besides, the young fry of Quixstar had the liberty of making for the open sea if so minded, and many of them had scattered themselves over the world, but hitherto nothing very like a whale had reappeared. The knowledge of this, and of their own mediocre lot in life, did not, as Miss Raeburn sometimes remarked, prevent every succeeding generation of parents believing that their children were likely to do something great, "Not an unnatural, and I daresay a blessed blindness," she said to good old Mrs. Gilbert when that lady spoke to her of her grandnephew's coming departure to do something somewhere. The old lady thought that Miss Raeburn could not know anything about it, but she did not venture to say so; she never entered the lists with Miss Raeburn, who had a reputation for being "clever," and an unconscious (no doubt) trick of making people feel that she was not a dunce, for she was really humble, but always impatient of absurdity. Notwithstanding that her perceptive powers were a little opaque, Mrs. Gilbert frequently did not enjoy Miss Raeburn's cleverness, and as even the meritorious and laborious bee will sting if annoyed, if she had been heard to make the observation, "that any one might be clever who allowed themselves to say every impudent thing that came into their heads." What truth there is in that the reader may pick out for himself.

CHAPTER XXI.

CERTAINLY when Mr. Gilbert was in good spirits he foresaw great things for his son, and he had strong faith in him and them, but when desponding, when feeling that from no fault of his own he, a man of parts and ambition, was fixed to all appearance as schoolmaster of Quixstar for life, while men like Mr. Raeburn were carrying all before them, he wavered; but hope was still in the ascendant: he could not only brook the idea of being eclipsed by his son, but he could smile in glad anticipation of it.

John Gilbert had no particular vocation for anything, but he would have preferred being a gentleman, taking that word to mean a man who had plenty of money without working for it. That, however, he could not be, although he thought it hard. Why should he not have been born to wealth as well as the Cranstouns— the elder of whom would succeed his father, the younger having already inherited his uncle Mr. Singleton's fortune—or like the Raeburns? John had been educated solely by his father, and there was one lesson he had imbibed thoroughly, although it had only been given at odd times, and was not in the list of classes Mr. Gilbert taught, but it had fallen in good soil, and it was this—if people have not money, they are nothing. Not that Mr. Gilbert worshipped money, far from it. In most cases he looked down on rich men—looked down on them from a height. It was men of ability and character apart altogether from wealth and position that he held in esteem, but somehow or other his son gathered from his father the lesson that has been mentioned. He did not gather it from his mother. The dyer's hand gets subdued to what it works in; but there are in this world people—and it is a mighty privilege to know such—who can lie among the pots and yet appear like doves; not that there was anything about Mr. Gilbert that could actually smear, very far from that, but there was much that could corrode; yet the circumstances of Mrs. Gilbert's life had neither soured nor narrowed her nature, she could afford to esteem her rich neighbors as well as her poor ones.

John Gilbert's going away was not an era in Quixstar any more than Peter Veitch's had been, and it was less so in his father's house than Peter's had been, for he was only going to enter a merchant's office in Eastburgh, and was to come home every Saturday, therefore there were no set speeches, or tears, or even kisses,—the occasion was not too trying, and it was hopeful in the extreme.

Then Tom Sinclair began to get restive under Mr. Doubleday. He took his mother into his counsel, and told her "he had made up his mind what he was going to be, and he would need no more education. Latin and Greek were all nonsense, and people were beginning to see that. If Bell wanted to go on with Latin she might as well do that as nothing, which was what girls generally did, but he could not afford to lose more time."

"You're right there, Tom," said Bell; "I know what you want to be, and the sooner you begin the better."

"In what direction does your taste point, my son?" asked Mrs. Sinclair.

"I'm going to be a banker," said Tom.

"A banker, my boy! That is a line of life in which there is but small scope for ability."

"I don't know that," said Bell; "in emergencies bankers have been Prime Ministers—at least in France, and it's a wide field, Finance."

"But you would need to take care, Tom," said Effie, "or you might do mischief."

"And get into a biographical dictionary this way," said Bell: "'Sinclair, Thomas, a Scotchman, born of respectable parents, organized the great Quixstar Bubble Company, which brought ruin on thousands of his countrymen. Died abroad; date uncertain.'"

"Bell," said her mother, "that's carrying your joke a little too far.—But you'll think better of it, my boy, and we'll see what your uncle says."

"I've made up my mind," said Tom.

"It must be awfully monotonous, Tom," said Bell.

"It's mere mechanical work. You'll get no say in the management till your head is as bare as a turnip. I've been in various banks, and could see that. You would not need to dirty your hands, though, and they always have capital pens—quills that make it a treat to sign your name."

Effie said, "A bank clerk once told me that they have periodical burnings of bank-notes."

"Yes," said Tom; "the dirty ones that are withdrawn from circulation."

"Are you sure of that, Tom?" asked Bell. "Is it not done to teach the young men the fleeting and worthless nature of the article they work among."

"How will they feel when they are actually burning thousands of pounds?" said Effie.

"Like Cleopatra when she drank dissolved pearls, perhaps," said Bell.

"The notes are kept in by a grating," said Tom, "that there may be no mistake."

"Well, Tom," said Bell, "if you are determined, I'll give you a lot of thin paper which you can cut into squares, and a damp sponge to wet your finger and thumb, and you can begin to practise your business. It must take some practice to count notes so cleverly, and I wouldn't like you to be awkward among the rest."

"But Tom is not determined," said his mother. "I really think, my boy, it would be a burying of your talents to go into a bank. I would not by any means force your inclination, but I won't deny it will be a deep disappointment to me if you do, and we must consult your uncle."

"What do you want me to be, mother?" said Tom.

"I think, my boy, that we are bound to let our light shine in the world—that it is wrong to bury our talents. —But here comes your uncle, we'll hear what he says. Adam," she said, "my son has just been talking of his wish to begin life—to be doing something in the world, in short—"

"Tired of your lessons, Tom, are you?" said his uncle.

"What's the use of learning things I'll never need— wasting time!" said Tom.

"What do you wish to do?"

"I mean to be a banker."

"Then be a banker. I see nothing to hinder you."

"But, Adam, only think a moment. There is no scope for ability in banking."

"The less the better," said Mr. Sinclair.

"But it's a mere throwing away of Tom," urged Mrs. Sinclair. "If he had even gone to sea like the boy

Veitch, or studied for the bar like the butcher's boy, he might have made a name; but what can he do in a bank?"

"Peter Veitch had a taste for danger, and the boy Johnson may inherit a sweet persuasive tongue; but if Tom wants to spend his life counting money,—if it is his deliberate choice, let him have it. I don't think he will disgrace you."

"Disgrace me!" gasped Mrs. Sinclair.

"No; he is honest, and will be proof against temptation, I don't doubt."

"I am painfully disappointed, Tom," said his mother, after Mr. Sinclair left the room. "Your uncle has no idea of parental feeling. One would have thought he might have taken the place of a father to you all. If he had been capable of that he would have felt some natural ambition that your talents should not at least be buried. But it is only what I might have expected. Well, I'll consent that you try banking; you'll not like it, you'll feel your powers cramped; but it won't be too late to change, and it's gentlemanly, not like a trade, still—"

"Not like a trade, mamma!" said Bell; "it's the very root and essence of trade,—buying and selling money. But Tom won't have anything to do with that part of it; he'll only be a calculating-machine."

"Wisdom will die with Bell," said Tom.

"Quite so," said Bell.

When Bell went to the schoolroom, she said to Mr. Doubleday—

"Tom's going away!"

"Going away?"

"Yes. He's taken it into his head all of a sudden that he'll be a banker, and says he won't need any more lessons; and uncle says he can get him into a bank at Eastburgh at once."

Mr. Doubleday was at one of the windows cutting a quill, and said nothing for some minutes. Then he said—

"In that case I'll have to go away too, I suppose?"

"You would not think it worth while staying to teach girls only, would you?"

"Worth while?" he repeated, turning round.

"Yes," she said. "I wish you'd stay. Mamma speaks of sending us to a boarding-school; I hate the very idea of a boarding-school."

"Your mamma does not wish me to stay, then?"

"Mamma is good: say you'll stay, Mr. Doubleday, and I'll manage it."

"Stay?" he said. "I don't want to go—I'll never want to go."

"Then you must like being here; I wouldn't have thought it. What do you like it for?"

"I don't know—I really don't know."

"It must be the *tout ensemble* of the whole," said she laughing. "Do you not like your own home better?"

"No."

"But you have friends, haven't you?"

"Yes."

This was a topic on which Mr. Doubleday never enlarged, and Bell felt she had been thoughtless in touching on it. She feared his home and friends must not be very delightful, or he would speak more of them.

When this little conversation was repeated to Mrs. Sinclair, she said—

"He doesn't know what he likes to be here for? He might know that he never was as well treated in his life. Few people—very few, would have had the patience with him I have had; and as for your uncle, you would think he makes him of fully more importance than he does me. But I have got him to dress decently; and since you are so anxious, he may stay, although I consider myself foolish in indulging you so far."

Four of these Quixstar school-fellows were now in Eastburgh, living very innocently as yet, and one was sailing on the sea, and one was sleeping the long sleep in the churchyard at Ironburgh—a grand churchyard, where all kinds of absurdities were perpetrated in stones and shells, and flowers and words over the dead, and which on a summer Sunday was thronged by crowds in gay clothing, as if it were a fair. Did they go to mourn, or meditate, or what? A strange concourse of the living and the dead, enough to make a fastidious corpse yearn for a lone hillside and waving grass.

CHAPTER XXII.

Mrs. Sinclair accompanied her son to Eastburgh, and saw him settled in a way suited to his circumstances and prospects.

"Tom," she said, looking round the handsome rooms she had got for him, "I desire that you should be as comfortable as possible, and that you should cultivate good society. You have excellent introductions; and people should try to be acquainted with those above them rather than below—those who are better than themselves, and they are sure to improve both in mind and manners."

"But if a lot of fellows insist on improving themselves by sticking to me, what am I to do—that is, fellows below me?"

"You need not encourage them. There's no difficulty in that, Tom."

"Shake them off? And if the people better than me shake me off?"

"They won't do that, that's entirely different."

"I don't see it. I've read in books that we should always choose the best society. Pity the best society; it would need to strengthen its rails."

"Tom, I earnestly trust that with these good rooms, and your introductions, and the tastes I have tried to instil into you, you won't disappoint me in this, after I have yielded to all your wishes."

"Don't be frightened, mother. I won't need much society, and what I have won't be wicked—I promise that; but I'm not ambitious."

Mrs. Gilbert also went with her son, and handed him over to the care of a decent elderly woman she had long known, and with whom John declared he would get on famously.

"You won't feel dull, John, when you come in at night?" said his mother anxiously; "you'll only have five nights a week, and you can amuse yourself with a book."

"Dull! I don't know what dull means. No fear, I'll get on."

"And, John, I think I may trust you not to get into extravagant habits."

"How could I be extravagant if I wished it?" asked John.

"I am not afraid of you, John."

"I'm not afraid either," said he.

It is certain John was not afraid, and it is equally certain that his expenses at his outset in life were extremely modest, and that if he had any wishes beyond them, he kept them in curb. Was it not his intention to make money? only all his intentions were young and very loose in the fibre, and, nothing preventing, those would flourish best that were indigenous.

The Quixstar lads naturally met occasionally, especially Tom Sinclair and John, although they had not much in common; but their sisters were a bond between them, and the intimacy was encouraged on both sides at home—not that Mrs. Gilbert admired Tom deeply, or that Mrs. Sinclair considered John of sufficient mark to make his friendship of the least consequence to Tom, but each felt that her son might have a worse companion.

John's first essay at hospitality was on Tom's behalf. Mrs. Auld, John's landlady, was a just woman, but not genial—not by any means genial. She felt that John had in a manner been committed to her care, and she cared for him conscientiously; and he, having been accustomed to authority, endured it for a time, till getting more fully fledged, he took to flight.

On principle, Mrs. Auld objected to him having company, and, generally speaking, when a woman has it in her power, if she does not make her sentiments heard, she makes them felt.

When John saw his tea table, he felt it was not by any means furnished as he would have liked it to be for his guest. He lifted a small vessel about the size of a humming-bird, which his landlady called a cream-pot, and tasted the contents. When Mrs. Auld came in, he said—

" Couldn't you give us a little better cream ? That does not seem just the thing."

" No' the thing ! What ails it ? " and she brought her nose swoop down like a hawk on the humming-bird. " Weel, it may be a wee thing turned. What's the callant's folk when he's at hame ? "

" His uncle lives in Quixstar. He is a retired tobacconist."

" A retired tobacconist ! The milk'll do. I'll warrant he's used to naething better."

" I can tell you he is used to the very best of everything."

" Then it'll be a gude change to him no' to get the best. Changes are lightsome."

This might be true, and it was true that Mrs. Auld was a good, honest woman, trusted by Mrs. Gilbert, but it was not likely that a youth getting daily more versed in the ways of the world was going to stay with her longer than he could help—he, a young man rejoicing in a cane and a ring, which last article of luxury he transferred to his pocket from Saturday to Monday, the homage which his youthful vanity paid to good sense. His example commended itself to Tom Sinclair, who, although slow and fond of his ease, gratified his mother by careful attention to his toilet.

In the matter of changing his lodgings, John went mildly to work. If he had said to his mother that he wished to do so, the likelihood is she would have made no objection, but he began by dropping hints at a distance, that he was not quite comfortable, and so on, leading the way gradually.

Then he amused himself of an evening writing such an epistle as this, in a scrapy feminine hand: "SIR,—In answer to your advertisement, I am a widow without family, but with an airy bedroom and well-furnished sitting-room; would be happy to let the same, with coals, gas, and attendance. Rent 5s. per week inclusive. Entry immediate. Early answer will oblige." This he would stick into a book as a mark, perfectly certain that his landlady would not fail to read it—to how many landladies are the written documents of their inmates sacred? Mrs. Auld read, and burned with indignation. It never entered her mind that she was being played upon, and she was between the horns of a dilemma: either she must take no notice, or she must stand convicted of having read the note. John arrives to see the success of his stratagem. He instantly knows that it has taken effect.

"I hope nothing is annoying you, Mrs. Auld?" he remarks in mild tones.

"What mak's ye ask that?" says Mrs. A. snappishly.

"I thought you looked a little as if you were."

"Weel, I havena lived till this time o' day to be annoyed wi' trifles."

"A trifle! Is it anything I could put right?"

"Ye didna leave that letter there for me to read?" says Mrs. Auld, unable to contain herself longer.

"What letter?" says John innocently.

"I read it. I mak' it a duty to read onything that's lying aboot, as your mother gied me a charge o' ye. I took ye mainly to oblige her, and ye're free to leave when ye like; but tak' my word for it," pointing to the note, "that woman'll mak' her rent oot o' ye in some shape."

Mrs. Auld withdrew, shutting the door with a bang, not having her feelings soothed by hearing her lodger burst into hearty laughter. John was not long in getting out from under Mrs. Auld's watchful care. And the boys continued their weekly visit to Quixstar till Time stole them away, and quietly and effectually put men in their place.

In these years Peter Veitch had only been home once, and then his visit had been limited to a day and a night, and the only person he saw out of his own family was Mr. Kennedy, whom he met on the street and accosted. Mr. Kennedy looked at him, and did not know him. Peter introduced himself.

"Oh," said Mr. Kennedy; "I see; and you've tired of the sea, and have come back to take up the spade and the hoe again? All right."

"I have not tired of the sea. I am going back tomorrow."

"Indeed? Ah, well, see and behave yourself," and Mr. Kennedy shook hands—he was rather in a hurry.

CHAPTER XXIII.

WHEN Time stole the boys, he took the girls too, not however before a snatch had been made at them from a most unlikely quarter. The Gilbert girls had been singularly pretty in the bud, so as to alarm their mamma for their future fate, but the flower did not by any means come up to the promise of the bud, which shows that people ought not to eat sorrow with a long spoon. However, they were well enough—better than the average; but John's good looks had gone on improving with the years. Scripture writers tell us of people who were well-favored and goodly to look upon, as if it were rather an advantage than otherwise, and there were persons in Quixstar and elsewhere whose eyes rested with great enjoyment on John Gilbert,—his father and mother, his grandaunt, and even Miss Raeburn was weak enough to come under the spell; and younger eyes than theirs were fascinated. Mr. Gilbert felt that John was the ladder by which the family was to rise to fortune, and his mother—well, she did not think less of her daughters, but she thought much of her son.

At this particular time, however, there was a pair of weak spectacled eyes that never saw John Gilbert without the sharpest pang of envy. What had befallen Mr. Doubleday? There were times when he would have given his right hand, nay, I verily believe his hope of salvation, if only his soul could have been clad in such a body as John Gilbert's. Mr. Doubleday was still at Old Battle House.

"He was harmless and inoffensive," Mrs. Sinclair said, "and as the girls objected point-blank to being sent to a boarding-school, and got on well enough with him, she would rather have him than a governess—indeed, she would not have a governess on any consideration. Besides, there was Mr. Sinclair in the house, and you never could tell what might happen, and they had all got accustomed to Mr. Doubleday, odd being as he was—singularly harmless; but he was not quite a fixture, he would have to leave some day," etc., etc.

It was Maddy Fairgrieve who first discovered the impending calamity. One morning she went into the schoolroom to finish her dusting. She had a light foot; and Mr. Doubleday, who was standing in one of the windows, did not hear her. He was holding a glove in his hand, and he kissed it repeatedly. Turning round, he became aware of Maddy's presence, and not being quick-witted, he looked caught, and hid the glove in his pocket. At this instant Bell came in, and spied one of her gloves.

"Did I leave my gloves last night?" said she. "Here's one—where's the other?—Maddy, did you see it lying about?"

"No," said Maddy; "I didna see it lying about"—which was the truth.

"It must be somewhere, though," said Bell, and she proceeded to hunt for it.

No doubt Mr. Doubleday felt as if he had been guilty of theft, and he slowly drew the glove out of his pocket.

"There it is," he said simply.

"Out of your pocket! Did you mistake it for your own? The last instance of absence of mind!" said Bell, her face as clear as day. It was evident the tutor had never told his love.

Maddy retreated to her own quarters, and laughed. "He's no blate," she thought. "Aside Bell he looks like naething but a skinned rabbit. Wait till her mamma finds it out, and it will be a business! And the woman that writes to him so often—I'll warrant she has him tied neck and heels. It's aye the way wi' student callants; they entangle themselves before they've had time to draw their wits up frae their heels. But I dinna think Bell'll interfere wi' her rights. I wonder if he kens what like he is!" and Maddy laughed again, judging, as women are apt to do, and men also, by mere externals, and feeling herself certain that Mr. Doubleday was making a terrible breach in his honor by repudiating a prior claim.

Bell was nearly a grown-up young lady, and no doubt there were people who described her as bold and bouncing. If an angel were to descend, some one would find fault with the poise of his wings, and discover that he was either over fluent or over reticent. Bell was large —not too large—and bold with the boldness of a free, well-set nature, that thinks no evil. It was a pleasure to watch her eyes, or to meet them. They were not of that blue which is reckoned so soft and womanly; nor that black which glitters and scintillates so beautifully by mere force of the coloring pigment—for as often as not they are like the sham drawers in a druggist's shop, apparently full of wares subtle for life or death, but having actually nothing behind the appearance. Bell's eyes were grey, that clear calm grey, at which to look merely gives you a feeling of rest when they are at rest, but that kindle at the least friction of heart or soul, like a lucifer-match drawn across a rough surface. Her nose was straight, good, and unobtrusive; she had a clean-cut mouth, which opened well, and showed a row of teeth—not small, to be sure, perhaps a little too big for beauty—but white and regular as no dentist could make them, and giving the impression of high health and strength without a particle of coarseness; she had a good forehead, as became a mathematical student, with fair hair and plenty of it.

Alas! that beside her Mr. Doubleday justified Maddy's comparison is too true. But he had fallen in love. Love, you see, can kindle his torch in a turnip lantern as well as in a silver sconce, and even spectrum analysis would reveal the combustible material to be very much alike in both cases. Think of Mr. Doubleday in this state of incandescence. How he would have manifested his feelings if he had never learned the A B C cannot be known, but it is not very likely it would have occurred to him to kiss a glove and put it in his pocket if he had never read of such a thing being done, although love does a good deal in the way of inspiration.

What was pretty well known to him,-having lived so long under the same roof with Mrs. Sinclair—even to him, innocent of anything like keen worldly wisdom as he was—was the likelihood that she would not smile on his wishes in the matter of her daughter, and he was in a strait between two, whether to ask Mrs. Sinclair for her permission to win his love, or to woo without it. Mr. Doubleday never hated any one, it was not in him to do so, but he had a conscious overallish feeling toward Mrs. Sinclair which made him always more comfortable in her absence than her presence, and it is a very difficult matter to go and lay open your deepest feelings to a person for whom you have no more regard than this; and as it is easiest, when you are perplexed but not pushed, to do nothing, Mr. Doubleday would probably never have thought of doing anything, had not cruel fate kept the wound of love open by laying the blister of jealousy over it. John Gilbert came often to Old Battle House. John Gilbert was goodlooking and clever. Mr. Doubleday did not think humbly of himself; he was conscious of powers of some kind, but he knew he had neither the clear sight nor the agility which springs to opportunity, and till now he had never felt the want. Often as he had heard Mrs. Sinclair discourse to her son with the view of stinging him to exertion, on the number of clever people in the world who never got any benefit from their cleverness because they did not know how to use it, could not dress it for the market, and by the pricking of his thumbs had known that while Mrs. Sinclair was seeking to rouse her son, she was also speaking at him, he had never winced. What could such a woman know of the bliss of pursuing knowledge for the sake of knowledge? When he had hinted at such an idea she hooted it. "That's all very well, Mr. Doubleday," she said, " but if you carry out that notion you'll crawl through the world a poor man."

"I don't object to crawling through the world a poor man."

" Very well, you'll get no respect."

" I can do without respect."

" Oh, if you come to that, you are independent, to be sure."

" No, ma'am, I'm not so independent; next to my own approval, I value that of a good man."

" And you think a good man will approve of laziness."

" You said poverty; you did not say laziness."

" Well, people are poor because they are lazy."

"If that is your conviction, ma'am, I'll not disturb it."

What was he to do? He could still forget himself in his books—his first love—but the next lesson in mathematics came, and John Gilbert came. True, it was a natural enough thing that John Gilbert should come, he had always come, he was a friend of Tom's, and besides, there was Effie,—"But what," thought Mr. Doubleday, "what could she possibly be in any one's eyes compared with Bell?"

Now many people thought Effie the better-looking of the two. She was less every way than her sister, she was pretty, did not look into things too high for her, and was not strong-minded; her mamma said she was quite a sensitive plant, and always had been, and John had teased Effie from their childhood up.

Sometimes Mr. Doubleday thought of opening up the matter to Mr. Sinclair. He liked Mr. Sinclair. Mr. Sinclair was his friend, and oftener than once he had tried to do it, but failed; he had led a life so out of the crowd that he had a womanish shrinking; it seemed as if it would vulgarize a sacred feeling to talk of it, so the sweet and the sour stuff went on burning together, no one being the wiser except Maddy. It needed a lively imagination to originate the idea of Mr. Doubleday being in love.

But, grievous to say, Maddy was not Mr. Doubleday's friend in this matter. She was a just woman, and she was indignant at the wrong done to the tutor's supposed betrothed; still, if he had been a fine-looking youth, of frank and genial bearing, perhaps her sense of justice might not have been in the ascendant.

"But," she thought, "I needna distress mysel'; Bell will never tak' up wi' the like o' him." She sounded affairs, however, and took an opportunity of bringing the tutor in as a topic. "Would you call Mr. Doubleday gude-looking, Miss Sinclair?" she said.

"No," said Bell," I would not, nor any other person."

"Puir man," said Maddy.

"Do you pity a man because he is not a beauty, Maddy?"

"No—no' if he has other things."

"Mr. Doubleday has plenty of other things. He is good, and he is learned, and he never despises ignorance, but he should not use his hands. It's a very funny thing that with such a mind he should not know by intuition how to fold paper and tie a string, but it actually puts me in a fever to see him try to make up a parcel."

"He's a stupid body," said Maddy.

"That he is not," said Bell emphatically. "It is a pity he is so handless, but it is not so bad in a man as a woman."

"I dinna ken," said Maddy; "there's heaps o' bits o' jobs about a house a man can do if he has hands. What use would Mr. Doubleday be at a flitting, think ye?"

"None," said Bell, laughing; "I would never engage him to help at a flitting."

"Weel, I like a smart, look-active man far afore a dungeon."

"Dungeons are good in their place. You can draw a great deal out of a dungeon. First and last, I have got more good from Mr. Doubleday than almost any one." Bell stood up for her tutor warmly, but, even to Maddy's experienced eyes, as calmly as if she had been speaking of old Peter Veitch.

CHAPTER XXIV.

THERE are people who having got a startling piece of information do not burn to impart it,—who having made a discovery by their own unaided wisdom can yet refrain from publishing it,—thereby abstaining from giving a skeptical world triumphant proof of that wisdom. There are such people, although they are rather thinly sown, and you could hardly expect that Mrs. Sinclair's old and valuable servant would forego the pleasure of a mild and respectful crow over her mistress.

Some changes were being made in the household arrangements, and Mrs. Sinclair remarked to Maddy, " We could make use of Mr. Doubleday's room now, if we had it. He'll have to be leaving some day."

"It's high time," said Maddy, with a mysterious snort.

"I should think I am the best judge of that," said Mrs. Sinclair loftily.

"Maybe; but he's dune a' the gude he's likely to do here."

"He's not going to do you any harm, is he, Maddy?"

"Na; there's nae fear o' me. I wadna tak' up wi' the like o' him."

"Who's taking up with him?—not Mary (one of the servants)? But Mr. Doubleday has more sense. You imagine things, Maddy."

"Maybe. When Miss Bell runs off wi' the tutor I'll maybe imagine that too."

"Really, Maddy, you should think twice before you speak. You're an old servant, but there is a limit to freedom."

Maddy snorted, and held her tongue. Mrs. Sinclair, however, had intended the remark to draw out all she might have to say, and her sudden and complete silence was provoking.

"There is a limit to freedom, and therefore, Maddy, I can't think a person of your sense would have said what you did say without grounds," Mrs. Sinclair said, sure that a seasoning of compliment would untie the budget; but Maddy was disposed to play her fish a little longer on the hook.

"Oh, nae grounds but my ain imagination," said Maddy.

"Maddy," said Mrs. Sinclair, looking from the window at the garden, on which the sun was shining, "why should we indulge in bad temper when all nature is smiling?"

"I dinna ken your reason, but I imagine I do it out o' a spirit o' contradiction."

"It is a very bad spirit."

"Very."

"And one you ought to guard against, as well as setting reports afloat that have no foundation."

"I never did that."

"Do you mean to tell me you have the slightest ground for saying what you said a little ago?"

"Yes," said Maddy shortly.

"Then what are they? As a mother I have a right to know. What can they possibly be?"

Then Maddy thawed, and unfolded the glove scene and other tell-tale trifles.

Most people, who had been as long in the world as

Mrs. Sinclair, would have slept on information such as this before taking action on it. Mrs. Sinclair went immediately in search of the tutor. She looked into the dining-room, and found not him, but Miss Raeburn and Mr. Sinclair, they having come in from the garden as she descended the stairs. She scarcely had presence of mind for the ordinary greeting. "I'm looking for Mr. Doubleday," she said; "I thought after I got him polished a little he would be as harmless in the house as the cat; and what do you think I have just heard of him?"

"That he is in love with Bell?" said Miss Raeburn.

"Miss Raeburn! is it possible that you knew of—guessed of—such a thing, and never told me? I avoided getting a governess in case—in case," here she glanced at Mr. Sinclair, "anything ridiculous should happen; and now why, oh why, did you not give me warning?"

"I am innocent," said Miss Raeburn. "I made a mere random guess. Even jealousy did not sharpen my sight. I have seen nothing, although I'm in love with Bell myself."

"I'll give you Maddy's story," said Mrs. Sinclair.

When she had finished, her brother-in-law spoke first, and said, "It is nonsense. Doubleday is not such a sentimental fool. He looked closely at the glove to see if it was his own, and thinking it his own put it in his pocket—that is all."

"If I could think that was all, what a relief it would be! What do you think, Miss Raeburn?"

Being feminine and romantic, Miss Raeburn leaned to Maddy's view of the subject. "I suppose if it were the case, you wouldn't approve of such an attachment?" said she.

"Miss Raeburn, are you mad? Well, it is easy to

bear other people's calamities. I must question Mr. Doubleday or Bell, or both. What do you think, Adam?"

"Oh, by all means question them. If Bell wants to marry the man, let her do it; she might do worse."

"I'll not let her do it; I at least will stand between my children and ruin."

"Well, I know nothing about these things. Take your own way; but he is a good man and a scholar; and there's no accounting for taste"—and having given his opinion, Mr. Sinclair left the two ladies to manage such a delicate matter their own way.

"I declare to you," said Mrs. Sinclair solemnly, "I declare to you, Miss Raeburn, I would rather that Bell should live and die an old maid than marry Mr. Doubleday,"—then, catching a sparkle in Miss Raeburn's eye —" Of course you know I didn't mean—that is—old maids are often very useful, and I did not mean—"

"I know you didn't, Mrs. Sinclair; and I have not got a long nose. But if I were you, I would not question Bell on this subject. Most likely she knows nothing about it, and there's no need that she should know it."

"And there's no need that she shouldn't."

"She is very young," urged Miss Raeburn.

"Old-maidish caution," thought Mrs. Sinclair; and she said—"Perhaps the best thing would be to send away Mr. Doubleday immediately, without asking anything about it?"

"But where could he go to immediately?"

"Oh, a man can never be at a loss. One could hardly have turned a governess out at a moment's notice; but a man is different."

"Yes; but Mr. Doubleday has not the faculty of looking after himself most men have, and I doubt he has no money."

"If he had the impudence to think of Bell, he is able to look after himself; and he must have money. He has been well paid here, and what has he done with it?"

"Given it away. I suspect there is some drain upon him."

"Well, I am not bound to supply his drains. You don't see the thing as I do. Did you ever know such impudence? The more I think of it—"

"The cat may look at the king, you know; and a man of education and ability is any one's equal. You can't expect people to grovel in humility. But I don't believe Bell cares for him more than I do—at least it is very unlikely; yet if she did, he would be a good husband."

"I thought Adam unfeeling," said Mrs. Sinclair; "and I can only say, Miss Raeburn, that you can't know a mother's feelings—"

"Perhaps I can't; but I think you should give Mr. Doubleday a little while's grace—people never regret doing anything in a kindly way. Reverse the case, and suppose *he* had been your son."

"I don't think, Miss Raeburn, that I am in the habit of doing unkind things; but when one's child is threatened, really I must take my own way."

Mrs. Sinclair took her own way, and cited Mr. Doubleday to her presence.

"Mr. Doubleday," she said, "possibly it may come upon you by surprise: the intimation that owing to circumstances over which I have had no control, I must from to-day dispense with your services."

"I have been thinking of leaving for some time; I have wished to leave."

"I am glad of that,—that we are of one mind on that point."

"I have thought, Mrs. Sinclair, that I might better my position—"

"And I'm sure I don't object to your doing that—not at all."

"I'm not ambitious; but—"

"But you ought to be. I for one would be delighted to see you in a Professor's chair."

"Would that content you?" he said eagerly.

"Perfectly, Mr. Doubleday."

Mr. Doubleday for once in his life jumped to a conclusion.

"Then I may speak to Bell?" he said in agitation.

"About what?" asked Mrs. Sinclair.

Mr. Doubleday's fingers were playing nervously with one of the buttons of his coat, and he stammered, "I am—she is—that is—"

"You don't mean that you have been guilty of any imprudence, Mr. Doubleday?" said Mrs. Sinclair sharply. "I have been hearing—"

"I never told any one!" broke forth Mr. Doubleday.

"That's so far good," said Mrs. Sinclair. "I don't think I can blame. myself for want of vigilance. If I had taken a fluent good-looking youth into my house, it would have been different; indeed, I would not have done it; but with you I never dreamt of danger. I wouldn't for the world do an unkindly thing, but in the circumstances when will it be convenient for you to go, Mr. Doubleday?"

"To-day!" said Mr. Doubleday, suddenly and shortly, and he left Mrs. Sinclair seated on her throne of judgment, angry, vexed, and good-natured. How surprised she would have been had she known that the tutor cut the interview short from an instinctive feeling of repulsion!"

He went to the schoolroom to gather together the books that belonged to him lying there. Bell was sitting at the table writing. He did not speak, and she did not speak. At length she looked up and said—

"You're making a clean sweep. What are you going to do with all these books? and what's the hurry?"

"I'm going away to-night, and I'll take them with me."

"Going to-night! but you're coming back?"

"No."

"Going for good and all?"

"Yes."

"Nonsense! I don't believe it. You would have given us warning."

"I did not know I was going till a few minutes ago. Your mamma asked me to go."

"She asked you to go?" said Bell in surprise. "Why?"

"I suppose she thought me so ugly and so sunk in my books that I had not common feeling."

"Mr. Doubleday, what in the world has happened? I am sure you misunderstand mamma!"

"I am not so wretchedly dull!" he said bitterly.

"Neither is mamma so unjust and unkind. What is the meaning of it? Why does mamma want you to go?"

"She is afraid that you should learn to like me."

"That's not the thing. She knows well enough that we like you; we've liked you all along, so that can't be the reason," and she looked inquiringly at him.

"She is afraid," said he, turning over his books nervously, "that—that I like—love you too well."

"I see it!" cried Bell, with animation. "I was half thinking of that. Mamma is afraid that we'll want to marry! No danger! That's an idea that runs in mamma's head. The farthest back thing I remember is her saying she was afraid uncle would marry, and he's not married yet. Don't take offence at mamma, Mr. Doubleday; I can put her right about that in half a second. Marry! we would never think of it for a moment!"

"Would you not—would you really not, Bell? not if I were, as your mamma suggested, a Professor?"

"If I were going to marry, it would be the man I should think of, not his business. I would not mind much what his business was if it was something clean; not a chimney-sweep, for instance."

Mr. Doubleday laughed in spite of himself, "I must go," he thought. "It will be easier to go at once. Her mind awoke at my touch—I cannot reach her heart."

"I shall soon be forgotten," he said aloud.

"Not by me," said she. "I shall never open a dictionary without thinking of you, and when you're away, where can we go but to the dictionary, and it will be a bore. I'm lazy, and I like spoon-meat. But you won't really go to-night?"

"Yes. I may as well go to-night as to-morrow."

"Well, said she, "I have often thought you were losing time with us when you might have been doing something much more important in the world; but it was pleasant. I shall always look back on these years."

"Will you? And if we should meet again—"

"If? there's no if in the matter; you will surely come back and see us now and then; if you are near, you might come every Saturday, like Tom."

Mr. Doubleday smiled faintly and shook his head. He bade the girls good-bye in the schoolroom, and there was no word said but good-bye. Mrs. Sinclair met him in the lobby. "Now," she said, "Mr. Doubleday, if ever I can do anything for you, you have only to let me know. And I would like to give you two pieces of advice: cultivate ambition, and, Mr. Doubleday, act honorably to the—the person to whom you are engaged."

"To whom I am engaged?" said Mr. Doubleday, mystified.

"Yes. I have been told you are engaged to be married."

"Whoever told you that told you what is false, ma'am. Good-bye."

CHAPTER XXV.

MR. DOUBLEDAY walked on—walked out of his paradise; took his solitary way, no more intending or even wishing to go back than if an angel with a drawn sword guarded the entrance. It seemed to him the natural course of things. He had been so accustomed to be disappointed that the prosperity of his wishes would have dazzled him as the sun dazzles weak eyes. Besides, he carried his love with him as one carries a jewel in a case, and however often he might take her out and look at her she would still be the same—the scholar in whom he had had supreme delight, her face always alive with interest and fresh with youth. He walked on, strange to say, with a sense of elation. For months he had felt as if he had been living in deceit, in a false, feverish dream; now he was awake and free. Hope had not hung in the air when he was born, as genius is said to do at certain times of a nation's life, waiting to enter a favored newly-made body; he was not buoyant, and a half lifeless hope dies more easily; he abhorred anything like deceit, now that too was over. As Mrs. Sinclair said, "When all nature is smiling, why should we indulge in bad temper?" The sun was shining, and sending a long afternoon shadow before him, which he could neither overtake nor yet get quit of, any more than he could all at once get quit of the shadow of his vanished hope. He walked more quickly than was usual with him, but that was because when people are walking to a railway station they strike into a business pace whether they will or not, rather than with the view of walking down internal tumults. He came up to old Peter Veitch standing leaning over a gate at the entrance of a field.

"Fine day, sir," said Peter.

"Very fine," said Mr. Doubleday, and was passing on, when Peter said, "You'll hae heard the news?"

"No," he said, his tone implying that he did not care to hear it, but when Peter had got a startling bit of news, like many people he was fond of telling it.

"Lord Winkworth died this morning," he said. (This nobleman had some estates in the county, and a residence not very far from Cranstoun Hall, a favorite residence, where he mostly lived, and where he had died.)

Mr. Doubleday was not so struck as Peter expected; he said, "Indeed," somewhat absently.

"Sudden in the end," Peter continued; "he had been no' sae weel, off an' on, for a while. Eh, Mr. Doubleday, it's a blessing that great folk dee."

"You're surely not pleased at the man's death, Peter?"

"No, no, sir; but when ye see puir folk fechting on a' their lives, and living in damp houses, wi' a wind blawing through them fit to tak' onybody up the lum, and getting the cauld, drapping into the ground like a broken leaf, it looks hard; but when the like o' Lord Winkworth's ta'en away, that had doctors frae a' parts, and everything done for him that could be done—the house and the very passages, they tell me, were heated up to an equal temperature a' the year round,—it brings things to their level. When their time comes the rich maun gang, they canna creesh the hand o' death."

"I envy him," said Mr. Doubleday.

"He had a gey and easy billet, ye wad think," said Peter; "but I'm no sure I wad hae changed wi' him. To be flattered and made o', and hae a' body takin' off their hats to ye, and hae your pouches fou o' siller frae the cradle to the grave, is trying—very trying; I'm no sure how I wad hae come out o' sic an ordeal."

"Be certain he had his own share of evils," said Mr. Doubleday; "no man comes into this world and goes out of it without them; it's not his life I envy, it's his death."

"Are ye tired o' life, sir—ye're young to hae gotten that length?"

"There's not much worth living for," answered Mr. Doubleday ; "and think what he'll know now."

"Dear kens—that's ayont me. I canna say I want to dee—it's no' natural; but I've enjoyed life; I've wrought hard, and had my ain trials; but working wi' your hands keeps body and mind in order, if ye're no' ower sair wrought—how you folk that work wi' your heads come on I dinna ken. Weel, I tak' a dook in the burn every morning, and that's ae thing worth living for, for ye're just a laddie when ye come out; and I often get a hearty laugh and that's anither thing worth living for; but ye dinna look in a humor for that. Ye haena the toothache, have ye, sir?"

"No, I never had toothache in my life."

"Then be thankfu'; it's no' every ane that can tell the tale."

Next morning Mr. Sinclair looked over the edges of his paper at breakfast, and said, "Surely Mr. Doubleday is late to-day?"

"Do you not know?" said Mrs. Sinclair; "he is away."

"Where to?"

"I don't know; his boxes are addressed to Eastburgh. If you had not been out driving, he and they might have been sent to the station together."

"You don't mean that he is not coming back?"

"Most certainly I mean that."

"Impossible! you could not turn him out at a moment's warning?"

"He proposed going, and I must say I did not press him to stay."

"But I did," said Bell. "I did not want him to go in such a hurry; we liked him, and although we gave him so much trouble, he liked us. I'm very sorry he is gone; I feel like a fish out of water."

"I think, Adam, you'll allow that my prompt action was hardly misplaced," said Mrs. Sinclair, with a knowing smile.

"It's done at any rate, and can't be undone," said Mr. Sinclair, and he did not think the more of his sister-in-law for her energy, which savored of heartlessness.

"I'm glad, for Mr. Doubleday's sake," said Bell. "I always felt he was wasting his time here."

"That's something like sense, Bell," said her uncle. "Well, what do Effie and you propose doing now? But perhaps your education is finished?"

"Except as regards music," said Mrs. Sinclair; "they will go on with it."

"I know, uncle," said Bell, "that you are laughing at us about our education being finished, and I don't like it. Mr. Doubleday once told me that the greatest of all reverence is reverence for what is beneath you."

"And you claim reverence as being beneath me?"

"I am a good deal younger at least."

"That's undeniable, I must allow."

"But, Bell," said Mrs. Sinclair, "it was quite natural of your uncle to suppose your education finished. By the time I was your age," at this point Mr. Sinclair retired with his newspaper, "I had not only finished my education, I had refused more than one offer of marriage, and good ones too."

"Why, mamma," said Effie, "did you refuse them?"

"Because, my dear, I was kept for your papa."

"But, mamma, tell us the particulars: I would like to hear them of all things?"

"Tell us about papa," said Bell. "What kind of man was he?"

Bell, when she thought of her father, always pictured him to herself as a man among men, the fact being that he was nothing worse and nothing better than a solemn goose.

"The most excellent of men, my dear."

"Was he like uncle?"

"No; not at all. What your uncle might have been if he had early in life married a superior woman we can't say. No; your father was not like him," etc.

Bell, as her uncle allowed, showed sense occasionally, but her wisdom was not of the kind that could smartly discern a want of that quality in the opinions and acts of her elders. It could not enter her mind to criticise her mother or her uncle. A woman must be bad indeed before she loses her prestige, and in the eyes of her children Mrs. Sinclair was eminently wise and good.

When Mr. Sinclair had finished his newspaper he sat for half an hour or so meditating, and the subject of his meditations was his nieces. "His attention had been called" to them pointedly by the schoolroom-quake that had taken place, and he had looked at them particularly that morning, critically and disinterestedly, and had discovered that they were grown up, and that each in her own way looked well, but he preferred Bell upon the larger pattern. "Doubleday has taste," he thought, smiling, "if he has not wisdom." Mr. Sinclair smiled, so that if there was any similar episode in his own life the probability is he had come to regard it from the elderly point of view as a piece of romantic nonsense, otherwise —one would think—he might have sighed in token of sympathy for Mr. Doubleday, and in memory of his own young self.

Then he thought, "Their mother is not overgifted with sense, I'll have to mount guard;" whereupon he called them into his room,—" Now," he said, "I know you have nothing to do—"

"We intend—" said Effie.

"Yes, yes, you intend. Well, I daresay, but if you'll come here two hours every day I'll see that you do something, as well as intend to do it. What do you say?"

"Oh, we'll come. What are we to do?"

"Anything you like, except trifle.—See, Effie," and he took from a shelf Robertson's History of Charles the Fifth, an abridged edition, "if you would read such a book as that you might be the better for it; but I suppose you wouldn't?"

"I've read it," said Effie; "ask me questions, and you'll see?"

"Oh, I don't doubt you, and I'm glad you can read a book of that class—very glad."

Next he examined Bell as to her mathematical acquirements, and said, "Not so bad; well, you can go now, and come here every morning at ten. I'll see that you make some use of two hours out of the twenty-four." This was all the encouragement Mr. Sinclair vouchsafed his nieces.

When Tom came home the following Saturday, he said to his sisters, in his usual laconic fashion, " What's the row been ? "

" What row ? " asked Effie,

" We met Doubleday on the street in Eastburgh yesterday, and we could not make him out. He has left, it seems, for good. Have we tired of our mathematics, Bell ? "

" Who was with you when you met Mr. Doubleday ? " asked Effie.

" Answer my question, and I'll answer yours," said Tom.

" Thomas, my brother," said Bell; " ask first, was there a row ? "

" Doubleday didn't leave at an hour's notice without a row."

" He left without a row," echoed Bell.

" Effie," he said, " how was it ? why did he leave ? You may as well tell me. I'll get it from mamma at any rate."

" Tom," said Bell, " it's a long story. You have heard of cumulative force ? "

" I say, no nonsense. What was it, Effie ? "

Bell said, " Mr. Doubleday took his shoes to the mending; Mr. Doubleday stayed at home; Mr. Doubleday went to the post for a letter, and Mr. Doubleday sometimes got none: cumulative force—and mamma said he had better go, and he went."

" Effie," said Tom, " can you speak sense ? "

" I fancy," said Effie, " mamma and he differed about something, I don't know what, and he went off in a hurry; that's all I know.—Now, who was with you when you met him—John Gilbert ? " Tom nodded.

" How was Mr. Doubleday looking ? " asked Bell.

"Through his spectacles," said Tom.

"That is very satisfactory," rejoined Bell.

"Is John coming over to-night?" Effie asked.

"Yes; and his sisters."

CHAPTER XXVI.

BELL seized an opportunity in the course of the evening to pay a hasty visit to Miss Raeburn.

"Miss Raeburn is not out, I hope?" said she to the servant who opened the door.

"No; I'm not out. Come away, Tibby," cried Miss Raeburn from her sitting-room.

"I was afraid, from the blinds being down, that you were out."

"I was reading a book for which I wanted a dim religious light," said Miss Raeburn; "and also to feel alone, which you can't do so thoroughly with open windows."

"I have interrupted you, then?"

"If you had not been you, you would have interrupted me; but being you—child, I could wish to have you for the prop of my old age."

"You're not old," said Bell.

"Just so old that when I go into a druggist's shop for anything, I get it wrapped up in a document setting forth the merits of an unguent warranted to make thin hair grow thick, when all other means have failed."

"But that's by chance," said Bell; "I don't believe the common run of shopmen are so clever as to pick and choose what will suit each different customer."

"There are clever ones among them, though. I saw a circular the other day from a man who has invented a specific, offering his portrait—a first-class thing, he said, both as a likeness and a work of art—to every shopkeeper who would put it in his window, and sell his specific with a percentage; besides, he remarked, the portrait and the specific would be the means of indefinitely extending the exhibitor's usual business."

"People must be fearfully fond of money," said Bell, "that act with such consummate impudence to get it. If that man could sell impudence at so much the ounce, I would buy some of it to give to Mr. Doubleday as a parting gift. He would be much the better of it. You know he has left us?"

"Perfectly. Everybody in Quixstar knows."

"I daresay. It was to speak about him I came. I haven't long to stay."

"Speak then, Tibby"—Miss Raeburn generally had a name for those she specially liked, other than that by which they were commonly known.

"What do you think will become of him, Miss Raeburn?"

"How?"

"Do you think he'll be able to look after himself? I always felt as if he were a creature that needed to be taken in and done for; and to think he was sent off at a moment's notice! Mamma won't hear reason, and I don't like to speak to uncle about it, so I came to you."

"To ask whether I thought he was likely to sink or swim? I think he'll swim, or get some strong swimmer to take him in tow."

"I would like to hear of it."

"Oh, he'll write; be sure of that."

"Whom will he write to?"

"Your uncle or Mr. Gilbert. probably."

"I liked him, and he is such a helpless being; positively he couldn't wipe his own spectacles properly. I used to take them from him and do it; and yet he wrote beautifully, and he is so simple. One day he met a knife-grinder on the road, and got his knife sharpened. He had no change, and gave the man a one-pound note. The man was to get change and bring it to him at the house in the evening, not to keep him waiting. He never saw either man or money again, at which he wondered, he told me."

"We must hope he won't fall among thieves, then," said Miss Raeburn; "only, if he should, he would have the happiness of not knowing it."

"I doubt," said Bell, and she sighed, " happiness and he have never had much to do with each other. I know he had an uncomfortable home, although he never exactly said so."

"I hope we'll hear of him getting into some congenial post soon."

"I am very sorry for him," said Bell; "but it has been a comfort to speak of him to you."

"I wonder," thought Miss Raeburn when her visitor was gone, "if she really cares for him; it would be a piece of amazing luck for him, and they are complementary to each other. Pity is akin to love, they say, but is love akin to pity? I trow not. Pity is the poor relation that claims kindred with the rich; love is the rich relation that forgets the poor; love likes to glory in its object, not to pity; it is hardly possible, but stranger things have happened."

Mr. Doubleday wrote—wrote both to Mr. Sinclair and Mr. Gilbert, regretting he had not seen them before leaving. His letters were dated from a provincial town, and stated that he had got the place of classical and mathematical master in a school there, and little more. A faint dropping fire of letters was kept up for a considerable time, then one of Mr. Sinclair's letters was returned to him, marked "Not found," and Mr. Doubleday was lost sight of and apparently forgotten, or nearly so, by the inhabitants of Quixstar. They kept the "negative," however, so that fortune had only to throw a strong light upon him for good or evil, and they would be all able to supply his portrait immediately.

And Mrs. Sinclair had rest, and those that were in the house with her. And the girls spent two hours every forenoon in their uncle's room, he not interfering much with them, only seeing that they did not trifle, and giving them help when they needed it, and he could give it; for when he couldn't he never hesitated to say 'so—a touch of greatness to which every one is not equal—and exerted himself to hunt down the information wanted, and they came to know each other better, and to respect and like each other—not love. The truth is, when one person has been in the habit of snubbing, and another of being snubbed, no conditions more unfavorable to love ever existed. Not that there had ever been any really bad feeling on either side; there never had been anything worse than indifference, which gradually gave place to an interested regard, so that by the time another summer came round, and Mr. Sinclair was of a sudden left alone in his house, he woke up at least to a partial sense of their value. The stillness was oppressive, and he caught himself counting the time till they should be home again, not that he was at all without resources, or that he needed company, but that, unknown to himself, he had got trained to listen to his nieces' tongues, and watch their looks.

CHAPTER XXVII.

THE reason of this temporary eclipse at Old Battle House, or the motive power rather, was Tom. He liked fishing, and he liked loch-fishing. He had spent his holidays often in this way alone, but on the present occasion his mother thought it well to accompany him, and they all went to Lochside, a place in the West Highlands, so out of the way that Mrs. Sinclair, who did not appreciate scenery, and liked conveniencies, said if she had known the difficulty of getting the necessaries of life she never would have gone. She allowed her daughters— "being always," as she said, "far too good-natured"—to ask the Gilbert girls to visit them there.

"I wouldn't let them go," said Mr. Gilbert to his wife when he heard of the invitation.

"Why not?" asked Mrs. Gilbert.

"Well, for one thing, Mrs. Sinclair is always speaking down on people; and after all, who is she? Her husband was a mere nothing. No doubt she has money. Without it what would she be? I don't like her."

"But she is not asking you to visit her?" said his wife.

"No; I daresay she knows better than that."

"I don't see the difference between visiting them at Old Battle House, and visiting them in the West Highlands."

"She'll let you know it some day, though; she'll think she has done you a great favor."

"Well, I think it is very kind of her to ask the girls

to go with them; and they are very anxious to go. They have not very much change, you know."

"Oh, I know that well enough. I don't need to be told that we are poor." Mr. Gilbert had come out of his school in a bad mood.

"I neither think nor feel that we are poor;" said Mrs. Gilbert cheerily, and she diverted the conversation to other topics. His was a trying occupation, and we are all poor creatures. But what a remarkable thing the love of a good woman is! After having for years tacked, and humored, and managed, and kept down her own infirmities of temper and temperament, all to soothe, and cheer, and "keep up" her husband, she loved him now, when he was wonderfully real, as much as when she married him, thinking he was her ideal. Surely this is instinct. It is said women don't reason; if so, many a man ought to be thankful.

After Tom's furlough was over the Gilberts went, according to Mrs. Sinclair's arrangement, for she explained, "When my son is with us we'll not have room, our accommodation is so limited."

"Why did the woman ask them, if she hasn't room?" said Mr. Gilbert.

It was good-natured of Tom Sinclair to consent to this invitation being given, for when he came, as he did regularly at the end of the week, he had to betake himself to an inn in which great ease could not be had—not a modern palace dropped at the foot of a mountain, but a little primitive Highland public-house. Oftener than not he brought John Gilbert with him, and John was an acquisition in any company, both useful and ornamental.

"What a lovely sunset!" Effie exclaimed, when they were out one evening on the loch.

"Oh, the sunset is well enough," said John; "perfectly well."

"Can anything in nature equal it?" pursued Effie with enthusiasm.

"Something in art is very like it," said John. "You've seen a red bottle in a druggist's window at night?"

"John, you are a Vandal," cried Bell. "I feel moved to capsize you into the water." John was leaning over the boat, and it would not have been difficult to make him lose his balance.

"Do," he said, "and I'll take you with me. I like pleasant company."

"Thank you," said Bell; "I don't like my pleasure damped."

"What's the use of going off in spasms about a sunset?" Tom remarked. "Jack is right; that round disk is very like the red bottle in a druggist's window."

"But wandering oft with brute unconscious gaze, man marks not thee," declaimed Effie.

"Oh, Jemmy Thomson, Jemmy Thomson — oh!" chanted John.

"I wish you would look to your oar, Jack," said Jane Gilbert; "you'll land us all in the water yet."

"I can't work miracles," said John. "I'll hardly *land* you in the water."

"Suppose you tumble us in?" Jane said.

"Well, suppose it, if it gives you any enjoyment."

"Sit still, Jane, and we're all safe," said Tom.

"Oh, I can trust you perfectly, Tom; if you had not been here, I don't think I would have come," Jane said.

"Tom does not speak, Jane," said Bell; "his feelings are too deep for words."

"Here is little Mary in the corner," Effie said, "does

not speak either.—Come, what are you thinking about? are your thoughts also too deep for words?"

Mary Gilbert, the youngest of the group, answered, "No, they are not; but I never can get room to speak, you all speak so much."

"Stupid thing!" said Bell. "Can you not bounce in whether any one is speaking or not? But we'll all hold our tongues for two seconds, and give you a chance."

"I was thinking," said Mary, "that it would be delightful to stay out on the loch all night."

"I second that motion," said her brother. "The truth is, I'm frightened to go in."

"Why?" asked Mary in wonder.

"The pillows in my bed are so hard. I wished I could take off my ears last night, and fling them on the table, they were so much in my way. My head felt all ears together."

"Are you sure it was not a crumpled rose leaf, John?" asked Bell.

"What are the pillows stuffed with?" Effie inquired.

"Road metal, so far as I could judge," replied John.

"I could weep to think of it," said Bell.

"And Tom," Jane Gilbert said, "it is on our account you are subjected to such hardships."

"Entirely on your account that we are subjected to hard pillows."

"Well, I won't forget it," said Jane.

"Neither will I," John said, "unless I get concussion of the brain some night."

"Oh, there is the moon coming over the hill!" cried Effie.

"Let her come," said John; "give her time; don't hurry her."

"Hurry!" Effie answered. "How calm and majestic she looks!"

"She has nothing else to do," John said. "If I were up there I could look calm too."

"But not majestic, John," Bell said; "not majestic. 'Uneasy lies the head,' you know."

"One gets accustomed to it," said Tom.

"To the moon?"

"No; to the hardness of the pillows."

"Tom, you are not romantic," said Bell, "and it's a pity."

"I don't know that it is," said John, "I'm too romantic—too easily touched up, and it's trying; for instance, at this moment, I don't envy the man who could look at that moon without tears."

"There they are—the tears," said Bell, as a shower came pattering down with little warning, just as Mary Gilbert's voice struck in, singing,

"Oh had we some bright little isle of our own,
 In a blue summer ocean far off alone,
 Where the bee banquets on through a whole year of flowers—"

and "there are never no showers," her brother added. Amidst laughter they made for the shore, and all hands helped to draw the boat up on the beach.

CHAPTER XXVIII.

"DEAR MISS RAEBURN," Bell wrote to her friend at Quixstar, "if you were on the loch, and from that point of view saw the house in which we are living, you would think it was a place where Virtue attired in white muslin should have her dwelling. It is heavenly. Quixstar is good, but I doubt we shall miss the loch sadly when we return. Somehow water seems to scenery what the eye is to the face. We could fancy ourselves in Eden here. Mamma does not like it; she says we can't live on scenery. Isn't it a humbling thing, Miss Raeburn, that we can't do without food? I remember Mr. Doubleday used to get impatient of his body. I begin to sympathize with him, although it is difficult to imagine what we'll be without it. There is a postman passes our door on some long round, and hands in our letters. If we could shut out him and the newspapers there would be almost nothing to desire. Effie and I don't look at the newspapers; but mamma and Jane Gilbert will read them, and speak of the news. News are quite out of keeping here. By the bye, mamma has changed her opinion of Jane Gilbert. She did not care much for her, but now she thinks her remarkably pleasant and obliging. I always thought her good-natured, but not bright. Mary is my favorite, only she is so shy. I am positively thankful when it is a wet day, that I may get rest with a clear conscience, and I hibernate on these days. If it is only mist, I must be out. Mist is a beautiful creature, whether lying or trailing, or flying before the wind, or climbing the mountains like a living thing with the sun's rays glittering on its back. Effie and I were on the loch in a boat by four o'clock yesterday morning. The mist was writhing in the glens, on the far side of the loch the mountains were standing dark as night, and on our side the sun picked out every scaur and cranny. The boat sat like a duck on the waters, that sparkled and glittered. Water always looks young and fresh, even when its face is wrinkled by a breeze, and a dark cloud above quenches its light; it may look angry, but it does not look old. We seemed to be the only human beings in possession; it was singularly delicious. We were fishing, and it is astonishing how you get into the spirit of it. I am not sure that it is right to fish for amusement; but we eat all we catch, so that is not so bad. John Gilbert says fish grow unconscious whenever they are taken out of the water, and don't suffer. I hope that is true. Tom always breaks their necks to make sure their misery is over, but I don't like to see him doing it. I have been out all day, and am a little tired, so I mean to do nothing more than sit in the window, and watch the moonlight on the loch and the hills. When it is a dark night it has a strange eerie effect to go out and listen to the intense silence. We'll not be long of being home now.—I am yours, T. B. SINCLAIR."

"MY DEAR TIBBY," wrote Miss Raeburn, "I am glad you enjoy scenery. I can do with it too when there is a sufficiency of appetizing food, and mist is very nice to people who have not got rheumatism; but what is scenery compared with the things that have been taking place here? What do you think of Mr. Kennedy having gone over to the Roman Catholic Church, actually entering a convent, and leaving his poor invalid wife to make the best of it? For my part, I am prepared for your uncle turning a Mahometan. Then we have had a murder, or what promises to be one; and the eldest Miss Smith has run off with a dancing-master. And we are to have a prize-fight; but don't tell, for I got it in confidence. Dear Tibby, I was innocently bursting with my news, but as you say news of any kind is quite out of place in Paradise, so rather than write another note I'll just draw my pen through what I have written, and hope you'll excuse my thoughtlessness. Your uncle is wearying for you; so am I. What a fine touch that is: Tom twisting the trouts' necks from extreme tenderness! I think I'll make a picture of it. Peter Veitch is at home just now; and your uncle having once tasted the sweets of pedagogy hankers after them again, and has Peter in training an hour every evening. There—I am trespassing again, so no more. J. RAEBURN."

"Well," said Mrs. Sinclair, when she heard this missive read, "they speak of women doing unaccountable things, but of all unaccountable beings commend me to an old bachelor. Peter Veitch at Old Battle House every evening! What is your uncle thinking of? But of course, it's a far more natural thing to take an interest in a boy out of a cottar's house than in his brother's children."

"I think," said Jane Gilbert, "that is not nearly so remarkable as Mr. Kennedy turning Roman Catholic. I have a letter from mamma, but it is strange she does not mention it."

"Nor the murder, nor Miss Smith's runaway match, nor the prize-fight either, I suppose?" said Bell.

"Leave old maids alone for news," said Mrs. Sinclair.

"Most people like news, mamma."

"Yes, Effie; but people who have had no experience view them differently. For instance, Miss Raeburn evidently enjoys telling about Miss Smith. Now, I have no feeling but the most profound sympathy for Mr. and Mrs. Smith."

"But how do you feel for Mrs. Kennedy?" asked Jane Gilbert. "For my part, it seems incredible. Gone into a convent! He was the last man I would have expected to do that."

"Oh," said Bell, "don't you see it is all a joke? Miss Raeburn has been amusing herself a little at my expense."

"Has she? and how do you like it?" asked her mamma. "If I were you, I would ask her to amuse herself at her own expense next time."

"I like a joke, although it is at my own cost," said Bell. "I wonder you take it so seriously, mamma. I thought you would have laughed."

"Why? I don't see anything laughable in stringing together untruths. Probably Miss Raeburn thinks it clever, but I don't see it. At her age she might have more sense."

"But," said Tom, "is it necessary to suppose she is joking?"

"Not necessary, Tom, but expedient," answered Bell.

"Why? People as good as Mr. Kennedy have gone over to the Roman Catholics before now," he said.

"Better, I believe," rejoined Bell. "Fancy Mr. Kennedy with a hair shirt, and a discipline."

"Nonsense!" said her brother. "Monks live comfortably enough, and are not overworked. I know Miss Raeburn is right about the prize-fight. Why should she be wrong about the other things? Miss Smith is a sensible person, and if a man was willing to keep her she knew better than not to have him."

"I have a line from your uncle," said Mrs. Sinclair. "If he were like any other person, he might have told me what was going on, but he says nothing.—What do you know about the prize-fight, Tom?"

"Merely that such a thing is to be."

"You have nothing to do with it, I hope?" said Mrs. Sinclair.

"Thank you; no."

"Who has?" asked Effie.

"Walter Cranstoun is the mainspring," answered Tom.

"How vexed Sir Richard and Lady Cranstoun must be!" exclaimed Mrs. Sinclair. "I feel for them, and it makes me doubly thankful for my own mercies."

"There's John coming," cried Effie, "He was in Quixstar last night, and will be able to tell us.—John, has Mr. Kennedy turned a Roman Catholic—become a monk?" she abruptly asked whenever he appeared in the doorway.

John was quick and ready. "Catch him," he said. "Wouldn't he have to get up at two every morning to say his prayers?"

"What would mamma say if she heard you, John?" said his eldest sister.

"If she said what she thought, she would say I was right."

"Has Miss Smith run away with a dancing-master?"

"Not that I heard of."

"I never doubted Miss Raeburn was joking," said Bell.

"A poor joke," said Mrs. Sinclair. "My dear girls,

whatever you set up for, don't set up for being clever women. A clever woman is no comfort to herself or any other person."

"But I don't think Miss Raeburn sets up for being clever, mamma," Bell remarked.

"I'll tell you what it is, Bell," said John. "Cleverness, like murder, will out. I know it by myself. I have often made conscientious efforts to be stupid, but it won't do. Whatever happens, I hope my friends will not forget that—mind, I'm serious."

"More than serious," said Bell; "melancholy and morose. We'll hear of you in *la Trappe* shortly."

John burst into a curious laugh. "You've hit it," he said, "sure enough. I'll be in a trap if I don't look out."

"What kind of trap, John?" asked Effie. "What do you mean?"

"That's another way of being clever, my dear," said Mrs. Sinclair, "to speak in riddles, and see a joke where no one else sees it.—You may depend on it, John," turning to him, "no one enjoys that kind of thing, and it had better be dropped."

"Thank you," said John, "I'll try."

CHAPTER XXIX.

"JOHN," said Tom, when they were waiting in front of the house for the girls to walk in the evening, "I can only say that if you are getting into another mess I'll not help you. I have done it once, and I won't do it again. I have regretted doing it once—you understand?"

"I hear, at any rate, but it is bad taste to introduce disagreeable topics here, and now—"

"It is worse taste to act like a fool. Mind, I warn you I won't be soft twice."

"How lovely the sands look from this point, with the evening sun on them!" Effie said as she came out.

"Exactly what I was saying to your brother, Effie, but I doubt that sort of thing is lost on him. He does not care for it."

"But you do," she said, "although you sometimes pretend not. Why don't you always speak so that one may know what you mean?"

"I'm sure I always look what I mean, Effie," he said, in a soft aside that made her blush like the little pools on the sands, which had reddened under the western sky. He went on, "'Oh had we some bright little isle of our own,' as Mary sang the other night."

"Come, Jack," said Tom, "don't be sentimental. We have enough of that without you chiming in."

John Gilbert had been coming out a little in the

world, and had overstepped his income. Being cashier in his office he helped himself, not largely, and with the intention of replacing the money before it could be missed. To accomplish this he had thrown himself on Tom's mercy, and not in vain. It was a touch-and-go business, and as the French say it is the first step that costs, he took it lightly. However, he might be quite sure that Tom would keep his word, and let him find his way out of such another scrape—if he got into another—without his assistance.

Bell was the last to come out, and she found only Mary Gilbert waiting for her.

"Have they really gone off and left us?" she said.

"Yes; Tom and Jane went first, and then Effie and John."

"We'll not follow. I don't care about walking. We'll sit down somewhere and dream. See, yon little toy yacht that came in sight a while ago has cast anchor. How innocent and pretty it looks!"

They crossed to where the stump of a tree lay by the brink of a mountain stream, which after a heavy rain shot down its rocky bed so white and frothy that it looked like a band of frosted silver gleaming in the dark breast of the hill, but now it was gliding quietly past with only a drowsy gurgle like the purr of a sleeping cat.

"Now," said Bell, "we'll sit here where we can see everything, and let the music of the burn creep in our ears."

"Shall we sit long? I wish I had brought a book," said Mary.

"A book! Oh Mary, it would be a sin to read in a night like this. Dream, I'm going to dream."

It was a place in which to dream, if quietness and

beauty induce day-dreams. The skies were very bright and the blue concave seemed so near, that the birds floating aloft looked as if they would brush against it, and come down glittering in the dyes of heaven. The water was still, and the mews flying on its surface might have been taken for silver rings jointed in four places, and set rolling on a crystal flood. The trim little yacht sat on the loch, her image so thoroughly reproduced that if she had been a living thing she would have sniffed about it, and made advances as a kitten does when it sees itself in a mirror. The land too was taking advantage of his brother sea's good humor to lock his hand in his, and they appeared one. It was difficult to distinguish them, and tell where the water ended and the shore began. The very mountains were trying to look at themselves in the glass, and the downy gold-tinged cloudlets changed places in the water as they did in the sky with a slow, lazy grace of movement.

The girls sat silent for a long time, when Bell said suddenly, "Mary, you are the very thing for an evening like this."

"Why?"

"Because you can hold your tongue."

"Any one can do that. It's not difficult."

"Not very many people can do it well." Mary laughed.

"But don't you know, Mary, that there is a silence that is oppressive, and a silence that is delicious?—the people that are silent, not meaning in the least either to soothe or irritate you."

"Then it must be you who are either in a good or bad humor."

"Perhaps, possibly; I don't know," said Bell musingly."

"Oh!" cried Mary, in a tone of alarm; "there's a man coming down the hill above us."

"Are you frightened? The people are not savages."

"No; but we are far from the house, and he may be a sturdy beggar."

"If he is a beggar, I hope he is sturdy, poor creature. People that beg would need to be sturdy, I think."

"Bell, I don't believe you know what fear is."

"Oh, I could be as frightened as any one if I saw good cause, but the man coming is one of the men belonging to that yacht. I have watched him all the time: two landed, one went along the shore, the other up the hill, and now he's coming down again, and we'll have the pleasure of gazing at a human being other than ourselves."

"I hope he'll pass and take no notice of us."

"To be sure he will! You are easily frightened, Mary."

The man in passing looked very broadly at them with a half smile on his face. It seemed as if he would go on, then he stopped, turned and said, "I suppose you don't know me? My mother was not sure of me."

"Peter Veitch!" cried Bell, starting up and laughing with pleasure. "Your mother must not have had her spectacles on; you have grown a hairy creature, but I would know a Quixstar face looking out of a bear's skin."

"I would not have known him," said Mary.

"But how are you here?" Bell asked. "I heard uncle was teaching you, and I know he does not allow trifling; and how did you know us—we are a little changed I should think?"

"I'll sit down before I tell you, although you don't ask me."

"Oh, yes. Share our stump; Mary, can you—"

Peter was just putting his foot on a grassy knoll, when Bell cried—

"Not there; don't set your foot down there. Oh, it's done."

"What is it? What is done?" he asked, puzzled.

"Look here," and she went on her knees on the grass, while he did the same, "do you see what you've done now? You have bombarded a city, made a volcanic eruption, an earthquake." It was an ant-hill into which he had crashed his foot, making an awful commotion. "These creatures will have a third edition of their newspaper out to-night—how do you think you'll figure in it?"

"The ants were hurrying hither and thither in terrible confusion, those of them that had escaped destruction wildly asking what had happened, and the news spread in a way that might have made the telegraph blush for its deliberation, then gangs of the little shiny brown and black insects set to work to bury the dead and repair the ruin.

"I have made fearful havoc," said Peter, looking up from the curious sight and meeting Bell's eyes, "and I'm very sorry."

"So am I, but it can't be helped," and at this very moment across the ant-hill a look printed a thought between these two that never might remove—printed it, however, in invisible ink.

"We can't do anything to help them, I suppose?" said Mary.

"Stand out of their way, that's all," said Bell. "I wonder if the little atoms can feel grief?"

"I hope not," said Peter, "or I must have caused lamentation and woe."

"Well, now that the hubbub is over, what have you to do with that fairy ship lying on that fairy ocean?" Bell asked, pointing to the yacht.

"I am a visitor on board; it belongs to Walter Cranstoun."

"I commend his taste; to glide about on a summer sea in such an ark as that must be a very charming thing."

"He finds a week or two enough at a time, though," said Peter, "and so it is."

"What—don't you like the sea?"

"Yes, the sea; but I don't call that pretty pond the sea; at sea we have work as well as enjoyment—that's all enjoyment, and one tires of it."

"Do you enjoy a storm at sea?"

"Enjoy is not the word. I don't know that I could make you understand it; it is something deeper and higher than enjoyment. I wish you had been in a storm, you would not forget it; you would know what I mean."

"Tell me true—are you not frightened?"

"No," he said.

"Oh," said Mary, "it is as safe on the sea as on the land. God is everywhere."

"Yes; but it is not as safe on the sea as on the land," said Bell. "You don't think, Mary, that sitting in the parlor at Quixstar on a dark windy winter night is not safer than being on a ship in the Atlantic? If one place were as safe as another, where would courage be? You used to be a bold little urchin, Peter; I suppose you are that yet."

"An urchin? You can judge for yourself." They looked at him, and laughed. He was rather tall—not dark, however; his hair was lightish brown and still unruly—no treatment could take the curl out of it; his skin was brown with the sea tan; he had an open goodlooking face, keen grey eyes, with sight like a vulture's, a hearty laugh, and a frank manner, which bridged the interval since he and these girls had been school-fellows with the agility of a cat.

"What are you and uncle studying—mathematics?" asked Bell. "I thought so, that is his hobby, but sometimes I think he is not very bright, at least he seems so astonished at me understanding a thing readily that either he must have had great difficulty himself, or he must have thought me next thing to an idiot. I suppose you need mathematics to take the latitude and longitude?"

"Oh, I could do that before I knew mathematics at all; but I like to get to the bottom of things."

"That's very like you; but the worst of it is one never can get to the bottom of things.

"Well, as far as one can get."

"But don't you feel worried when you're baffled? I feel as I do when I am listening to intense silence,—my very external ears seem to stand up, but you make nothing of it. By the way, why are you not in white ducks and a blue jacket—isn't that the proper sailor rig? For anything I see, you might be a mere landlubber."

"That's what I am at present; you should see me at work."

"What do you do? Is it hard work, hauling at ropes and singing Dibdin's songs? I love Tom Bowling. I really would like to go a voyage to see into things."

"Would you?" said Peter with enthusiasm. "When you do, I hope it will be in my ship."

"Bell does not know what fear is," said Mary. "I would not go a sea-voyage if I could help it."

"What! when it is as safe on sea as on land?" said Bell.

"Oh, I forgot," said Mary.

"Has uncle been telling you yet that mathematics is pure poetry, Peter?"

"No, we have no poetic flights; we stick to business."

"I have not been able to see the poetry yet, but I may in time. Uncle does not talk much; how do you get on with him?"

"Oh, well enough."

"You'll have plenty to speak about; for my part, I can never think of anything to say."

"I would never have guessed that."

"Ah, when I am beside people that I can say anything to that comes into my head I get on, but with uncle I always catch myself thinking what to say, and when you do that nothing seems worth saying."

"I'm glad I'm not Mr. Sinclair," said Peter. "Are you going to be here long?"

"Till Friday."

"That is the day I arrive in Quixstar too. Do you see that man down there? He came ashore with me in search of milk or eggs or something, and he is getting impatient to be off."

"But you'll stop and go to the house with us and see the others?—we're all here."

"I'm sorry I can't wait. Tell them so, will you?" and he bade them good-bye, and strode down the hill with nothing of the porpoise-roll of the conventional sailor in his gait.

"He is changed," said Bell, "but very like himself."

"He seems to have stood hardships well."

"I hope he has not had many hardships, Mary."

"They waited till the boat pushed off, leaving a trail behind it as of arms stretched out to clasp some loved one and say farewell. Then the yacht spreading her sails glided away, and was lost to view round the nearest point. Still they lingered; it was a night that did not seem made for sleep, yet the deep rosy sleep of youth was not out of keeping with its exceeding beauty and majesty.

CHAPTER XXX.

When Bell and Mary went in they found the others assembled.

"What became of you?" said John.

"Rather, what became of you?" Bell answered; "why didn't you wait for us? But we have had an adventure which you have missed."

"I had a kind of adventure too," said Mrs. Sinclair. "A man, something like a sailor, passed the house; when he saw me sitting in the window he came forward and held out his hand. I said, 'No, no, I don't want any.'

"'Any what?' he said.

"'Shells or silks, or whatever you are selling,' I said.

"'I am not selling anything. I am Peter Veitch, the son of Peter Veitch at Quixstar.'

"'Well,' I said; 'what do you want?'.

"'Nothing,' he said, and went off quickly.

"I thought how true the words of the poet are, 'The child is father of the man!' He used to be a very forward boy, and it was certainly impudent enough of him to accost me as he did. If I had not checked him, no doubt he would have pushed himself in when we go back to Quixstar, especially as your uncle patronizes him."

Bell listened, her face red with vexation.

"Why were you so unkind, mamma?" she said; "it is not like you."

"Unkind, my love? It was true kindness to let the lad know his place at once."

"Oh, mamma, I believe he came ashore chiefly to see us, like the warm-hearted sailor he is. What will he think?"

"Don't be foolish, Bell. I had no intention of hurting the lad's feelings. He would see that well enough."

Bell said no more, but her spirits hung fire the rest of the evening, which Tom at length observing, said—

"Something must be going to happen. I have not heard Bell's voice for half an hour."

"I have been in silent thought," said she; "I read somewhere the other day that silent thought is electricity in abeyance. There's a grand name for holding your tongue, Tom. You keep a good stock of electricity in abeyance."

"You are distressed about the sea-king, I perceive," said John Gilbert.

"Yes, I am; very," she said.

"He had not felt the snubbing deeply, do you think?" said Mary "or he would not have spoken to us."

"He could not help feeling it," said Bell; "but he has a fine nature. He always had, and he overlooked it."

"Do fine natures swallow a snubbing easily?" asked John.

"I should think," said Tom, "fine natures that have come to maturity in the forecastle of a ship would; but you have not told us your adventure yet, Bell."

"Merely that we had half an hour's talk with Peter on the hillside; that's all."

"And discovered the fineness of his nature?"

"Rediscovered it only."

"Jane," said Bell next morning to Miss Gilbert, "you

must have had a dull walk last night with Tom. Effie says she and John never made up to you."

"How do you think it would be dull?"

"Oh, Tom has so little to say. I don't mind, because I'm his sister, and am fond of him, and know his good points, but it is different with you."

"I can't know him quite so well as you do, still—"

"What do you and he talk about? I sometimes tell him if ever he gets a wife she'll have to do the courtship, for he won't take the trouble."

Jane blushed and said, "Do you really think so? What do we talk of? Various things. He has a very sound judgment, I think, and he is steady and well-behaved—"

"Steady and well-behaved!" cried Bell, laughing, "I should think he is."

"Well, you should be thankful. I know people whose brothers are not that, and it is a great thing to have to do with men you don't need to be anxious about."

"It is a fine negative pitch of bliss, certainly."

"Negative or not, what can you enjoy if you are always anxious?"

"Now, I could imagine a case where anxiety would give a keen edge to happiness."

"Maybe. But there's mamma now;—to be sure papa and the rest of us are all she could wish, but she has had constant anxiety about money—how to make the most of a very limited income, and it is tiresome. Even if John had plenty of money I would not guarantee that he would not make ducks and drakes of it; but your brother will certainly never land himself in a disagreeable position."

"Not if he knows it."

"And he will always know what he is about. As I said, he appears to me to have such a sound judgment."

"Yes."

"You can't think how tiresome it is to have so little money! Mamma manages without losing her temper or spirits, but I couldn't."

"I think I could," said Bell; "it would be horrible if happiness depended on money when so few people have it."

"So mamma always says, but I have my own ideas about it."

It has been a custom among some semi-barbarous people to break all the beautiful dishes after a banquet, as a savage bravado of wealth, or perhaps to prevent them ever being put to less worthy or noble uses; but when the Sinclairs left this fair scene on which they, or some of them, had been feasting for weeks, they left it as fair as ever. The greatest vulgar man alive can't fold up the mountains and the tarns when he goes away, and have them unfolded and specially arranged for his own use when he returns. Possibly if he could do it he would. No,

> "the pomp that fills
> The circuit of the summer hills"

goes on without the faintest reference to him; nay, it makes the rude masses from the heart of a city as free of its glories as majesty itself can be.

On the day the Sinclairs left, just as they got out of the loch a steamer entered it, freighted to the water's edge with an excursion party. It passed quite close. The decks were crowded; there was singing and laughter, and fiddles playing, and babies crying. The sea was strewn with nut-shells, orange-skins, and empty paper bags. The day was hot, and on board there seemed to be a general swelter. It was enjoyment in the very rough.

"These," said Tom, "are going to spend the day at our late quarters."

"What desecration!" said Effie.

"Why desecration?" asked Bell. "I like to think of all these lungs being filled with fine air and these eyes with beauty, even if they are not very conscious of it. I saw one man, at least, with hard hands and corrugated face, who was laying his very ears into the scenery. If you had seen him! He was gazing and gazing with a perfect dream of delight in his face."

"Probably thinking where he would get a light for his pipe," said Tom.

"Well, there is no law against a blending of enjoyments,—is there, Tom? You and I ought to have a respect for tobacco," said Bell.

And the steamer churned on its way, leaving the water behind it a wide belt of white angry foam, over which the sea-gulls hovered and circled, dipping into it with their dainty pink feet curled up as if to keep them from being wet, and seizing any remnants of food thrown overboard. Was ever dirty work done by such graceful-looking scavengers?

CHAPTER XXXI.

PETER VEITCH had walked into his father's house unannounced on a Saturday afternoon. His father and mother were sitting at a table at the window, he reading a newspaper, she with one of her hands buried in the foot of the stocking she was darning. The house was resting from its usual Saturday forenoon scrubbing, the fireside was white as of old, a big pot was simmering over a clear glow of cinders in the grate,—except for an odor more rank than savory that escaped from it, it might have been a painted pot upon a painted fire, both looked so unlike any bustle of human affairs.

Peter stood for a second; then he said, "Mother! father! do you not know me?"

"Gude guide us! Peter, is it you, bairn?" said Mrs. Veitch, seizing his hand and stroking it.

"Man, Peter, I wadna kenned ye!" said his father, gazing at him. "Ye're nae mair like what ye was than a full-grown puddock is like a powowit."

"Maybe," said Peter. I don't think I had a tail to lose, had I?"

"I'm sure if ye had ye wad hae lost it," said his mother, "for ye was a wild laddie. I thought if your head hadna been weel fastened on, ye wad hae come in without it some day," and the tears glittered in her eyes.

"But it's on yet, you see; and I'm back all right—neither drowned nor wrecked; and the scent of grumphy's supper comes over me like an old song."

Peter's father and mother were proud of him—he was their son; but he was not the little urchin in baggy moleskins that had left them, and about whom they had agonized at parting, and who had promised to come back unchanged. The thing was not possible.

We part with our dearest friend, and Time instantly begins to insert a fine wedge, and by degrees splits our interests, our cares, our feelings, our occupations, all that makes our lives. We meet, but they will not dovetail again. The son of this pair had come back to them a stranger almost, a full-developed man who had seen something of the world, with different ideas and aims and education, and even a different language, only his heart was in the right place still. His father cross-examined him about his business, and his mother about himself.

"Bairn," she said, "I'll warrant ye hae had a heap o' hardships. Mony a nicht I couldna steek an e'e for thinking o' ye."

But Peter wouldn't confess to hardships. "I've roughed it a little," he said; "that's all.—And now I'll go out and take a look about the place, I think, for auld lang syne."

"Ay, do so," said his father; "and, man, if ye're passing Mr. Kennedy's door, wad ye look in and tell him I canna come on Monday, but if Tuesday'll do I'll come? He sent a message when I was out that he wanted me in the garden on Monday."

"Hout, man," said his wife, "Peter'll no' care for gaun errands now."

"Just as much as ever I did, mother. I'll report myself to the minister, and give the message."

Peter strolled about for a while,—not sentimentally at all, not as a man after the lapse of half a lifetime looks at the haunts of his youth, but in joyous mood, for he had life before him, and was in high health and spirits.

Being Saturday evening, he found Mr. Kennedy in his study. It was the gloaming; and Mr. Kennedy, seeing what he supposed was a rustic in his Sunday clothes, thought to himself, "Some young fool wanting to get married."

Peter introduced himself, and gave his father's message.

" So you are Peter Veitch ? " said Mr. Kennedy, not visibly struck by the intelligence. " Well, I hope you are behaving yourself. And you have tired of the sea, and are going to take to the spade and the hoe again ? "

This was precisely the remark Mr. Kennedy had made the last time he saw Peter; but when memory begins to get just a little blurred, the same circumstances bring up not merely the same ideas, but the same words.

" No, I am not tired of the sea. I like it better than I did at first."

" Ay, indeed ? Well, there are not many who can say that.—You've grown a good deal, Peter."

" Yes, I have been long away. My father and mother have been telling me of a good many changes here—"

" Yes, yes, changes. Change is the great law of the world, and we must all submit," Mr. Kennedy said, half speaking to himself.—" Well, my lad, I'm glad you are liking your calling and behaving yourself; it is always a comfort to hear of a lad behaving himself. This is Saturday evening; but I'll see you again." Holding open the door, he continued, " You'll find your way out, I daresay; —and tell your father Tuesday will do as well as Monday. Good-night.—I'm very glad to know that you are behaving yourself.

Thinking over this interview after he retired to his

chamber, Peter laughed. Peter found his sleeping quarters in his father's house exactly as he had left them, not that from romantic devotion the door had been locked, and the apartment kept sacred in his absence—that was impossible, owing to the simple fact that it had not a door. It was reached by a stair, the stair being a ladder laid against what appeared to be a hole cut in the roof of the passage. A bed canopied by the sloping rafters, a chair, and two *kists*—big blue-painted boxes—which had contained the whole worldly wealth of Peter and his wife when as yet they were serving man and maiden, made up the furniture of the room, but the sailor had not been accustomed to very luxurious quarters, nor did it matter to him. After he was in bed he had an opportunity of watching the heavens from the four panes of glass that shone like an eye in the roof of his nest, till he fell asleep with the imaginary dash of billows in his ear.

When he awoke it was Sabbath morning, and labor knew it, and was still. He opened the sky-light, and looked out. The smoke of the household fires was beginning to steal from the chimneys, and lose itself in the pure morning air. He could see in the garden the little hut of divots he had made for a rabbit-house still standing, the top of it grown over with the minutely wrought rich little flower called None-so-pretty,—almost a weed, yet the workmanship and the tints are exquisite: anything more perfect than the coloring, shaping, and arranging of the leaves into the bright green rosettes clustered so humbly on the ground need not be seen; dear it is to every man and woman who has ever been a child in an old-fashioned garden. The water glided past from the upland glens where all night it had been singing a quiet tune to the sleeping woods. Some horses were in a field on the north side of the water, and of all rural sights on a Sunday, horses at large are not the least pleasant. Birds are pleasant. They may have their trials; it is said that they feel bereavements deeply, but one can't believe that their coquettish little noddles were ever made for anything but enjoyment. If labor is a curse, it has not alighted on them. Do they have twinges of rheumatism? do the small wings ever feel stiff? do the tiny throats ever crave a lozenge? are they ever in low spirits? It cannot be; they are always having change of air and scene. I am persuaded their lives are all holiday, or why should they hop, sing, and dance as they do? Therefore, although they are a sight passing pleasant, you are not so much *en rapport* with them as with the hard-worked horses. The horse that on Saturday laid its whole mind and strength to dragging a burden, on Sunday saunters leisurely in the park, twitches his tail, cocks and uncocks his ears twenty times in a minute, picks out the dainty morsels in the field, and eats in the society of his intimates, or lays his neck across a dike and has an interview with a neighbor, or takes a canter or a roll on the grass as if intoxicated with the air of freedom. Swift must have been contemplating horses at large on a Sunday when he conceived the idea of that remarkable kingdom where the horses were the masters, and the yahoos did all the dirty work. Bees are commonly supposed to have no regard for the Sunday, but that is a mistake. Like the Jews, they have a Sabbath of their own, and keep it. Winter is their resting-time, and the whole summer is a preparation for it. On this Sunday they were away travelling through the air, and alighting on a tall French willow in the garden, passing from pink bloom to pink bloom, with a low hum of satisfaction, gathering taxes from Flora, who makes no resistance to the diligent civil little officials.

Of old, Peter had been accustomed to wash his face at the back-door, as less favored or distinguished members of the family were expected to do still, but he found now that his mother's care had given him the means of making his toilet before he descended. It was a brief inartificial process. Also his mother stayed in from church to cook a dinner, which was not her custom—not that they went without dinner on Sunday, only it managed to cook itself on ordinary occasions; but Benjamin had come home safe.

On Monday morning Mr. Sinclair in walking past the gardener's cottage was hailed by his wife. "Ye'll ken what's happened, Mr. Sinclair?" she said.

"No."

"Was ye no' in the kirk yesterday?"

"Yes, I was there."

"Is't possible that ye didna see our Peter, the sailor?"

"I did not observe him; but," he said apologetically, "I don't notice people in church."

It was inconceivable to Mrs. Veitch how any one could have failed to see Peter.

"He cam' hame on Saturday, and his ship is repairing, so he'll bide a wee the now."

"Tell him I'll expect to see him to-day," said Mr. Sinclair.

"Thank you, sir; I'll do that."

Maddy Fairgrieve was in Peter's cottage shortly after Mr. Sinclair.

"I'm sure, Maddy," said Mrs. Veitch, "ye kenned Peter was come hame. How did ye no' tell Mr. Sinclair? He didna ken."

"Weel, he kens noo. I dinna think he is far ahint. What cam' o' you yesterday forenoon."

"I had the denner to look after. I ran out on

Saturday nicht, on the spur o' the moment, and killed a hen, and I was vexed after I saw how mony eggs was in't; but Peter's no' at hame every day," said Mrs. Veitch, trying to excuse herself for the extravagance she had been guilty of. "It wad hae laid on a' simmer, but it canna be helped now." Her habitual thrift was asserting itself in spite of her maternal feelings. Nor is it trifling (apart from the pleasure of a smile) to record this trait of Mrs. Veitch's character. Probably thrift has founded more families than soldiership or legal acumen: even royal houses have been built on this very homely and fast disappearing quality.

Mr. Sinclair and Peter entered on their mathematical studies at once, and resumed them immediately on Peter's return from his visit to Mr. Cranstoun on board the yacht—a visit accounted for by Mr. Cranstoun's anxiety to have the opinion of a practical seaman on his new toy, Tom Sinclair alleging that Mr. Cranstoun was short of hands, and had asked Peter to stop a gap, but Peter never worried himself seeking for reasons why kindness was shown him, but was always ready to take it for kindness pure and simple. A nature like this keeps wonderfully free from the vexatious dust that clogs the movements of more complicated machinery.

CHAPTER XXXII.

"Oh, Miss Bell," said Maddy Fairgrieve when the family returned, "I am glad you're come back. I've just been like a fish out o' water the time you've been away, and so has your uncle, but he doesna let on."

"I rather think, Maddy, he has enjoyed our absence."

"He couldna do that—wha likes an empty house?—and even now that ye're come hame, I dinna seem o' much use."

"What, Maddy! do you want me to say we couldn't do without you?"

"I never want folk to say what's no' true; but I like best to work among bairns, and there's nane o' ye bairns now."

"That's a melancholy fact. I dearly love my own little disappeared self, that you used to order about so."

"Me order! I was far ower simple wi' ye a'; but I whiles think if I could just fa' in wi' a widower with a young family I wad hae naething to wish for."

"Oh, Maddy, what a pity widowers don't know! We'll advertise. Plenty of people do that," said Bell, laughing; "I'll draw up the advertisement, if not for your sake for that of the young family, in whom I'm interested already. What shall we say? We'll begin with 'Widowers'—then 'respectable' in brackets. Come, help, Maddy; it must be short and to the point. 'A kind-hearted and experienced woman wishes to marry a man with as many small encumbrances as possible; references and cartes exchanged.' Will that do? How many words is it? twenty-four, I declare. Now you get eighteen for sixpence; what can we strike out? I think the person who invented that system invented a powerful educational engine. We could just say, 'Woman wishes to marry man,' etc., and leave him to find out your good qualities at his leisure, and then he'll only cost you sixpence. Cheap, if good. You must get your carte taken again, and in a new gown; and when your head is between the tongs, just look pleasant, will you? remember what is at stake."

"Ye're a daft lassie," said Maddy; "wad ye really send a thing like that to a paper?"

"Why not?"

"And bring a' the riff-raff o' the country down on a body. Na, na! we'll leave it to Providence."

"But Providence works by instruments, Maddy."

"That's true; but we'll no' put an instrument like that in his hand.—There's the door-bell ringing; that'll be Peter Veitch to his lesson wi' your uncle. I was diverted wi' his mother. She was angry Mr. Sinclair didna see him in the kirk the first Sunday he was at hame."

"Well, it was not unnatural; he is the apple of her eye."

"Apple! but folk needna be silly, they micht haud their tongues; I think I could hae done that."

"Ay; but everybody is not you."

"That's true; and Peter is a fine-looking laddie, and just as free and frank as ever. When he cam' in the first time, he says, 'Ha, Maddy, is that you? You're not a day older; and how's the keeper?'"

"What did he mean by that?" asked Bell; "what's the keeper?"

"He wad ken best himsel' what he meant," replied Maddy, laughing.

"I wish uncle would ask Peter to stay a little after his lesson is over."

"He'll do that some nicht likely," said Maddy.

"I wish he would," echoed Bell.

Left to the freedom of his own will, that is what Mr. Sinclair would have done, but he was specially warned by his sister-in-law not to do it.

"No good ever comes of taking people out of their own stations," she said; "and it may do evil. The girls have good sense, and have been well brought up, and I can trust them perfectly, still—".

"I'm sure," said Mr. Sinclair, with a tinge of irony, "if they come to grief, it won't be your blame. Well, I'll keep Peter to myself."

"I'm glad you see and appreciate my views; if you were to bring the lad in for a little just before he sails I would not mind; his parents are decent people, and deserve to be noticed, perhaps."

"I don't appreciate your views," said Mr. Sinclair, with customary bluntness, " but, as I said, I'll keep Peter to myself."

And Peter came and went without being admitted into Mrs. Sinclair's dovecot; but the doves were to be met elsewhere, and they were met, and the ink in which the thought was printed across the ant-hill began to grow visible to two pairs of eyes in the warmth of these meetings, and when Mrs. Sinclair and her daughters were sitting together of an evening, and Effie would remark, "Peter Veitch is with uncle; I heard him come in," and Mrs. Sinclair said, "Yes, my dear," Bell said nothing; but as the hour wore on, she would lean her head on her hand, or, putting her hands on the table, would lay down her head altogether. When her mother would ask, "What's the matter, Bell; have you a headache?" "No, I haven't a headache; I'm listening. I like to listen, even if there's nothing to hear. If you train yourself to listening your hearing gets very sharp." And by this system of training Bell heard her uncle going to the door with his pupil, and making such an uncommon and valuable remark as this, "It seems a fine night," and the rejoinder, "Very; good-bye, sir," and felt her happiness sensibly increased.

Peter had keen eyes and ears also, yet even his sight could not pierce a stone wall nor see through a door; but we have all heard of the miser who upbraided his son for rubbing his allowance of bread on the locked door of a room, in a closet of which there stood cheese, as a most luxurious extravagance; so Peter found it a great luxury to have the chance of sending his eyes along passages where Bell might possibly be, and of passing the door of a room in which she likely was. To see her standing at a window as he approached the house was—it is not good to overstate a case—but it was very apt to confuse his ideas of the old Egyptian's problems, and give Mr. Sinclair an opportunity of demonstrating the whole thing to his own satisfaction principally.

CHAPTER XXXIII.

THERE were blackguards in Quixstar, not many or great to be sure, still not to be despised in their own line. Advancing civilization has not left the blackguards behind, at least those capable of taking the arm she holds out to them, and keeping pace with her. From these she has taken the ruffian bearing, the bludgeon, and the crape, and substituted an oily tongue and a pen, which may make them less mischievous, or more so. But about this time there was a revival of the brutal type, and Mr. Cranstoun had got two young athletes, not very bad yet, but with fine possibilities of undeveloped blackguardism about them, to enter a protest against the effeminacy of the age, and to give an exhibition of the noble art of self-defence. This was the one grain of truth among Miss Raeburn's fictions in that letter which any one who liked her would have called amusing, and which one who did not like her would have called foolish, and even wicked. Walter Cranstoun specially invited Peter Veitch to be present, an invitation which was accepted. This was not a very great honor, as any one in the secret of the hour and the men was free to go to it; and it was curious to observe the kind of people among whom the mystery of the impending event had been whispered.

The theatre of operations was a field of Sir Richard's, chosen near the railway station for convenience, and out from the station gate came most of the spectators. They were not like people going to a sheep or cattle market, nor like brokers on their way to a displenishing sale, nor like guests for a wedding, nor mourners for a funeral, and yet they had a dash of all these characters in their less respectable phases, but if told they were going to a prize-fight you would at once have recognized the fitness of the thing, and there is always a certain beauty in fitness—they were the men for the occasion, and it was the occasion for the men.

It was not a sight good to look upon, but Peter Veitch stood and looked at it; so did John Gilbert. John had come from Eastburgh on purpose to be present —he enjoyed seeing life; but he returned to Eastburgh as soon as it was over, so that if his own family heard he was there they might be pretty sure that report was a mistake.

Mr. Cranstoun and more than a dozen kindred spirits retired to the inn at Quixstar to dine and settle their bets. It is a rational thing to dine—a wise thing to dine in company—a right genial thing to dine with old friends—therefore Peter Veitch accompanied them; he had no dislike to seeing life any more than John Gilbert.

Old Peter Veitch and his wife sat long by the fire that night, she audibly wondering " what was keeping that callant," and he prolonging his usual smoke, filling his pipe oftener than once; but they were not anxious. " He's nae ill gate," his mother said, and Peter sat, his eyes half shut, and with that pleased idiotic look on his face peculiar to people in the act of smoking.

At length, convinced that Peter had found a night's quarters elsewhere, they rose to go to bed, when there came a dull thud against the house-door.

"Preserve me! what's that?" said Mrs. Veitch.
"We'll look and see," said her husband.

They opened the door, and sitting on the step with his back to them and his head bent forward was a man. Mrs. Veitch stooped to look at him, and even in the gray light she recognized her son.

"It's Peter," she cried, "and something has come ower him."

The old man put a hand on his son's shoulder and peered into his face.

"He's drunk," he said, "the first thing is to get him in."

Without another word, and with much exertion, they got him into the house; to get him up to his own bed was impossible—he was drunk and incapable; they placed him on a chair, and there he sat helplessly, his mother at his shoulder supporting him. She and her husband gazed at each other; not only had they hitherto had perfect confidence in their son, they had looked up to him as to a superior being, and the mingling of love and pity and grief and amaze in their faces was wonderful. They got him to lie down on the bed, where he soon fell asleep, while they took their seats on each side of the fire again, saying never a word. They had made an idol of Peter, and they were struck dumb; fallen greatness men handle gently, even when they are not connected with it.

Before six the gardener went out to his daily labor, and Mrs. Veitch went into her garden to lay some clothes on the hedge to dry; when she came in again the bed was empty, she got a great start, but immediately a' voice from the upper regions cried, "Mother, I am here." She went up and spoke to him; he only said, "Leave me alone, mother."

Peter Veitch had not spent the last years of his life in a sheltered seclusion; but it is one thing to see other people in a state of drunkenness, and another to behold yourself on that beastly eminence. He hunted all round for some excuse, some palliation, but found none, nor the shadow of such a thing, so with a frightful headache he lay in misery and humiliation. It came into his mind, What if Mr. Kennedy should meet him, and ask how he was behaving himself? and in the midst of his wretchedness he laughed, then he rose and shook off his sin, so far as genuine repentance will do that, and, clothed in his right mind, he went down when his mother called him to dinner.

There was an awkwardness, although Peter and his wife exerted themselves to talk jauntily about various things, and Mrs. Veitch, by way of drawing her son out of his own thoughts and into the stream of conversation, asked cheerily, " What o'clock are ye, Peter? The knock was standing this forenoon, and I'm no sure that she's richt."

Then Peter had to reveal that on the previous night he had been robbed of purse and watch—the watch that had been his grandfather's, which had been given to him by his mother when he went to sea.

" Robbed ! " cried his father in the excitement of the moment; " that beats a'."

" Weel, weel," said Mrs. Veitch, " it was o' sma' value. Ye wad hae gotten naething for't but the price o' auld silver."

This watch, that had for many a year told off the hours of a good man's life, was by this time in the melting-pot.

It was not native talent that committed the robbery, although it must be allowed that there were natives equal to it, but a deputation of professional metropolitan thieves that had been sent that day to Quixstar on business, and a good deal of property changed hands, and did so with safety—no efforts were made by the owners to recover it.

"That was a fine affair at the station yesterday!" said Tom Sinclair to his sisters when he appeared next day. "The field is trampled as if a herd of buffaloes had been in it. I'm told that the very game was scared; and by the way, the sea-king was crapulous."

"That's the name John Gilbert invented for Peter Veitch," said Effie; "but what does crapulous mean?"

"What! You learned ladies don't know what crapulous means? Go to the dictionary."

"I know," said Bell; "it's from the Latin—*crapitas, crapitos, crapitorum*, to use obsolete long words."

"Oh, a little learning is a dangerous thing," said Tom.

"Drink deep," said Bell, laying her hand on her brother's shoulder; "and that is exactly what Peter Veitch did not do."

"Crapulous," said Effie, who had gone to the dictionary, "means sick with drunkenness."

"You have it," said Tom.

"Peter Veitch was not drunk," said Bell. "You may have been told so, but it is a mistake."

"If it's a mistake, all the better for him," said Tom; "but it's a common thing among sailors, especially when they get a run on shore. Very likely he's used to it."

Bell did not trust herself to speak again. A drunken common sailor! "It's a lie," she said to herself emphatically, "and I'll make sure of it. Whom can I ask? There is no one I can ask but himself, and I'll do it this very evening."

As the man who plans murder fixes his eye on what

he will have, revenge or booty, and loses sight of the means and their consequences, so Bell thought of nothing but the straightest road to her end, and as the door opened in the evening to admit Peter to his lesson, he lifted up his eyes and beheld her come sweeping down the staircase, her figure, especially her head, framed in a sheaf of bright rays which the autumn sun sent through the window behind her, and he was dazzled. What if this wondrous vision had hailed him with the unminced question, "Were you drunk last night?"

But it came on and said, "How do you do? Yes; I think uncle is waiting for you," and disappeared through a door.

If Bell had asked that question she would have proved herself her mother's daughter, which she was not. Nature in making her had taken a leap back among her ancestors to select the materials, and in coming down the stairs it had flashed on her, "If it is true, have I any right to humble him before me? and if it is not true, have I any right to insult him?" which correct instinct produced the very tame interview recorded, although one would really have liked to know how Peter would have taken it. It is to be feared that, humbled in his own eyes though he was, it would have gone far to prove the goddess mortal. As it was, he went away with the picture set in rays hung up in his memory for ever.

When Mr. Sinclair came in from seeing his pupil to the door he said, "Peter leaves to-morrow to rejoin his ship. He is a fine young man."

"You might have asked him in for a little," said Mrs. Sinclair.

"I might, but probably he'll be busy to-night, and I did not ask him."

CHAPTER XXXIV.

So Bell held her faith in Peter Veitch unshaken. Faith and love go hand in hand all the world over, and anything more terrible than their divorce human nature is not called upon to endure, yet just such an engine of torture as this was being slowly but surely prepared for nerves of the finest in Quixstar.

How many people must come into this world, and go out of it, without encountering genuine sympathy. Not the kind of people who lift up their voices and cry aloud for it, who meet with nothing congenial, and tell you of their very fine and delicate feelings—when you fall in with such, look out for some extra piece of selfishness, and you'll not likely be disappointed; but those whose fineness of feeling shows itself in care for others, and in freedom from selfishness, the good and the humble, whose humility is not a creeping self-conscious thing, leaving them liable to be trampled on, but a quality that is always clad in dignity and self-respect. Such a person was Mrs. Gilbert. It would need a fine touch to draw her truly. Her daily life was a repetition of details too trifling to be dwelt on, but which had to get her best attention, or the domestic machine would have begun to creak and groan. She did not delight in them, but she attended to them well and ungrudgingly. Many women would have become smaller and narrower in such circumstances, but she had capacity to guard against that—only this very capacity, and the high tone on which her nature was pitched, if they increased her enjoyments, laid her open also to keener suffering.

Despite her love—and it was deep and true—she could not help taking the measure of her children in some degree. She saw the hardness, the want of elevation, the worldy shrewdness of her eldest daughter, and had done her best to combat them. If Jane could have been infected, smitten, with some higher qualities, no doubt she would have been; but you'll not teach a drumhead cabbage to shrink by putting it alongside a sensitive plant. Still, love made the best of it. Jane would be able to stand her own ground. Mrs. Gilbert had less anxiety about her than about Mary, who was shy and dreamy, with little force of character. But John—she had every reason to feel satisfied about him. He had got safely over the most perilous time, the first years of being out from under his father's roof. Yes; John's conduct and prospects were all that could be desired. She and his father believed that, but there were people who could have told them otherwise; and the wonder is, that some one with a conscientious love of carrying evil tidings had not made known to them that their son was spending money faster than he made it. He liked to do this, and he did it; but he came home every Saturday as innocent and as carelessly ready to enjoy himself as ever. He was not bad—not depraved, that is; if he had been possessed of a sufficient private fortune he would have acquired a good name, for he would have been under no temptation to do wrong, at least wrong of the kind he fell into.

"Are you going out, Bell?" Mrs. Sinclair asked. "And where are you going?"

"To Miss Raeburn's. Will you come?"

"Not to-night, thank you. I daresay you have fallen in love with Miss Raeburn?"

"Long ago. I do like her!"

"Well, I don't object. I don't think you'll get much harm from her. She often says unfortunate things; but my influence is greater than hers yet, although tact is not quite a thing that can be taught."

The shortest cut to Miss Raeburn's house was past Peter Veitch's cottage, and Bell took that way. While the sailor had been at home she took the other way out of deference to herself, for certainly no other person would have charged her with passing his father's house because he was there; but conscience makes cowards of us all. Now however it was different; different indeed!—all the difference between keen vivid interest and blank dulness!

As she was passing the door, Mrs. Veitch came out. They spoke.

"And Maddy's leaving ye?" said Mrs. Veitch.

"Leaving? I never heard of it," Bell said.

"She'll be ower blate to tell ye, likely."

"Blate!" said Bell; "what should make her blate? Nonsense!"

"She's gaun to be married. I wonder ye dinna ken."

"She must have been wooed by proxy, surely. I can't believe it."

"It was made up the time ye was awa'. It's the gamekeeper—the man whose wife died eighteen months syne, leaving a lot o' wee bairns. I dinna think but Maddy'll mak' a gude stepmother."

"First-class!" said Bell, laughing. "I remember she said something one day she no doubt intended for a hint, but I was dull, and did not take it up.—Providence indeed!" Bell said to herself.

"I've just gotten a letter from Peter," said Mrs. Veitch, speaking on the theme nearest her heart. "His ship is to sail the morn."

"You'll miss him after having him so long."

"Miss! miss is nae word for't! Eh, Miss Sinclair, be glad ye hae naething to do wi' sailors."

"It's to Melbourne he's going, isn't it? That's often a pleasant voyage, and not dangerous."

"Maybe; but it'll be a weary time ere we see him again, if ever."

"You should not look at the dark side," said Bell cheerily, as they parted; and Mrs. Veitch thought, " It's easy speaking. It wad mak' nae odds to her if Peter was at the bottom o' the sea; but oh, the difference to his faither and me !"

"Ah, Tibby," said Miss Raeburn, " I'm always glad to see you. Come and tell me how the world's using you. You look a little glum; what's amiss?"

"Nothing, except original depravity, if I am looking glum. The world uses me too well; that's the only thing I have to complain of."

"It is not a common complaint."

"Well, you see, I have nothing to do but enjoy myself, and I have done that remarkably well yet."

"Is there anything to hinder you going on doing it?"

"Nothing; but I would like to have work—something to do."

"Send away the housemaid and beat the carpets."

"That would be turning her out of a situation."

"But you don't mean to stand idle till every other creature in the world has got work, do you?"

"I can beat carpets, and I like it—it is very exhilarating; still, that's not the kind of work—"

"There it is," said Miss Raeburn. " Now, Tibby, I

thought you had more sense than join in that stupid cant about having nothing to do. If you really can't get anything to do, be content to do nothing, and hold your tongue."

" It's all very well for you, Miss Raeburn, who have no care that you want to divert—"

" And pray what care have you that you want to divert? This is something new. Out with it, Tibby!"

" It's nothing very great; but I don't want to think too much about it, and as it concerns another person I can't tell it."

" How very, very mysterious! And you want something to drive dull care away? I could give you some hours' work in my garden every day, if that would do. I'm going to have Peter Veitch, and you would be under his orders, and his conversation might divert your thoughts."

" He is a good old man!" said Bell warmly.

" Excellent among the excellent," said Miss Raeburn, looking straight into her visitor's face; "and you could sympathize with him on his son's departure."

" I couldn't—I think he was right to go. I wonder at Tom, for instance, our Tom—do you know what he is going to do?"

" Something rational, I don't doubt."

" The bank he is in at Eastburgh is going to open a branch here, and they have offered Tom the management, and he means to take it. Think of it! at his age, when he might do anything! Why, he might as well be a horse in a mill."

" I think Tom is right; he is not a dunce. A man that can take the correct measure of himself is no dunce."

" Of course, Tom is not; if he were a dunce I would

not wonder at it, or if he were compelled by circumstances—but his own free choice!"

"You approve of Peter Veitch going to sea; that's generally thought a monotonous life!"

"It can't be monotonous to a person with any mind. Peter does not find it so; he told me if he had his choice to make now, with all the experience he has had, he would still go to sea."

"I am glad to hear it, very glad that he has not mistaken his vocation; still, I must say I sympathize with Tom preferring to stay on dry land at the kingly occupation of counting out his money, and he'll have exercise for his mind in dealings with his customers; it won't do to hand out money to any one."

"Oh, he'll need to know their circumstances, whether they have money, and how much;—very interesting!"

"To know these things is very interesting to most people who are not babes in the wood suffering from mysterious cares which they cannot reveal. I have been young, and now I am old—"

"You're not old, Miss Raeburn."

"Oldish, and I think it is well when the average shoemaker sticks to his last; he is likely to do more good and less ill by that than any other course."

"Have you had a visit from uncle?"

"No."

"I thought you were reproducing his ideas in different words."

"Great minds jump," said Miss Raeburn. "What does your mamma think?"

"Oh, she thinks Tom is burying himself, but is reconciled to it because she'll have him beside her."

"And having him always at home may be the means of lightening your load of mysterious care."

"Ah, you may laugh. Have you ever known care, Miss Raeburn?"

"Have I ever known anything else? Have you never guessed? But it is a sad story—"

"Ah, I am sorry if I have touched on—you really always look so happy."

"Looks! what are looks? When I think of my husband—"

"Oh!" cried Bell, with a start, "have you a husband?"

"No; that's the point. I ought to have one—there's one born for every woman, but he and I have missed each other, and either he is gone, or he is wandering in lonely wretchedness, or he is tied to the wrong person. Conceive what I suffer sitting here in helpless ignorance. Talk of care, indeed!"

"And he may be suffering as much on your account," said Bell.

"True; I did not think of that."

"I'm vexed I have suggested it; it was very heedless—"

The door-bell rang. "That," said Bell, "is a man. I saw him pass the window. Perhaps Mr. Phantom, your husband?"

"Not Mr. Phantom, my husband, but Mr. Raeburn, my brother," she said as Mr. Raeburn entered.

CHAPTER XXXV.

It was fine moonlight, and Bell took the roundabout way home. Two people in different parts of the world, both looking at the moon, have in all ages and nations been supposed by this act to have communion at once ethereal and comforting. Bell gazed at the moon, and Peter Veitch gazed at it—he saw not only the moon in the heavens, but half a dozen moons floating about on the inky waters of the harbor. Possibly five thousand pairs of lovers were looking at the moon that night, but she carried no distinct messages. Nature is like a deaf and dumb mother — she is infinitely tender, she will soothe and comfort, and smile and weep, but she does not hear, and she cannot answer. In the midst of the rude and civil bustle on the ship's deck before departure, the moon showed Peter the red tiles of his father's cottage, and the gravel in front of Old Battle House whitened by her rays, contrasting with the straight line of deep shadow thrown across it by the building, and made his heart glad, while she enveloped Bell in a happy reverie broken in upon by a voice that said, "Whither bound?" She started, but it was only John Gilbert.

"Homeward bound," she answered.

"You neither saw nor heard me coming," he said. "Where have you been?"

"I was at Miss Raeburn's, and I left when her brother from Ironburgh came."

"Mr. Raeburn—indeed! are you sure?"

"Quite sure; is it of any consequence? I both saw and spoke to him."

"Then you are right. I am on my way to see Mrs. Gilbert."

"Is it not too late to go in on the old lady?"

"No; I'll be in time for supper, and I can make myself useful conducting the orgies."

"I hope they are not too boisterous?"

"I try not to go to sleep at least. By the bye, I'll give you something; I got a bunch of them the other night from her," he took out his pocket-book; "I forgot all about them."

"What are they?"

"Not pound-notes," he said, taking out some slips of paper, "it is a copy of verses. Mrs. Gilbert has a lot for distribution; you'll see it's 'Lines by a Pious Idiot.' Of course lines by pious idiots are not scarce, it is the artlessness of the confession I admire. Give one to Effie, and here is one for yourself, which you'll keep for my sake; you may as well think of two idiots when you are about it."

"John, you are a regardless mortal, I doubt."

"I'm glad you doubt it; but I must tear myself away, or Mrs. G. will have put on her night-cap."

When Bell got within the gates of Old Battle House she stood for a little, enjoying the stillness and the moonlight. As she stood she heard a sound as of suppressed sobbing among the thick dark bushes. The bushes were high, and she saw no one, but wondering who or what it could be she turned into a narrow footpath and went to the place the sound seemed to come from. She stood, and getting accustomed to the darkness a figure appeared leaning against a tree. She instantly recognized her sister's dress. ."Effie," she said in astonishment, "is it you? What are you doing here?"

Effie sobbed again.

"What is it? What in the world is it, Effie? Tell me?"

"John Gilbert is going away," said Effie between sobs.

"Never mind John Gilbert, but tell me what you are crying about."

"I tell you he is going away to Van Diemen's Land or Australia, or some of these places, and we may never see him again."

"Nonsense! I parted with him only a few minutes ago, and he said nothing about it."

"He does not wish it known."

"Not known! How can he help it being known? and why did he tell you if he does not want it known? I don't understand it."

"You mustn't tell. Even his mother is not to know till he is off."

"What has he done? and why does he tell you only?"

"I've known him all my life," sobbed Effie; "and—and—we are engaged."

"Engaged! To be married do you mean?"

"Yes; and it may be years before he comes back—if ever."

"Oh, Effie, Effie!" said Bell in a tone of profound tenderness, "I am sorry for you. Does mamma know?"

"No; and you must not tell her. I did not intend to tell you, but I could not help it."

"You have done wrong, Effie, and John Gilbert has done wrong in getting your promise, and binding you not to tell, and he must have some reason—not good I doubt—for going abroad in this way."

"Right or wrong, I love him," said Effie proudly and passionately, "and you must promise here to keep our secret."

Bell was surprised at such force of will in her sister, who had hitherto appeared always glad to follow rather than to lead. She was effectually diverted from her own cares whatever they might be, but she would not give her sister an unconditional promise to keep her secret. While she was soothing and comforting Effie, Miss Raeburn was saying to her brother—

"How long are you going to stay this time, Jamie?"

"I must be in Ironburgh to-morrow forenoon."

"Then we'll hardly have time to thaw. Isn't it curious how you and I should need thawing when we meet now-a-days?"

"I did not know that, Joan, but I'll break the ice boldly. I came to speak of John Gilbert. Do you know anything about him?"

"Do I know about John Gilbert? How know?"

"Do you see him often? Does he come home regularly?"

"Yes. What do you mean? He was often at Lochside with the Sinclairs in summer. They are intimate, more so of late than they used to be. John is clever."

"Too clever, I am afraid."

"What is it, Jamie? He has not been doing anything bad?"

"He has put my name to a bill, and got it cashed."

"Forgery!" said Miss Raeburn.

"Yes; that's the name for it. I have not denied my signature yet."

"Don't do it," she said earnestly. "It would kill his mother."

"It is entirely on her account I have paused. Even

Jane does not know of it. Thank God it is none of my sons."

Miss Raeburn was silent. She had more personal affection for John Gilbert than she had for any of her nephews, except the boy who was drowned, and the eldest, who had been much with her as a child, and with whom she kept up a close correspondence now that he was in India in some civil capacity. She knew little of the others, the intercourse between Ironburgh and Quixstar had grown more and more slack as years passed. Mr. Gilbert imagined he was undervalued by his wife's relatives, as well as by the world in general, and this small jealousy worked its natural effect. Then Miss Raeburn did not particularly affect her brother's wife. If blame, or how much, attached to either party, it cannot be known, but so it was. Time can bring this state of matters about in the best regulated families, and whereas in early life Mr. Raeburn and his sister blended like two drops of quicksilver, it had come to pass that now, as Miss Raeburn said, they needed a little time to thaw when they met.

"It will kill his mother," repeated Miss Raeburn.

"I don't know, Joan. It is amazing what people will live through."

"But she need not know. Take up the bill as genuine."

"But what dependence can you have on him in future? I think if it had been one of my own sons, I would have let the law take its course. It might be better for him in the end."

"That you would not. Is the sum a large one?"

"It is quite large enough; but I don't mind the loss to myself. It is the depravity of the boy."

"I don't believe he can be depraved. He may be foolish."

"Don't defend him, Joan."

"But you'll not expose him? You'll give him another chance for his mother's sake?"

"That is what he calculated on."

"But he can't be hardened. I don't believe he is hardened. See him. I'll ask him to come here in the morning, and you can judge what had best be done."

When Miss Raeburn sent, inviting him to breakfast, John Gilbert was supping with Mrs. Gilbert, and accommodating himself to the lady's ideas with the same facility with which he suited himself to less worthy company.

Mrs. Gilbert had unbounded faith in her grandnephew. She considered she had had a hand in his training, and she liked to look at her handiwork. He was always ready to manage any little business matters for her, and she had much pleasure in a staff for her old age, which was at once useful and ornamental. On this night he told her that he had been distributing the "Lines" she had given him, and she said he would never regret being so well employed. He waited kindly on his old friend, for he really liked her, and he had a pleasure in doing it. No; he was not depraved, but he was very easy-going. Before he left he asked his aunt for a loan, not quite an insignificant one, and she gave it without an instant's hesitation. His conscience smote him, but the pang was momentary. He would repay her shortly, without doubt; as for his uncle Raeburn, he would never miss the money. It was merely a loan without his knowledge, and before long he would speedily repay it too. When he went home and heard of Miss Raeburn's invitation, it did not give him unmixed enjoyment, it confirmed him in the plan he had been maturing for some time, but he said, "Well, I'll see. If I'm not lazy in the morning I may go."

"In the morning, Mrs. Gilbert not hearing her son moving, knocked at his door, and getting no answer went in, but he was not there. "He has not been lazy," she thought; "I wonder I did not hear him go out." None of them had seen or heard him go out, but it was concluded he had gone to Miss Raeburn's, and without further remark they had breakfast, and Mr. Gilbert went away to his labor of teaching his part of that large section of humanity which, being shut into schools day by day for long hours, wonders how the rest of mankind spends its continual holiday; when a message came from Miss Raeburn to say that "If Mr. John could not come to breakfast, would he come up for a few minutes after?"

"What can have become of him?" said Mary. "It makes me think of the morning James Raeburn was drowned."

"Nonsense," said Jane. "He has remembered something he wanted to do in Eastburgh early, and has gone off without thinking. At all events, he is quite able to take care of himself."

Jane was of opinion that most people were quite able to take care of themselves.

Mrs. Gilbert was surprised, but not anxious. She had confidence in her son, and that does not shake and fall at once. In truth, she had no misgiving. Tom Sinclair came in for a minute as he passed the door on his way to the station, and undertook to make John send an account of himself whenever he reached Eastburgh.

Tom had his suspicions, which were verified when, on reaching Eastburgh, John Gilbert was *non est inventus*. He was angry; "He has not taken my advice," he thought, "and he must stand the consequences. Well, I did not undertake to tell his mother if I got him; I only undertook to make him report himself. They'll hear of it soon enough," and Tom went about his usual business not greatly ruffled.

CHAPTER XXXVI.

As there is a pause in nature before the crash of a storm, so a stillness came over the schoolmaster's dwelling, waiting for what might be dreaded as evil tidings. John's absence without explanation was so unaccountable. They did not send here and there inquiring for him—they waited. When Mr. Raeburn made a brief call, there was no particular allusion made to John's absence; and he went home, paid for, and concealed his nephew's guilt. The Gilberts kept quiet—that was not what Mr. Gilbert would have done,—he was not self-contained naturally; he would have asked everywhere if any one had seen his son; he would have given up his school for the time, and perhaps taken to bed with grief, but his wife's strength of mind came to his help. " Why compromise John in the eyes of the public?" she said; and he was persuaded to go on as usual. Moreover, Jane's constant iteration that Jack could take care of himself had its effect on her father. It also had its effect on her mother: she shrank from it—it was a coarse view of the case.

Whether John's absence was the result of thoughtlessness merely, or folly, or something darker, he had no idea of the suffering he caused, as day after day went past till nearly a week was gone, and nothing was heard of him.

Mrs. Gilbert was sitting alone one evening brooding

over the subject. The tide of love for her son swelled within her—her thoughts hunted round him and round him; and feeling the terrible strain, she had said to herself, " How cruel he is! how cruel!" at the same time shrinking from her own words, when suddenly Effie Sinclair slipped into the room and said abruptly—

" Have you not heard yet from John, Mrs. Gilbert? You should have heard by this time. He was to write before he sailed."

" Sailed!" said Mrs. Gilbert.

" Yes. Oh, he did not want it known, but he told me. He was to write, and I have not heard yet."

An incontrollable pang shot through Mrs. Gilbert, and the blood rushed to her face. He had told this girl, and left her—his mother—in ignorance and anguish!

" He was to write to me to the post-office in Eastburgh, and I have been there to-day and there is no letter; and I am so anxious—so anxious," pursued Effie. " I didn't mean to tell you—my own mamma doesn't know; but I thought you would have heard from him, and I am so anxious."

By this time Mrs. Gilbert was seeking excuses for her son, and Effie's eyes and her blushing face pleaded for her.

" Effie," said she, almost trembling as she spoke, " do you know why he went? Has he done anything wrong?"

" No, oh dear no! He said he would get on better in the colonies; that was all."

Mrs. Gilbert saw that was all Effie knew. If only she could be sure that was all!

" And where has he gone?"

" To Australia; he wasn't sure what part. Are you angry at him going away without telling, Mrs. Gilbert?"

"I am grieved—grieved in a way you can't understand."

Mrs. Gilbert had known Effie all her life: that she should ask if she was angry at her son going away as he had done was quite the kind of question she would have expected her to put. But there are times when any kind of human sympathy seems very poor and inadequate.

While Effie sat, the postman came to the door. She ran for the letter—John's writing was on the back of it— it was to his mother. Mrs. Gilbert opened it and read—

"DEAR MOTHER,—I sail to-day for Melbourne. I did not tell you, for if I had, neither you nor my father would have let me go. Now, a man has a far better chance of getting on in a new country than in our old crowded island. I hope you have not been uneasy. I mean to come home before long with a fortune. My love to you all.—I am your affectionate son,

"JOHN GILBERT.

"*P.S.*—Write to the post-office at Melbourne; I'll call there when I land."

Mrs. Gilbert held the note in her hand like one in a dream. Was this her son, her very son in whom her life was almost bound up? He hoped she had not been uneasy!

Effie started up.

"My letter will be in Eastburgh. I'll go for it the first thing to-morrow," she exclaimed. "You'll keep our secret, Mrs. Gilbert? I only told it through stress of anxiety. You'll keep it?"

"Yes," Mrs. Gilbert said, hardly knowing what she was saying.

"Good-bye," cried Effie; and she went as abruptly as she had come.

The first member of the family to come in was Jane. Mrs. Gilbert was sitting, still with the note in her hand. She was not thinking, she could not think, she was hardly feeling, she was almost beyond that with this thing that had come upon her.

"From John!" Jane cried, seizing the letter. After she had read it, she sat a moment without speaking, then she said slowly, "He is more foolish than I thought him, if he has gone in this way from no cause; yet I think if there had been anything wrong, anything to make us ashamed and affronted, we would have heard of it by this time."

"Jane!" Mrs. Gilbert said, in a tone which meant, "Have pity."

"It is true, mamma. It is a great trial, but it might have been worse. Plenty of people go to Australia. He is likely enough to get on."

When Mary read John's short farewell she burst into tears.

"It's a relief to hear of him; but oh, why has he left us? Surely he does not know how we love him?"

"No, Mary," her mother said; "I think he does not."

Mrs. Gilbert's voice sounded dry and hollow.

"Mary," Mr. Gilbert said, coming beside his wife's chair when their daughters had left the room; "I always thought your son would do something for you. I have never been able to do much, but—" here his voice faltered, and he left her abruptly, and for an hour walked up and down the garden.

"There's papa walking," said Jane to her sister, looking from their bedroom window; "to look at him just now one would not think he wanted energy."

"And does he?" asked Mary."

"I daresay you know that as well as I do. I love

papa, but one can't be blind to facts. Would he ever have dozed on here all his life if he had been energetic?"

"I never thought of it," said Mary.

"But I have. Papa is a very good man, but he has done little or nothing for his family, beyond keeping them alive. Jack is different; he may do well, or he may not; he has the energy, and he is clever, but he wants balance. I would not like to be tied to his chariot-wheels; one would never know what to expect. Papa and mamma are surprised at him going off; I am not, although I would never have expected him to do it in such a foolish way."

"You don't surely think yourself wiser than papa and mamma, Jane?"

"No, not wiser; but I have a faculty of seeing things as they are; they haven't. Many people live in a delusion from first to last, especially about themselves and their friends."

"I think," said Mary, "I would prefer living in a delusion. If any amount of wisdom or sense could make me see mamma as a mere ordinary woman, I would not have it at any price."

"I was not speaking of mamma; but I say while we are in this world, we can't afford to shut our eyes to facts; we can't believe we have been living in ease and luxury when we have had the utmost difficulty to make ends meet. You must know that?"

"Oh, I know it; but I have never felt it."

"But I have, and it's galling and tiresome. Look at the Sinclairs and Raeburns, and even the Smiths—although I don't envy the Smiths, I like to feel secure, —all rolling in money; it makes a wonderful difference."

Perhaps if Mrs. Gilbert had heard this conversation

it would have pained her as much, if not more, than her son's unforeseen flight. Her family life, happy as she esteemed it, noble as it really was, reduced to the measure of pounds, shillings, and pence, and by her own daughter!

Perhaps the most touching thing in all the history of cruelty is the story of the woman who was accused of witchcraft, and whose husband and children gave evidence against her. She denied the crime to the last, but said " Let me die. Since my husband and my children believe me guilty, I have no wish to live." To such a woman as Mrs. Gilbert, the bitterness of being disappointed in her children could not be much short of the bitterness of death. She sat still in her parlor-window, the place where for so many years she had sewed and worked for them, and determined to lock all her grief and anxiety up in her own mind, to throw her care on God and not to darken her dwelling with it, and she did it; and Mr. Gilbert, who leaned on his wife with all his might although he did not know it, seeing her cheerful as usual, began to think that it was not such a calamity after all, John having betaken himself to a new country—that it might turn out to have been for the best,—in truth, the very high-road to fortune.

CHAPTER XXXVII.

THE sudden flight of the schoolmaster's good looking son did not pass without remark; on the contrary, it was the subject of much comment of a nature readily imagined.

Next to his own family and his old aunt, the person who put most heart into the interest she took in it was Miss Raeburn. She wrote a letter to meet him on landing, telling him what his uncle Raeburn had done; how no one but he and herself knew of the matter, and beseeching him to act wisely in the future. "You should do this from the highest motive, John," she wrote; "but surely you will do it for your mother's sake; don't make her suffer more than you have done already. There are not very many people in the world to whom I look up, but positively I am never beside your mother without feeling little; she seems to live in a purer atmosphere than other people; all the small spites and jealousies and worldliness that abound seem smaller and more hateful in her presence; don't wound such a nature, for the wound will be terrible, I warn you."

His father and his mother, his sisters and Effie Sinclair, all wrote to welcome the voyager on his arrival, such was the profusion of love thrown at his feet, and the boy did not know how to value it.

Miss Raeburn was mistaken in thinking that the secret of John's flight lay between her brother and herself. One of the clerks in the bank, an amateur " expert," had detected, or thought he detected, the forgery, and he was not to be done out of his conviction because the bill was paid as genuine and passed into oblivion. He, the clerk, was intimate with one of the Smith young men, and mentioned it to him, the Smith young man mentioned it to his mother, and his mother mentioned it to Mrs. Sinclair, and in this fashion the story was propagated and whispered about.

Mrs. Sinclair did not regret John Gilbert's departure herself; no doubt he was very good-looking and clever, but he was only the schoolmaster's son, and, what was a great deal worse, penniless. But that did not prevent her sympathizing with his family; and as she believed they would never be much the better of John, she thought one or both of the girls ought to be doing something, and the sooner the better; so having heard of a family at the Cape of Good Hope wanting a governess, she thought she would call and offer the post to Jane Gilbert.

Happily she found Jane in and alone.

"I am sorry Mrs. Gilbert is, not in," said Mrs. Sinclair.

"I am very sorry too, and mamma will be vexed at missing you; we are always so glad to see you."

Now Jane was not a hypocrite; she was always glad to see Mrs. Sinclair or any of the Sinclairs at this time.

"I wished to see your mamma, to sympathize with her on her loss. How you must all have felt Mr. Raeburn's kindness!"

"Mr. Raeburn's kindness?" said Jane.

"Yes," said Mrs. Sinclair, who never for a moment doubted that the Gilberts knew the whole circumstances, or perhaps even she would hardly have introduced the subject to them. "Yes," she said, "in paying the money and saying nothing about it — giving him another chance."

Jane felt her face burn—she had always suspected something; but she was equal to the moment.

"I think you must be under some mistake, dear Mrs. Sinclair; so far as I am aware, uncle Raeburn did nothing."

"Mistake!" cried Mrs. Sinclair, "there can be no mistake; I had it almost directly from the bank-clerk who detected the forgery."

"Forgery! Oh, Mrs. Sinclair, you are most completely mistaken—forgery!"

If Jane had felt sure of her ground, sure that she could refute the charge triumphantly, she would have said a great deal; but she was not sure, it tallied with her own suspicions, and she dared say nothing more, and still her face burned and her heart beat.

"Well, well," said Mrs. Sinclair good-naturedly, "if it is a mistake, so much the better.—I came with a message for you particularly."

"A message to her—from whom?" Was the shame of John's doings to blight and change her own lot? So Jane hurriedly thought, and sickened at the possibility.

"Yes, my dear, a message; I have been thinking, as you can't look to your brother now, and will have little or nothing in event of anything happening to your father (Jane must have enjoyed this, it was not shutting her eyes to facts), that it would be well for you to begin to do something for yourself. We'll hope your father has many years to live, but an elderly woman turned out on the world can hardly find a place, and I don't wonder —so now is the time for you to try to make a little money; and, as I heard of a situation I could get for you, I thought I would let you know."

During this speech Jane had gathered her senses and regained confidence.

"You are exceedingly kind, Mrs. Sinclair," she said.

"Oh, don't mention it; I delight in doing anything to oblige; I thought of you, but the situation would suit either you or Mary, you could settle which yourselves."

"We are certainly greatly obliged."

"Don't speak of it; you can think over it, and let me know to-morrow perhaps."

"Well," said Jane, "I don't think mamma could want Mary—"

"Oh, I'm sure you are as dear to her as Mary; but your mamma will see it to be for good to one of you."

"Yes, oh yes; mamma will feel very grateful, but—"

"There need be no buts; we'll say it's a settled thing that one of you go; it's only to the cape—a very nice climate, I believe."

"Mamma could not do without one of us—"

"Well, it would be a trial of course, but it might be a good thing for you both to take situations; meantime—"

"I did not intend to make it public just yet, but since you are so very kind I think I must tell you that I am engaged to be married."

"Married!" cried Mrs. Sinclair.

"Yes."

"And may I ask who is the happy man? Do I know him?"

"No, you must not ask; I'll leave some other person to tell you that."

"Well, my dear, I haven't an idea; gentlemen are rather scarce hereabout, but I wish you much happiness. I'll set the girls to sew you a cushion. May I ask if he is in a good position? It's not curiosity, Jane, it's real interest in your welfare."

"Yes," said Jane, "he is in a very good position; I have nothing to wish for."

"You are not going far away, I hope?"

"Oh no; not very far."

"I am glad to hear that. It will cheer your father and mother, and they need something to cheer them after this sad affair of John's."

"We would have preferred having him at home," said Jane; "but there was nothing sad about his going away; we are all very hopeful."

"This will be news for the girls," said Mrs. Sinclair, as she parted with Jane. "They'll soon guess; they are better at guessing than I am."

"What a mercy," thought Jane when she was alone, "that there was nobody in but me; she'll surely never overhaul John to papa or mamma. I don't doubt she is right, but I'll keep it to myself; somehow I can bear things better than the others; I hope they'll never hear of this."

And they never did; that was one terrible grief spared them by a special providence, if we can call one providence more special than another.

It took Mrs. Sinclair only five minutes to walk home, but in that space of time she had every unmarried man she knew of within a radius of a dozen miles up in review before her. If Jane had not said he was in such a good position that she had nothing to wish for, it would have been comparatively easy to fix on one. If she had only had the presence of mind to ask if he were old or young! When she said the word "old," the idea of Mr. Sinclair suddenly flashed on her. "Can it possibly be

Adam?" she thought. "It is possible, but not likely. He can feel no want of company; and when a man gets into a set of habits he does not care for being put out of them, and Jane has no attractions to distinguish her from the common herd of girls. No; I am fairly at a loss."

When dinner was nearly over, she said, "Now, I have a piece of news for you, which is new and true. I saw Jane Gilbert to-day, and she told me she is going to be married."

Mrs. Sinclair kept her eye carefully on her brother-in-law as she made this announcement, but to all appearance he was completely unmoved. Observing her look at him, he said, "Is that so very astonishing?"

"Well, you know," she said, "Jane is not good-looking, and she has no money, and she has a brother who is no credit to her, by all accounts."

"Perhaps she is a fortune in herself," said Mr. Sinclair.

"Mary would have been my choice," said Bell; "but Jane will be a good wife. I hope the man is good, whoever he is."

"She said he was in a good position, and not far away. Can't you think who he is?" asked Mrs. Sinclair.

"I can't guess," said Bell. "He may be in Ironburgh; that's not far away, compared with Australia."

"Oh, but I understood he was in the neighborhood. —Can't you help us, Tom?"

"Tom must be chock-full of electricity on such a subject, but he holds it finely in abeyance," said Bell.

"I don't know," said Tom, "why women are always so interested and make such an ado about a marriage —men would be glad to get the thing done as quietly as possible. But no; from the first blush of it till it is fairly over, a hullabaloo must be kept up, or women wouldn't think it a marriage, I suppose."

11*

"Tom," said Bell, " you could do as Mr. Drysdale the baker here did, who married his housekeeper. When told the minister was come, he put off his apron, went up stairs for a little, was married, came down and put on his apron again, and went about his business."

"Well, that was rational," said Tom. "He must have had a sensible woman to deal with. For my part, I hate an uproar at a wedding."

"I agree with you, Tom," Bell said, "but the custom of all times and nations is against us, so I doubt we must be in the wrong. At least, two people can hardly set up against the voice of the whole race."

When Mr. Sinclair went away as usual Mrs. Sinclair said—

"I don't doubt your uncle thinks me silly in being so taken up about Jane Gilbert's marriage, but I would really like to know who the bridegroom-elect is. I have a great curiosity."

"Well, mother," said Tom, "you may soon know that, for I am in a position to tell you. *I* am going to marry Jane Gilbert.—I'm going out; I'll not be back for two hours; get familiar with the idea, and have the talking over in that time, will you, and oblige me?"

Having thus thrown his shell on the carpet, Tom retired, not waiting for the explosion—thereby showing his wisdom.

It did not seem as if the talking were to be done immediately, for the three ladies sat in blank silence, struck dumb with surprise. Whom the gods mean to destroy they first blind. Poor Mrs. Sinclair felt this in her inmost soul—she had been blind indeed; but any one, she argued, would have been blind. Tom had known the Gilbert girls all his life almost, and it is rarely that the familiar strikes. Then, according to her taste, they had positively no attractions, yet—yet this thing had come upon her, and she knew she could not set her foot on it so triumphantly as she had done in the case of Mr. Doubleday. If Tom had a quality, it was sticking to his point.

Effie was the first to speak. "I'm glad of it," she said. "I like the Gilberts."

"Liking them is one thing and marrying them is another. The daughter of a country schoolmaster, and the sister of a man who has had to flee for forgery!" said Mrs. Sinclair.

Effie turned from white to red, and back to white again.

"Even if that is true, mamma—" Bell began.

"It is true, to my certain knowledge; though Jane Gilbert pretended she never heard of it, and denied it stoutly. There is more in that girl than I thought."

"You know, mamma," said Bell, "you'll never change Tom's determination."

"I was infatuated to take them to Lochside with us —not that I wanted them, but you and Effie would have it. See what's come of it; and he might have had the pick of the young ladies of the county!"

"Hardly, mamma," said Bell; "Tom is good and true, and all that, but he is not attractive. If I were not his sister, he is a man I would never wish to speak to twice. I am sure Jane will be a very good wife; but at any rate it is a thing we can't help, and we must make the best of it."

"I must say, Bell, you are cool. I'll get sympathy from you, at least, Effie. There's one thing Tom will find out in time, that he'll get the whole family to keep. I have no idea that John will ever come to any good— he'll just go from bad to worse, and that'll be seen."

"Don't, mamma! don't say that! I can't bear it!" cried Effie, and she ran from the room.

"She is very sensitive," said her mother. "She had always very fine feelings. She feels it more than his own sister; Jane braved it out very coolly, I must say."

CHAPTER XXXVIII.

IF Mrs. Sinclair could have despatched Jane Gilbert to a distance as easily as she did Mr. Doubleday, she would not have been very long about it, but like every other person in this world she had to submit to the inevitable, and when the time came she did it with what grace she might. She was too good-natured, and had too little real strength of character to stand out when her daughters were pleased and her son determined.

No one supposed but that Mr. and Mrs. Gilbert must rejoice in such a match for their daughter. Mr. Gilbert did. It pleased his vanity immensely, not to say that it relieved his anxiety as to the future and promoted Jane's happiness, but Mrs. Gilbert had not such unmingled satisfaction. No doubt Tom was a perfectly respectable man, but she knew him to be hard and selfish, and she feared that Jane and he would agree only too well, whereas under different influences Jane might have been improved and elevated; but like the other mother she had to submit to the inevitable. So Jane and Tom were married, and lived in a fine house on the outskirts of Quixstar, called, by the taste of its mistress, St. Hilda's Lodge.

When John Gilbert arrived at Melbourne he posted a newspaper to his mother, and that was the sole notice that came to Quixstar for many a day to show that he was in existence. The Spanish Inquisition in its moments of profoundest thought and ingenuity never inflicted keener torture than John Gilbert did in pure thoughtlessness, and there have been and are many John Gilberts.

Then came a letter—a long letter, written jointly to his father and mother—nearly filled with details of people he had met, whose name was legion, of all whom, if they did not know him, knew some one he knew or was connected with—his father, his uncles, his grandfathers. It seemed as if you only had to go to the antipodes to fall into not merely a centre, but a circumference, of interested friends. Very likely there were Ephraim Jenkinsons among the multitude, but as Mrs. Tom Sinclair justly remarked, " John took nothing with him, so he could hardly be fleeced." She thought of the possible stealing of his purse, while his mother thought of the possible contamination of his nature. Not a word did he say of what he had been doing, was doing, or meant to do,—how he liked the place, whether he was in comfort, or discomfort; not a word. Effie got no letter from him. His mother gave her this one to read, and she was not even named in it.

And in all this time Peter Veitch had never been home. His ship had been twice in London, but he had not had time to visit Quixstar.

" Time!" said Mrs. Sinclair when she heard of it. " Where there is a will there is a way. That lad is forgetting his duty to his parents, but it will let your uncle see that his sagacity may be at fault."

Mr. Sinclair did not see this at all. He thought the more of Peter for denying himself what would have been a very keen gratification, that he might do his duty. And Bell was of like opinion. She was given to think well of Peter, and his mother showed her his letters occasionally. She was rather fond of showing them. "I tell't him the last time I wrote to him," she said, "that ye whiles read his letters and thocht a heap o' them."

"Perhaps he may not like people reading his letters, Mrs. Veitch?"

"What for should he no' like it? There's naething in them he need be ashamed o', and ye see he aye speers after ye."

These messages coming from Peter, and going to him in this way, were a shade more substantial and satisfactory than those that came and went *viâ* the moon, although they were good too of their kind.

Poor Effie—she did not come out as a strong minded heroine; true to her *rôle* of sensitiveness, she lost heart and spirit. Bell soothed and comforted and humored her, but she refused to be comforted—that is, in private, for in public she seemed rather to forget her grief. After reading John's letter she came home, and wept bitterly. Then Bell said to her, "If I were you, Effie, I would not pine after a worthless man like a love-sick girl. I would rise and shake it off, and not let it eat into my life to make it useless."

"He may not be worthless," sobbed Effie.

"Well, stop thinking of him till he has proved himself worthy. Why, he does not even mention you," concluded Bell indignantly.

"People often don't speak of those they are always thinking about."

"You are infatuated, Effie. A woman may not, but what should hinder a man? What should hinder John Gilbert? It would have been the most natural thing in the world. So natural, that for him not to do it looks as if he had entirely forgotten you, or omitted you on purpose."

"You are cruel, Bell."

"I wish I could be crueller. I wish I could kill the idea of John Gilbert out of you. He will be the bane of your life, as he is of mine at present. Even his mother has nothing to say for him. Oh, how I pity his mother!"

Bell's love for her sister was great—all the greater that it was the love of a strong nature for a weak one —not that Bell ever for a moment thought her sister weak; quite the contrary, nature had most kindly denied Bell the faculty of seeing flaws in her friends.

She felt the responsibility of being Effie's sole confidant, and wished to tell her mother the story, but to this Effie would not consent, and Bell's post was not enviable. Thinking that change of scene might be beneficial, she eagerly accepted an invitation they got from a distant relative of Mrs. Sinclair's to visit her in Ironburgh. Effie hung back. She was a stricken deer that did not want to leave the spot she was on, but Bell carried her off, and found her reward.

Their hostess was rather a stiff, starched individual, with three daughters resembling herself; but Mrs. Raeburn came with her carriage very often, and took them to spend the day with her. Effie never disguised her eagerness to go, but Bell, out of courtesy to the friends she was staying with, often declined, and laid herself on the altar of duty, very thankful to see her sister looking like herself again.

One day when Bell was out alone, she seized the opportunity (for it was not often she was alone) of going to look at some parts of the town that she knew her cousins so-called would shrink from putting their foot in. She walked on, thinking and observing as she went, when she came up to a little boy in a perfect storm of grief. His face was all "begrutten," and he was sobbing as if his heart would break. Wondering what could be the cause of such extreme abandonment, she stopped to see if she could do anything in the way of consolation.

"What is it, my man?" she said soothingly.

"Oh, my peerie (top)! my peerie!" he sobbed.

"Is *that* all? What has happened to it?"

"It's gane down the cundy (conduit), an' I'll never see't again," and he pointed to a grating over a drain which had a gap in it wide enough to swallow his toy.

"Oh," she said, "never mind, dry your face and cheer up, I'll give you a penny to buy another."

His awful grief vanished on the instant, and she was fishing in her purse for the promised coin, when a woman came out of a door. "Mother," cried the urchin, "she's gaunna gie me a penny to buy a new peerie."

"Bairn," she said, "ye're fit to ruin a body in peeries, this is the second ye've lost; if ye loss anither I'll peerie ye;" then turning to Bell she said, "Ye're far ower kind, mem."

It began to rain, and the boy's mother asked Bell to wait a little in her house till the shower went off. As Bell sat waiting she heard a deep ominous cough, which did not seem far off, and she looked inquiringly at her hostess, who said, "Ay, it's a man that lives but and ben wi' us; he has been ill for a while, and he's no unco weel off."

"Is he not?" Bell said.

"He bides wi' a sister, and she drinks, and he has an awfu' time o't wi' her. He had been in a better way ance, for he keepit them a'—that's his faither and mother and her like—but she's the only ane left now, and he cam' hame ill a while syne, and tried to keep a bit schule as lang as he was able, but he's past that the now. I doubt his siller has melted away. I'm often wae for him.

I wish he may get his meat; when I'm makin' a bit denner, I gey an' often tak' him in some."

"Has he no friends?" asked Bell. "Can nothing be done for him?"

"Weel, I dinna ken, I'm sure."

"I can give some money; I don't know of anything else I can do."

"Money," said the woman, "would do him gude, if he could get the use o't."

"Perhaps you would take charge of it, and get what's necessary?"

"I think ye should gie him't yersel'; if I took it he would think I had been begging for him; now if ye gie him't, I'm no to ken onything about it."

"That may be true, but I have no pretence for calling. I could not justify my intrusion."

"Weel, mem, there's mony a leddy that doesna stick at bouncing into a puir body's house whether they have an errand or no'; but he's at a gey low pass, he may be glad o' a word o' sympathy."

"Would you go in then, and say I heard he was not very well, and would be glad to see him if he would let me?"

The woman immediately opened her neighbor's door, and Bell heard her say, "There's a leddy wantin' to see ye, sir."

"A lady! What lady?"

"I couldna say, sir; she's a stranger to me."

"And to me too. I know no ladies that could come here. Say I don't want to see her. Say anything you like."

There was something in the voice that made Bell listen.

"But, sir—" the woman began.

"She's not to come here," he said. "I don't want to see her."

In the face of this mandate Bell stepped into the room.

"I can hardly be mistaken," she said. "I really wish to see you, Mr. Doubleday."

Of a truth it was Mr. Doubleday, fallen upon evil days. He looked keenly at her, and his first act (showing wonderful presence of mind for him) was to raise his hand to his head and pull off a striped worsted nightcap; the blood rushed to his thin white face and receded again, while a smile faintly gleamed on it, like a single shaft of afternoon light on tarnished December snow.

"Miss Sinclair!" was all he said.

He lay back on his dirty cushions. Poor man, illness and poverty had not added to his attractions. Never celebrated for his attention to dress, he was worse now than ever. An old black suit, glazed and whitey-brown, hung on his shrunken body, the coat was fastened across his breast with a great stalwart yellow pin, the only vigorous-looking thing in the house; no shirt was visible; his eyes were as feeble and his hair as erect and scrubby as ever. Whether the one rapid touch he had given to his toilet by snatching off his nightcap was an improvement might be doubted. A small table was before him, covered with books, and he had been writing, or trying to do so.

Bell lifted a chair near him and sat down.

"Still busy among books, Mr. Doubleday," she said cheerily. "Do you know I was dreaming about you last night, but I did not expect to have the pleasure of seeing you to-day."

It would have been a trying thing for Mr. Doubleday to have met Bell in any circumstances, but here, in this squalid room, feeble and poverty-stricken, with the dread that his sister might burst in at any moment in any stage of drunkenness—it was too much for him; he could not speak.

Bell looked into his books and remarked upon them by way of making talk, for she hardly knew what to say; as to offering him money, that she could not do, although he seemed to want the common necessaries of life. On the only chair besides the one she sat on stood a basin of porridge and sour milk that had been the breakfast he had tried to eat, and there was no appearance of any other food in the house, although it was long past the hour when an invalid ought to have had some tempting nourishment.

"Miss Sinclair," he said at last, "it is very kind of you to come here, but you must not stay long in a place like this."

"Must I not? Do you remember how long it is since you left Quixstar?"

"Yes; it is five years past on the 17th of last September. This is November. I don't know the day of the month."

"It's the 15th. Why don't you ask what we've been doing all that time? You should ask what we've been studying at least? and do you know we've had a marriage amongst us; guess whom?"

"Not you?"

"No, not me. Jane Gilbert and Tom are married and settled in Quixstar. He keeps a little money-shop."

Bell looked at her watch, and Mr. Doubleday fain would have asked what o'clock it was, for his own watch having been disposed of from necessity, he had no means of knowing the hour, except by guessing; but he refrained lest he should betray his circumstances. And during the long hours of his sleepless nights he comforted himself by thinking that knowing the exact time would not make it go more quickly.

He trembled lest his sister should come in. What a man of his temperament suffered from this coarse woman, no one but himself knew. If she came in she would ask money from Miss Sinclair without an instant's hesitation, he was well aware.

Bell saw that for some reason he was impatient she should go, and she rose and said—

"I'll come soon back, unless you seriously object," and she laughed.

"Don't come," he said; "don't come to such a place as this."

"No," said she; "I really think I can't. I make it a rule never to visit an old friend unless he lives in a fine house."

"Go," he said, suddenly and eagerly as a coarse, repulsive-looking woman passed the window. He looked positively frightened.

Hurriedly saying good-bye, Bell passed out, and encountering Miss Doubleday, shrank from her. "And that is his sister," she thought; "how horrible!" then she turned back and went into their neighbor's house; she said, "Take that," giving some money, "and do what you can for him as soon as you can. I could not offer it to him."

The woman was surprised at the tones of her voice, thanked her, and went further into details of his circumstances, but Bell left her abruptly; she could hardly stand it; she would have wept but that she was on the street; the very depths of her tenderness and compassion were stirred.

In the dark hours of his life during the past five years, the idea of Bell Sinclair had many times gleamed on Mr. Doubleday as you have seen lightning play round the black shoulder of a hill at night, and instantly disappear, leaving a shadow of gladness in your mind. But it took all the hours of this wretched night to master the feelings which the sight of her had revived. Toil and disappointment had kept him company since he could think or feel, and now disease and poverty had joined the party; and when they were sitting round him like dogs of the desert waiting for their prey, that was the moment chosen to send the angel of his dreams to look at him.

In night and darkness, when the imagination is roused and the judgment asleep, how misery seems steeped in misery, and calamity descends into blacker blackness; with the morning sun comes a lightening of body and mind. After this wild night Mr. Doubleday looked his lot in the face, and, bad though it was, it was not really worse than it had been yesterday morning.

Why should all the lessons of faith and patience he had been years in learning be lost in a single night? He rose, and with trembling fingers got himself into his clothes once more. He was alone in the house, without fire or breakfast. He sat down and read his Greek Testament, a book he was fond of, for its doctrines were not foolishness to him as they were to the polite people in whose language it was written; and if ever he had found stumbling-blocks there, that time was past. In a little he heard a knock at his door, and his kindly neighbor entered. She had suspected he was alone, and had come to see what she could do for him. She brought him the never-failing cup of tea, but it had the bitter, stewed, sickly taste which belongs to coarse cheap tea that is always kept hatching in a pot by the side of a fire. He could not have relished it if he had been well, and he was at that stage of illness when he longed for something that had taste and substance. He swallowed it, however, and told the good woman that he did not know how he could ever repay her kindness, for his was an humble, grateful soul, and she left him with a motherly yearning towards him, determined that he should have a dinner of the best from the stranger's bounty. Feeling faint, he rose and looked into the press, where he found the porridge and sour milk that had been left the previous day. He ate that and felt refreshed, the sharp acid suited his palate ; and after his meal he bent his head in silent thanks.

CHAPTER XXXIX.

WHEN dinner was over in the respectable mansion where the Sinclairs were visiting, Bell went to her room to write a letter to Miss Raeburn.

"DEAR MRS. PHANTOM," she began, "Mamma's good cousin and her three daughters are very kind to us—oppressively kind, I may say; for they have the notion that they should entertain their guests from morning to night, and accordingly they never lose sight of us from the time we rise till we go to bed. It is comparatively easy for them, as they are four, and mount duty by turns; but imagine us being obliged to sit upright, not to yawn, to look pleased and even animated, and generally to behave ourselves for thirteen or fourteen hours a day. One good thing is, that Effie gets no opportunity to mope; she has given up writing poetry, which I take to be a symptom of returning health and spirits, and we have met many friends. If we had gone to Australia we could hardly have fallen in with more; we could nearly match John Gilbert. I had to apologize to the ladies for leaving them just now, by saying I was going to write a rather particular letter, and would like to be alone. The truth is, I expect to 'greet' before I am done, and that is a manifestation of the weakness of humanity which it is better should take place privately. I was taking a walk to-day in out-of-the-way places, and who do you think I discovered by the merest chance? Mr. Doubleday! Are you not hyper-astonished? I found him in sickness and want, tormented by a fearful-looking drunken sister. I am thankful I had the presence of mind not to look surprised or take any notice of his deplorable state. Their next neighbor told me, among other things, that they had not been able to pay for gas, and it had been cut off; so he sits mostly in the dark, but sometimes gets a candle. One night when this neighbor went in his sister was lying in a drunken sleep, and when Mr. Doubleday snuffed the candle he put the snuffers on a stocking he had folded and laid down for the purpose, that he might not risk making a noise and disturbing her by putting them in the snuffer-tray. Think of it! He is certainly too good for this world. Now, what is to be done? My impulse would have been to take him direct to Old Battle House, but I don't think mamma would like it; then I thought of writing to uncle, but it struck me you would see and understand the thing better. How would it do to subscribe among us money to send him to a warmer climate? I would give a year's income and more, and feel I had never gratified myself so much in my life. The difficulty would be to persuade him; only he must see that staying where he is, is next thing to suicide. I know you will throw yourself into this, and it must be done quickly. There is no time to be put off. It must have been this sister who wrote to him so often when he was with us—asking money, I don't doubt. He has had a hard life. I expect to hear from you immediately."

To whom Miss Raeburn:—

" MY DEAR TIBBY,—Gradually—insidiously and foolishly, I admit—I have allowed the habit of you to grow upon me till now that I am deprived of you, I feel like the drunkard who cannot get his dram. Does it become my duty to lay you down firmly now, rather than go on and be enslaved in all time coming? Say?

"It will be your turn likely to be hyper-astonished when I tell you that I do not pity Mr. Doubleday. It would be impertinent to pity him. Such a man is above the world. There are a great many people about whom one can't help thinking, when one hears of their death, that it will take some little time before they shake into the ways of heaven; but these won't be strange to Mr. Doubleday: he will fit in much better there than ever he has done here; and if it were not for the sixth commandment, the kindest thing would be to let him stay where he is; but it will hardly do to fly in the face of the decalogue, therefore by all means let us get him to a warmer climate, and there need be no difficulty. The proper object of pity is that wretched sister of his. You don't depict her as an angel of light; but could nothing be done for her? If we all got our deserts, who would escape a whipping? For myself, I feel wofully wicked, feeble, and fallible; but observe, Tibby, I don't say that to every one. The other day I was dining with the Smiths, and I was sitting beside Mr. Kennedy. There was some talk about a preacher who has made a little sensation by his preaching. Among other things he had said from the pulpit, one of the company remarked, was, 'that the devil heard every sermon that was preached.' I said, 'Poor wretch, that must be no slight part of his punishment.' The words were not out of my mouth when I felt my face burn; but as I had spoken low I hoped they might not have been heard. However, one of the Smiths, to whose juvenile bones it was of course marrow, called out—

"'Mr. Kennedy, did you hear what Miss Raeburn said?'

"'Perfectly,' said Mr. Kennedy; 'and I agree with her. I would not like to hear every sermon that is preached either'—which I believe; but it was a foolish speech of mine, and I have been sitting in the chair of repentance ever since.

"Mrs. Smith told me confidentially—but everybody knows—that her eldest son is to be married immediately to an Ironburgh heiress with £70,000, and they are going round the globe for their marriage trip. It is, she said, a marriage of pure affection on both sides.

"If the bride has £35,000 and they go half round the globe, or if she has £17,500 and they go to Paris, it will do very well. I am glad of this, for I like to see people happy after their kind, and this is a thing that will make the Smiths very happy. Mr. Johnston the butcher —Old Bloody Politeful, as the Smiths call him—gave me a New Zealand newspaper the other day, from which it seems his son John is making quite a figure there. How proud and happy his father looked! It was very natural, and I got into the spirit of it myself. Who knows but Quixstar may be famous yet through its great men?—'the obscure little town of Quixstar,' as the newspapers wickedly say when they have occasion to mention it.

"I see a cloud like a man's hand gathering over our little society here. It may increase or blow off; all I can say is, I am glad it is two men who are going to make fools of themselves, and not two women. I have. as much *esprit de corps* as that, and as much *esprit de race* as to be sorry two men I have a regard for—or whether I have a regard for them or not—should fall out by the way.

"I will be in Ironburgh the day after to-morrow, to get Mr. Doubleday excavated. If you and Effie give so much, I will make up all deficiencies, and you could present the money as a mark of gratitude. It will not be public at all, and he need have no delicacy about it; at least I hope not. *Au revoir.*"

Without doubt, whether she thought it or not, Miss Raeburn was clever in more ways than one. In the course of a few days she had Mr. Doubleday and his outfit packed and sent off *en route* to the shores of the Mediterranean, and his sister put into a retreat for the inebriate, hoping the best. By some she was called odd, and she was odd, so far as pursuing her way regardless of remark is odd.

There are people who tell us that oddities will die out; that the excessive attrition of modern times, the railways, steamers, telegraphs, and newspapers, will rub every corner down, till men and women are reduced to uniformity, as if they had been turned out of one mould. No fear! Nature has never yet been beaten out of the field by art; she has never yet shown herself so little fertile in resource. There will be oddities to the end of time; but the types may change, the patterns will be different; and Dame Nature has the new patterns in her pocket, all ready to be handed out as needed. The retired medical woman, for instance—will she be less worth knowing than the same type of woman whose energies never had an outlet, but who left perhaps a song or a proverb, or a ballad or racy saying, floating on society nameless, the only witness that she had ever existed? One would like to be the infant whose birth was announced in the newspapers yesterday, for he may live to meet her, and she will be worth meeting—only there are so many things one would like to meet and to see, and time is short.

When Mrs. Sinclair heard of Mr. Doubleday's reappearance on the scene, her maternal instincts flew to arms at once, but quite unnecessarily. It is true that Mr. Doubleday's love was of a kind that, like the herrings in Loch Fyne—if such a comparison may be allowed—could be nourished on invisible food; and men of his stamp are not keenly observant; still, even the snail has eyes at the ends of its feelers; and during the few days' intercourse he had with Bell before leaving, he knew by instinct that his love was hopeless. He would have liked to have died then, wrapped in the elysium of her presence; but people don't die when they like, and Mr. Doubleday went away, recovered a good measure of health, and returned; while many of the invalids who left Britain that winter, desiring to live with a very intensity of desire, who had much to live for—love, wealth, and all that the world can give — never came back.

Miss Raeburn returned to Quixstar as soon as Mr. Doubleday was fairly off, leaving Bell and her sister at her brother's (Mr. Raeburn's) house, where they were more at home than in the stiff establishment of their relative.

Mrs. Raeburn liked to have girls with her, having none of her own—a fact she often bewailed. Of late she had sometimes got Mary Gilbert for a week or two, but Mary was very valuable at home, and liked best to stay there. Since Jane's influence had been withdrawn, and she had become her mother's sole companion, she had improved and developed amazingly; and Mrs. Raeburn, in the kindness of her heart, thought what a good daughter-in-law she would make. If she had been eager to prevent any of her sons falling in love with her, it would have been the very thing that would have taken place; as it was, not one of them did so.

CHAPTER XL.

MISS RAEBURN was no sooner home than she had a call from old Mrs. Gilbert, who came with a letter in her hand she had got from her grandnephew, about which she wished to consult Miss Raeburn.

"You see," she said, "there is a letter enclosed in mine which I am to give to Miss Effie Sinclair, and say nothing about it, or my own either; but I like none o' these underhand ways, so I brought it to you to read, to see what you think of it."

The letter was dated about two months before, from a place Hongatonga by name, and was as follows:—

"MY DEAR AUNT,—Among the many kind friends that I left at home, after my own immediate family, there is no one I think so often about as yourself. How often I think of the tea-drinkings we juveniles had with you! I see the old fluted silver tea-pot with the island on its side, in which resided a big G, as distinctly at this moment as if it were before me. Is it still in existence?"

["What would hinder it?" interjected Mrs. Gilbert to Miss Raeburn, who was reading aloud.]

"I have seen a good deal of the world since I last saw it. This is a fine country, with a great future before it. The town where I am will be a large, handsome place when it is all built. Five years ago the place where it stands was bush; now it has ten thousand inhabitants—many, I may say most, of them Scotch. There is a man here who knew my uncle Gilbert. His father had a large tea-shop in Eastburgh in my uncle's time. Wilson was his name; his mother's name was Adamson. Do you remember them? He is married to a woman, or lady I should perhaps say, from the same place as Mr. Kennedy, and she knew Mr. K. very well when he was a boy. Speaking of Mr. Kennedy reminds me that we are not very well off for ministers here, and religion suffers accordingly. If you know any good preacher who can't fall readily into a berth at home, advise him by all means to come out; there is a good field, and he would meet with fair encouragement. Some earnest men here have set agoing revival meetings at present, and much good has been done. I have been at most of them in the evenings; and souls are being turned to Christ up to 11.30. [" O John! John!" ejaculated Miss Raeburn.] But I can't say I approve of such late hours, even for religious purposes. Mr. Wilson takes an active hand in these things. He has a large sheep run. Sheep are a remarkably good investment here; indeed, there are many good investments. You can get fifteen, twenty, and even twenty-five per cent., and the most perfect security—no risk whatever. I have just been thinking it is a pity your money should bring you such trifling returns, when it could be put out to such advantage here; so if you like to send it, or some of it—say £2000 or so—to me, I'll do my best for you; I'll send you a clear £400 a year for it at the least. I enclose a letter for Miss E. Sinclair; would you give it to herself quietly, and say nothing of having had a letter from me, so that no suspicion may be raised?—I remain your affectionate nephew, JOHN GILBERT.

"*P. S.*—Would you not think of coming out here yourself? Old Mrs. Adamson, Mrs. Wilson's mother, came out recently. She is eighty-three, and the likelihood is, by coming to the colony she will add ten years to her life. That is almost invariably the effect of such a change. I'll expect the money at all events. You know me well enough to know that I'll do nothing for you I would not do for myself.—J. G."

Miss Raeburn closed the letter with a smile on her face. She could not help it, and she thought, " Oh for dull mediocrity ! "

" Well," she said to Mrs. Gilbert, " what are you going to do ? Transfer yourself and your money to the antipodes ? "

" Na ; I'll no' transfer myself, although, if I would have done that for onybody, it would have been for John. Isn't it strange that the laddie says nothing about what he is doing, or how he lives, or about the ways and habits o' the folk, nor how he never wrote to me before, and writes so seldom to anybody ? "

" Yes ; it is strange."

" But I think I might send him the siller ? "

" If you lose £2000, can you still live comfortably ? "

" Na ; if I were to lose £2000 I would be next door to a beggar."

" Then don't send it."

" Do you think no' ? He's a clever business man, John, and he has a sense of religion."

" That may or may not be, but you have no right to risk bringing yourself from comfort to poverty in your old age. Take my advice, Mrs. Gilbert. I love John as much as you do, but I would not send him that money."

"Would you not?"

"Most decidedly not; and I would burn that letter in case his mother asks to see it."

"But I would like to keep it for his sake!" said the old lady, with a tear in her eye.

"Then you must not say anything about it. It would pain his mother exceedingly. As for Effie's letter, I'll post it in Eastburgh to-morrow if you like, and it can take its chance of falling into her mother's fingers. Like you, I hate underhand dealings."

And Mrs. Gilbert went away in the state people often are after taking advice, not very sure whether to act on it or not; but she decided to wait a while. Age is not impulsive. To do her justice, it was not the high interest she thought of chiefly. She considered that the money would give John some standing where he was—rightly judging that human nature at Hongatonga was much the same as at Quixstar.

Mrs. Sinclair forwarded John's letter to Effie without suspicion or remark, and she got in it Mr. Raeburn's dining-room when she and her sister were alone.

"Who is it from?" asked Bell.

Effie turned round, with her face slightly flushed, and said—

"John Gilbert."

"John Gilbert!"

"Yes; and it is impertinent," said Effie. "More than that, he has enclosed it to some one to post, and compromised me. Who in the world can he have sent it to, do you think?"

"I cannot even guess," said Bell, astonished at her sister's change of mood. "Do you mean to answer it?"

"Certainly not," said Effie, tossing the letter into the fire.

12*

"I'm glad that's over," said Bell.

"It is time it was over," said Effie indignantly.

"John is not so fortunate," Bell said, "as the man who threw off his friends as a huntsman his pack, for he knew when he liked he could whistle them back."

"He seems to have thought that though, but he'll never whistle me back."

Bell, while she was devoutly glad that this unfortunate episode was over, was as much surprised as glad. She would have expected that John's writing, his mere handwriting, whatever he might have said, would have been meat and drink to Effie: that she would cling to him through everything, but it seemed that happily she was mistaken.

When the Sinclair's went home they were escorted by George Raeburn, Mr. Raeburn's second son, who was young, good-looking, and a partner in his father's very lucrative business. Mrs. Sinclair threw no obstacle in the way of his crossing the threshold of Old Battle House and recrossing it, but when he had seen the young ladies safely under their mother's wing he went direct to his aunt's, Miss Raeburn's.

There he flung himself on a sofa and said, "Aunt, I want your help. You'll help me to get that girl for my wife?"

"Miss Sinclair, you mean?"

"You'll help me?"

"That I will not. It's a case in which a man ought to help himself. I'll not hinder you, though. Besides, if Bell thought you needed help of mine, and had asked it, she wouldn't have you. She likes people that can help themselves."

"Bell, did you say? It's Effie I want."

"Oh, it's Effie! That's different. Certainly there's no

accounting for tastes. Why, she can't hold the candle to Bell."

" Candle or not, I never cared for any one in the world as I care for Effie."

" Well, I don't think you need despair. Bell's knight might have to win his spurs, but if you want my candid opinion, I think Effie might be had for the picking up."

" Has she no lovers already? Such a creature as she must have lovers."

" She has one, I suspect."

" Oh dear," groaned the youth.

" But he is afflicted with a fell disease—"

" He must be intensely selfish then to think of marrying."

" A fell disease, known among the children of men as impecuniosity; but Effie has money, and not little. She would not be deprived of the necessaries of life though she married him."

" Do you know what she thinks of him—how she feels?"

" Not in the least, but I can guess how her mother feels if she knows of it—bitterly, I am sure."

" Effie is a gentle, sensitive creature; she will be guided by her mother."

" Well, well," said Miss Raeburn, " you can wait and see."

" Yes, I must wait; if I were too sudden I might do more ill than good."

" And how long are you going to wait?"

" Till I see I am sure of success. No woman shall ever refuse me."

" That is to say, to save your pride, you'll put her in the position you'll not put yourself in; she must as good as say yes before she is asked. If she's worth having, she won't do it; but I wish you success in your wooing."

"That's why you are not married," George said to himself. He thought he was wiser than his aunt, which perhaps he was, and he carried on his courtship that winter after his own plan, not impetuously nor conspicuously till he judged the fruit ripe enough to pull, when he pulled it, and it toppled into his hand very prettily, the parent tree making no resistance to being thus despoiled of one of its ornaments; but, for various good reasons, the marriage was not to take place till the close of summer. Every one was pleased with this arrangement; it carried pain to one heart only. Mrs. Gilbert thought of her son—not that it could be said there was a time when she did not think of him, sleeping and waking he was in her mind. She had been jealous of his love to this girl; now she was jealous for him; so soon and so utterly forgotten; but though he was her son, Mrs. Gilbert was just. Effie, she allowed, was right to forget him if she could, and it appeared she could. His mother could not; the form of the child, the boy, the man, seemed to be continually passing the window where she sat; but he was not there; he was afloat on a rough world, away out of her reach, possibly ill or in want, and a tremendous yearning of love came over her, followed by a sterner mood, when she thought of his heartlessness in going; in never writing; in writing that mere husk of a letter, and for a moment her reason judged him as if he had been another woman's son. "Ah," she thought, "I was unutterably thankful for his life when James Raeburn was drowned—how blind we are, how blind!" It was a terrible thing to see as clearly as she saw, and love as deeply as she loved; but, Mr. Gilbert appearing at the garden gate, her face smoothed, and her voice cleared, and she was ready to pick out the little thorns that gathered daily in his path. " Your mother," he sometimes remarked to Mary, " has got pretty well over John's departure. To be sure it was a greater disappointment and loss to me than to her. Well, he'll be coming home some day with a fortune."

CHAPTER XLI.

THE same law which causes an apple to fall, keeps the planets in their places, and fills all the little curves of a coast with a tide of waters, as well as the great bays where the navies of the world may float. As apples to planets are the persons of this story, as curves to bays the place where they played their parts, but the same laws governed them as govern greater people in greater places. The autobiographies of men of mark reveal a sad but most complete family resemblance in the rise, progress, and continuation of their quarrels to that which takes place among smaller men.

About the time Mr. Doubleday was rescued from his melancholy circumstances, the cloud the size of a man's hand, that Miss Raeburn alluded to in her letter to Bell, arose.

Mr. Sinclair was sitting by his fire reading one sulky November day, when a person wishing to see him was shown into his room. He was a little rough-and-ready-looking man, with glittering eyes and weather-beaten face; wearing a shaggy coat buttoned up to his neck; the sleeves of a sad-colored flannel shirt appeared at his wrists, and his gloveless hands looked hard and dry and not over clean; the thumbs were unmercifully bent back, as if each had swallowed a dose of strychnine on its own account. He put his hat on the table and sat down. If his manner had been of the subdued and resigned order you would have expected him to open down a bundle of soiled and miscellaneous stationery for inspection and purchase, but it was not; he seated himself like a man and an equal.

"My name is Miller," he said, "Miller from Ironburgh." Mr. Sinclair did not look as if he felt strikingly enlightened. "I used to know you by sight, sir, when you lived in Ironburgh; that's a good many years since now. You'll find it slow here, I should say, sir? I have a note of introduction to you, sir," and he handed it to Mr. Sinclair. "It's from Mr. Duncan; you knew Mr. Duncan, I think?"

"Yes, I knew him very well."

The note ran thus:—"DEAR SIR,—Mr. Miller is a worthy man, help him if you can.—I am, yours truly, J. DUNCAN."

Mr. Sinclair looked up and said, "Well?"

"The fact is, sir, I am a deputation from a Society in Ironburgh—The Rational Relaxation Society, it is called; our object is to promote the well-being of the working classes. People, sir, must have amusement, it is a craving implanted in us by the Creator. They get it in many ways questionable, or positively bad; our object is to beat bad forms of it out of the field by providing what are good and innocent; we are of no party, sect, or denomination, but we think we are the handmaids of religion."

"What do you do?" asked Mr. Sinclair.

"Well, we do a number of things. We select a place,' say Quixstar; we have meetings, we get hold of the young men, we elicit native talent, we have industrial exhibitions, we have lectures illustrated by diagrams of all parts of the globe; in winter we may have a popular exhibition of astronomy, in summer botany with open-air excursions, and so on. We vary things as we see cause."

"If people are interested—" Mr. Sinclair began.

"They are interested, sir; greatly interested. There are millions of good minds that never awake in this world because there is no one to knock them up. That's our business—to knock up sleeping intellect. Not an inglorious mission, I should say, sir?"

Now, it might almost have been taken for granted that Mr. Sinclair, having a contempt for humbug and a dislike to newfangled panaceas, would have snuffed Mr. Miller and his Rational Relaxations out on the spot. He was not a public-spirited man; and to be tied to the tail of a noisy society was not much to his taste—quite the contrary; but by the time a man—that is, a good man—comes to be as old as Mr. Sinclair, he becomes less selfish, more pitiful, far less harsh, and more lenient in his judgments, and thinks twice before he stamps out an effort for the good of his fellow-men; although, as we will see, there was quite enough of the old Adam in Mr. Sinclair even yet.

"You may do good," he said to Mr. Miller, "and there is plenty of room for it."

"There's one thing we want, to begin with," said the deputy, "and that is a place to have a meeting in."

"Why, there's Mr. Gilbert's schoolroom. You can't get a better place than that."

Quixstar was not overdone with accommodation of this kind. There was a large hall or room in the principal inn, which was used for public occasions, but at this precise time it was undergoing repair, after having been nearly destroyed by fire.

"No better," said Mr. Miller; "but we can't get it."

"Not get it! Does Mr. Gilbert object?"

"No, but Mr. Kennedy does. I have been at him both last night and this morning."

"There must be some mistake, surely," said Mr. Sinclair.

"No mistake that we're not to get it. He's the toughest old chap I've met for a while."

"He is a personal friend of mine. He has not understood fully. I have no doubt a word from me will set matters straight."

"Well, sir, if you think so—"

"Yes, I think so; and you may make any arrangements necessary, in the certainty of getting the schoolroom."

His visitor being gone, Mr. Sinclair wrote to Mr. Kennedy:—

"MY DEAR SIR,—I have just had a young man with me who tells me he has seen you about getting the schoolroom to hold a meeting in, and that you refused it. Allow me to vouch for the good intentions of the society he represents, and for his own respectability, in which case you will not hesitate to grant the use of the schoolroom. I will take it as a personal favor.—I am, dear sir, yours very truly, A. SINCLAIR."

To which Mr. Kennedy :—

"My DEAR SIR,—I wish you had asked any other favor within my power; I would have been too happy to oblige you. I don't doubt the respectability of the young man who called here; but he should attend to the proverb, 'Let the shoemaker stick to his last.' I am sorry to repeat my refusal, as I would do anything to oblige you personally.—I am, dear sir, yours truly,

"JAMES KENNEDY."

Mr. Sinclair rejoined :—

"DEAR SIR,—I hope you will reconsider your decision. I think you will allow that the proposed meeting is at least an innocent thing. I am sure that the humbler portion of your parishioners would enjoy such an evening's entertainment as this society proposes to give us; and if you will look into the matter for a moment, although your own views may be a little different on some points, you will hardly throw obstacles in their way.—I am, sir, your most obedient servant,
"A. SINCLAIR."

Mr. Kennedy put this last missive in his pocket, and going out, looked in on Miss Raeburn by the way, and showed her Mr. Sinclair's notes, telling her how he had replied to them.

"Think of Mr. Sinclair sending me a second application," he said, "as if I were a fool, and wrote without consideration, or did not know my own mind! He'll find his mistake."

"But why don't you let them have the schoolroom, Mr. Kennedy? What great harm could it do?" asked Miss Raeburn.

"Establish a precedent for one thing—a bad precedent. Why, the Mormons would be wanting it next to make my parish a recruiting-ground for the Great Salt Lake."

"Hardly," said Miss Raeburn.

"Then, set a lot of people in this parish spouting and thinking they can settle the nation, and where is it to stop? Intelligent, forsooth! a parcel of blockheads!"

"Now I think you hard on us, Mr. Kennedy."

"Not too hard. Besides, I know Sir Richard would be as averse to giving the schoolroom for any such purpose as I am."

"Is Mr. Gilbert agreeable?"

"Oh, Gilbert!" said Mr. Kennedy, in a tone which Mr. Gilbert might count it one of his many mercies that he did not hear—it would have unhinged him for a fortnight.

"Yes, Mr. Gilbert; he is in possession, and possession is nine points of the law. If I were you, Mr. Kennedy, I would not only let them have the schoolroom, I would head the movement. Take it in your own hands, and you may direct and mould it."

"But I highly disapprove of it, Miss Raeburn. Any intelligent man that wants to improve himself can easily get a book—I am always glad to lend books myself—and sit in his own house and read,—a far more likely means to the end than running to so-called entertainments."

"If a man can read he will do. He has his entertainment in his own hand; but what about the people who won't read, and want entertainment?"

"The best thing they can do is to go to bed early, and they'll rise the fresher for their day's work."

"I once told such a torpid man as that system produces that it was thought possible the stars were inhabited, and he said to me afterwards that he never slept all night thinking of it."

"Well, did the suggesting of such a speculation do him any good, or would his night's rest not have been better for him?"

"If you can make a man think beyond his daily round you have done a good thing, Mr. Kennedy."

"But even your thinking men, what do they make

of it? Peter Veitch, for instance, who is not the least intelligent of his class—"

"My old friend Peter the gardener?"

"Yes; I had an account sent me by him some time ago. The spelling is the most original thing you ever saw—laughable."

"Not a bit laughable, except to the eye. If you understood his meaning the end was served. Spelling is a mere conventionalism. It may be as well that people should all spell alike, but I would never measure a man's mind by his spelling. If I had left school at ten years old like Peter, and done a hard day's work every day since, I would never have attempted to spell at all, likely. Culture has not come Peter's way, except with the spade, yet he thinks for himself, and is not generally far wrong, but he has no instinct for the niceties of spelling, and I sympathize with him. I've never been able to spell myself.

"Indeed. Well, you see Peter has got creditably through life without being entertained in the evening. I'm going home to write to Mr. Sinclair. As long ago as when he came I had a presentiment he would work mischief, and I'm not often mistaken."

CHAPTER XLII.

As Miss Raeburn watched Mr. Kennedy's retreating figure she said to herself, "It's a pity they should quarrel, and about nothing."

It is always a marvellous pity when people quarrel. A quarrel is like that abominable weed the dandelion: allowed to flourish, it gives off noxious seeds all round; cut down, it leaves roots of bitterness that can hardly be dug out.

Mr. Kennedy wrote to Mr. Sinclair again:—

"SIR,—I have no occasion to reconsider my decision. I never decide, even on trifling matters, without full consideration.

"My views differ on every point from those of Mr. Miller and his society. I am as anxious for the welfare of the working classes as you can be, but to unsettle their minds and raise tastes they can have no means of gratifying is not, in my humble opinion, the way to improve them.—I am, etc., J. KENNEDY."

Mr. Sinclair wrote yet again:—

"SIR,—If you really have duly considered the matter, I am entirely at a loss to know what reasons have influenced you in persisting in your refusal to give this society the use of the schoolroom for an evening or two. I suppose it is hopeless to urge the request,—I am, etc.,
"A. SINCLAIR."

"Mr. Kennedy begs to inform Mr. Sinclair that he has received his note, which in his opinion does not call for a reply."

Just as Mr. Kennedy sent off this epistle—the last shot—one of the young Smiths paid him a visit, and Mr. Kennedy being full of the affair spoke of nothing else, and read the correspondence between himself and Mr. Sinclair. Mr. Smith thought the whole thing very laughable, and when he left Mr. Kennedy he sat down and whipped up an airy Punchified article, in which he inserted the letters of Mr. Kennedy and Mr. Sinclair *verbatim*, and sent it to the *Middleburgh and Quixstar Observer*, the local organ.

"Well," said Mrs. Sinclair a day or two after, as she finished her usual morning researches among the newspapers, "well Bell, your uncle has certainly come out at last. Just look at this."

Bell glanced over Mr. Smith's article. "I wonder who did that?" she said. "It is clever, but it will vex uncle. Would it do to put away the paper, and not let him see it?"

Before Mrs. Sinclair could answer Mr. Sinclair appeared, and she immediately said, "Bell wants to keep that paper out of your way for fear of vexing you; but I think if you like to mix yourself up in a thing like that you must just take the consequences."

"Mr. Sinclair read the article, while Mrs. Sinclair and her daughter were discussing a letter from Effie, who was on a visit to the mother of her betrothed.

"Ay, Bell," said Mr. Sinclair softly, for he was touched by this little evidence of his niece's consideration for him, "so you thought I could not stand that? I can stand that, and a great deal more than that, yet I think it is a very ill-advised thing of Kennedy to publish such an article."

"But, uncle, Mr. Kennedy never wrote it. He could not do anything like that."

"No; but he empowered some one to do it, else how could the letters have been given?"

"It's my opinion, Adam," said Mrs. Sinclair—"only you never ask my opinion,—that you had much better have let the thing alone. Within my memory the working classes neither had relaxation nor entertainment, and you got really good devoted servants, who stuck to their work and made that their entertainment. You don't get such servants now that there is a constant craving for change and excitement."

"It's a puzzle to me," said Bell. "I would like every one to be cultivated and refined, and to have as much enjoyment in life as I have; but, then, who would do the dirty work? I would revolt from it, and any one educated as I have been would, and yet it must be done; and even work that is not dirty is often frightfully heavy and monotonous. When we went to see Mr. Doubleday off, the steamer was behind its time in sailing, and we waited on board. I watched two men loading the next ship with pig iron. One on the quay fixed a rope round so many bars of iron, swung the crane round, and lowered the iron into the hold. The man in the hold put the iron in its place, and sent up the rope. That went on without variation the entire day I suppose. Even to look at the monotony was wearisome. The men were beginning to get old, and they had kindly, patient Scotch faces; no want of mind in them. In my circumstances these men might have shone; and here am I, with every privilege, and I don't shine. Why should they be there, and I here? There is no end to puzzles."

"None," said her uncle; "meantime we must do what we can. I don't suppose all we'll attempt here will make the people victims of culture, but it may give them an idea of something higher and better than mere animal enjoyment.—By the bye, I had a call from Peter Veitch last night."

"What did old Peter want?" asked Mrs. Sinclair.

"It was not old Peter; it was his son, the sailor."

"And does he resume his mathematical studies with you?"

"No; he is only to be here a day or two. He is captain now; he has got a fine ship to command, one of a line between Liverpool and Melbourne."

"The old people will be proud," said Mrs. Sinclair. "He'll be quite by way of a gentleman now."

"Peter was born a gentleman," said Mr. Sinclair. "He is one of Bell's puzzles."

"My puzzle?" said Bell, with a terrible consciousness, and wondering what her uncle meant.

"Yes; he should have been born in a palace, and he was born in a cottage."

When Mr. Sinclair left the breakfast-table he said to Bell, "I would like if you would come to my room for a little when you are ready; there's no hurry."

This was an unusual request. What could he want? Could it be anything about Peter Veitch? Bell thought, and blushed, and felt ashamed of her own silliness, remembering the proverb, "As the fool thinks the bell clinks." She went to her uncle's room, not without some perturbation, and was thankful (as people often are) that no one knew her thoughts but herself.

Her uncle said, "Come here, I want to show you these," and he unrolled some papers that were lying near him on the table.

"You see," he said, "as the schoolroom can't be had for any purpose except such as Mr. Kennedy approves, I have made up my mind to build a hall, and have got the plans here."

"Oh!" said Bell, suddenly recovering the full use of her senses. "And have you got a site?"

"Yes, I have got that too, and a very good one; but do you approve of the thing—of its being done at all?"

"I have not had time to think."

"Take time."

"It's a thing that's much needed here—it will be a public good."

"That's what I think, and I mean to make it complete." Here he was interrupted by the room-door being opened and a visitor coming in. Bell was standing at the table with her back to the door; turning round to see who entered, she met Peter Veitch. Both were taken by surprise, so much so that their greeting was rather constrained, and Mr. Sinclair looking on said, "Surely you've met before since you were at school? Bell, you know Peter Veitch?" "Can it be possible," he thought, "that she is of her mother's opinion, and does not think he is good enough company for her?"

"Oh, yes, I know Peter very well, but I did not expect to see him here."

"Roll out the plans then, Bell," said her uncle, "and I'll get Peter's opinion of them as well as yours."

"Plans of what?" asked Peter.

"Did you see the *Middleburgh and Quixstar Observer* this morning?" Bell asked.

"Yes, I saw it," said Peter, "and I know so little of the people here now, that I could not even guess who wrote yon article."

13

"It was not written without Mr. Kennedy's knowledge, that's clear," said Mr. Sinclair with emphasis; "and I, for one, don't envy him the authorship."

"From seeming evil still educing good," said Bell. "Uncle is going to build a hall to make us independent in all time coming, and here are the plans; will you look at them?"

The three drew their chairs to the table, and Mr. Sinclair went into his plans really with enthusiasm, while his two young friends did not listen with the profound attention they might have done; the great and the little problems of life had suddenly disappeared, and they were conscious only of being together.

"Well, now that I have explained them all to you fully, what do you think of them?" asked Mr. Sinclair, with the tone of a man who feels he has done his best.

"Nothing could be better," said Peter, cloaking his ignorance in vagueness.

"Which of them could not be better?" said Mr. Sinclair, "which of the three plans?"

Knowing nearly as much of them as when he sat down, Peter was rather at a loss, but thinking that Mr. Sinclair had dilated more on the merits of No. 2 than the others, he said. "Taking everything into consideration, I should be inclined to give the preference to No. 2."

"And you, Bell?" said Mr. Sinclair.

"That's what I think too."

"Then, I think you are both right, according to my judgment. It is neither too plain nor too ornamental, and it is commodious. Well, I think we've spent time enough over them," looking at his watch. "I'll take a walk with you, Peter, if you have nothing better to do. I dare say, Bell, you're tired of us."

It was too tantalizing the cutting short of this unlooked-for meeting, but Mr. Sinclair had no notion of his own cruelty, not the slightest, he was as innocent as possible. He went into the lobby to get his hat and coat, and Peter was idiotic enough to let that momentary opportunity pass without saying a word, from sheer want of the necessary impudence; by the time, though, that he had walked to the gate with Mr. Sinclair, the thought that he would be away many months, that when he came back he might hear of Bell's marriage then, as he had heard of her sister's now, gave him the courage of desperation, and he said to Mr. Sinclair:—

"I'll be back immediately. I want to speak to Miss Sinclair."

It could not occur to him to use any subterfuge to say he had left something behind, and he returned to the house, and going straight in, he met Mrs. Sinclair in the passage. They exchanged some sort of greeting, and she said—

"Have you forgotten anything?"

"No; I want to speak to Miss Sinclair," he said.

"I'll take any message. She's engaged, I think."

"Oh, not much engaged, mamma," said Bell, emerging from her uncle's room. "I'll go with you to the gate, Peter," she said, taking a shawl from the lobby-stand.

"Let me put that on," he said; "I'm accustomed to unfurling sails, you know," and he threw it round her shoulders.

They stepped out of the house.

"Bell," he said hurriedly, "I can't do things smoothly, or in a civilized fashion, but make allowances. I'll be away for months—say you won't forget me."

They were just at the gate, where Mr. Sinclair was waiting.

"No," she said, as they shook hands, "I will not."

Peter felt light in the head, and answered Mr. Sinclair's remarks rather at random. Bell stood a minute or two fastening the gate very securely, then walked round the garden unconscious of every external thing.

> "Oh, how this spring of love resembleth
> The uncertain glory of an April day,
> Which now shows all the beauty of the sun,
> And by and by a cloud takes all away."

CHAPTER XLIII.

MR. SINCLAIR'S intentions were soon public property. In the newspapers appeared this paragraph:—

"QUIXSTAR.—We understand that the wealthy and philanthropic Mr. Sinclair of Quixstar has secured a site on which he means to erect a hall and other accommodation, including library and reading-room, for the use of the people of Quixstar. The plans have already been drawn out by the eminent architects Messrs. Black and White of Eastburgh, and we have had the pleasure of inspecting them at their office. The design is at once substantial and elegant. Too much praise cannot be awarded to the noble and public-spirited gentleman who has thus come forward at once to supply a long felt want, and to add an interesting and ornamental feature to the town."

Some men enjoy having their trumpet blown, and, on an occasion such as this, could move in their little sphere to the music of it, thoroughly convinced that they were doing a great public good from exalted motives. Mr. Sinclair was not so blind. He believed that the hall would be a benefit to the place, but he also knew that to benefit the place was not his chief motive; he had determined not to be baulked by Mr. Kennedy. If it was a good work he had certainly been provoked to it —taking the modern sense of that word—and felt humbled in his own eyes, and he was annoyed at the paragraph and the writer of it, who was wholly unknown to him.

Mr. Kennedy on reading it at once attributed the authorship to Mr. Sinclair, and was seized with a deep and subtle pity for the man reduced to the abject shift of puffing himself.

Even the eyes of the inhabitants of Cranstoun Hall fell on this paragraph, and it was a subject of remark at luncheon on the day of its appearance.

"Sinclair," said Sir Richard; "Sinclair; that's the retired tobacconist, isn't it, that got that mole catcher for me? Knew him, I suppose, from filling his snuff-box for him. The man must have more money than he knows what to do with."

"Of what possible use can a public hall be in Quixstar?" asked Lady Cranstoun.

"It is to be used for the elevation of the working classes," said her eldest son; "to make them happy, intelligent, and so on."

"They are certainly not very intelligent," said Lady Winkworth, who had dropped in to luncheon; "at least I don't find them so."

"Don't you?" said Mr. Cranstoun. "What subjects have you tried them on, Lady Winkworth?"

"They were the wives of working men that I have called for chiefly, and I only tried to give them some hints about cookery. My cook had been telling me that excellent puddings can be made of the crusts of bread, and a most nutritive soup from the liquor of a boiled leg of mutton, and I tried to explain it to them, but they only looked stupid, and said nothing."

Mr. Cranstoun laughed.

"You did not say anything about catching a hare before cooking it, did you?"

"No; hare! Why, hare is game. Lord Winkworth used to be very strict about his game."

"I'll give a lecture," said Mr. Cranstoun. "There's not a better dodge going than the working classes. See if I don't give it to the women about cookery. I purloined one of your ladyship's tracts the other day, with cookery receipts at the end of it, and committed them to memory for the very purpose. One—How to make a leg of mutton dine a family of six, seven days; and another about rice. You take a quarter of a pound of rice, put in three gallons of water, one teaspoonful of salt, one half-teaspoonful of pepper, one large onion shred, simmer for twelve hours by the side of a clear fire, and you will be surprised at the amount of wholesome food. If I could drive these things home, I would feel that I had not lived in vain. Bacon's death from stuffing a fowl with snow would be nothing to it."

"I remember," said Sir Richard, "Mr. Kennedy speaking to me about the schoolroom being asked for some meeting. He refused it. I said he was quite right—quite right. What's the use of all this lecturing? If lecturing will make the world better, it should mend rapidly."

"To be sure it will," said George. "There won't be a topic nor an audience left for me soon. I shall have to assemble the birds, and give a lecture on nest-architecture."

"I think," said Lady Winkworth, "you should devote yourself to the development of rice—make it your specialty."

George laughed.

Generally at such crises the ladies of a man's household throw themselves into the mêlée with much zeal and devotion; but in this case the breach was not widened by feminine influence. Mrs. Kennedy, as we know, was not in a state to take an active part in anything. Mrs. Sinclair ignored the subject altogether, except when she lamented her brother-in-law's folly to Mr. Kennedy. "You know, Mr. Kennedy, if he had asked my opinion, he would not have entered on such a thing at all. But he never does ask my opinion."

"No," thought Mr. Kennedy; "his own opinion is perfect in his own eyes."

Or when she bewailed to her son and daughter-in-law his more than folly in spending money—money that ought to be kept for his brother's children—in a way that would do more harm than good. Tom said nothing—not an unusual way with him of expressing his opinion. Jane, however, eagerly agreed with her mother-in-law. Bell sympathized with her uncle, but in a quiet way; as for Effie, she was occupied with her own affairs; so that, when the first sensation made by the projected scheme blew over, the building went on during the winter growing steadfastly, and the only visible bad effect yet was a curious kind of blindness which had befallen Mr. Sinclair and Mr. Kennedy—when they met they could not see each other. How must it have appeared to those creatures who leave their silver bowers to come to succor us that succor want, and want it often very grievously? Couldn't they have whispered in the ears of these two men, "Don't quarrel; nothing your world can give is worth quarrelling about?" If they did whisper some such sounds it was in deaf ears, for even at a burial—across an open grave—where, if anywhere, the scales should have fallen from their eyes, they were as blind as ever.

It was about this time that there appeared an announcement in the newspapers of the intention of a young scion of royalty to visit Eastshire, where he was to be the guest of the Duke of Eastshire, and at the same time honor with a visit Sir Richard Cranstoun of Cranstoun Hall. Many people saw that paragraph; but into the minds of none of them did it sink except that of Mr. Miller, the active and energetic member of the Rational Relaxation Society. It flashed on him like an inspiration—royalty being in the immediate vicinity of Quixstar, why shouldn't it be asked to lay the foundation stone of the new hall? He pondered over it; and, not being above the weakness of wishing to get credit for his own bright ideas, he took no one into his counsel; and he wrote his letter of application, not without having duly considered what he was asking, and how he was asking it. If the request was granted, good and well; if it was not, still good and well in a minor degree,—in the first case it would be a grand triumph for the R. R. Society and for the pro-hall people of Quixstar; in either case it would be an advertisement of no secondary order. That would be a stern spirit, demanding more of human nature than it is capable of, who would deny to the good man a conscious satisfaction in his own good deeds; and Mr. Miller stepped about his usual business with considerable buoyancy, pending an answer to his request. The answer came; it was a refusal, declining for the boy the offered honor in the most courteous terms. Instantly Mr. Miller sent both letters to the newspapers, and Great Britain became aware that there was a Rational Relaxation Society, that there was a town Quixstar by name, where a Mr. Sinclair was building a hall. The inhabitants of Quixstar itself were variously affected by seeing themselves placarded in connection with royalty.

The milder and more easily pleased spirits, to whom
13*

fault-finding was neither a pleasure nor a habit, thought it well a hall should be built, good of Mr. Sinclair to build it, right that royalty should be asked to stamp it, and perfectly proper that royalty should decline or not at its convenience; and they were delighted that it should decline in such courteous and condescending terms. But there were the lean spirits—the men of the Cassius type, whom Cæsar did not fear, but said were to be feared— those who asked what royalty did to earn the immense revenues it drew from the thews and sinews of working men, and what right it had to refuse a request, however trifling, from the sovereign people; these were comparatively few though, and lean, chiefly through attending to public affairs rather than their own. There were people who laughed good-naturedly, and people who laughed in derision, at the clever Smith family. There was Mr. Kennedy, who was very angry, and was of opinion that he did well to be very angry. There were the Cranstouns, the elders of whom considered such a liberty taken with the throne from such a quarter not far short of high treason, and the younger, who thought it a pretty good joke. Miss Raeburn was amused, and Mr. Sinclair was vexed and annoyed more than he cared to show. He had called spirits from the vast deep of modern push, and found that they were beyond his control. As for Mrs. Sinclair, she told her daughters she considered this request for royal countenance the one redeeming point in the whole affair—a piece of good sense she would not have given their uncle credit for. Mr. Kennedy gave him credit for it though, and his pity for Mr. Sinclair waxed deeper and subtler and blinder than ever.

CHAPTER XLIV.

ABOUT this time the Gilberts' interest in public affairs was in some measure swallowed up by interest in their own. A letter had come from John, in which he stated his intention of being home about the beginning of summer. It was addressed to his mother, and made her heart beat not with unalloyed pleasure. He said,—

"MY DEAR MOTHER,—I have got all of your letters, I suppose, and a good bundle they would have been, if I had kept them [letters these in writing every one of which Mrs. Gilbert had shed tears]. You people who, like oysters, stay always in one place, suppose it something desperate to be so far from one's native town as I am, but those who move about the world think nothing of it. So Jane is married; well, Tom is very a decent fellow, and I congratulate them both; and Effie Sinclair proposes stepping out of the avuncular nest, and so the world wags. [Mrs. Gilbert had considered and reconsidered whether she would give him this piece of news, and deciding to do so, lest it should come upon him from a less sympathetic quarter, had done it in the gentlest way she could devise.] We have had an election here. Our elections are conducted by ballot, so that though there has been a good deal of excitement, there has not been so much commotion as on similar occasions in the old country. The contest was regarding Free-trade and Protection. There is a loud and stupid cry in the colony for protection for native industry, a most delusive and pernicious theory, which you would have thought might have been exploded by this time, but all over the globe you find people who block the way. Education is another question of interest here, as at home. I think I see my father cocking his ears at the mention of it. Well, it is in a wonderfully satisfactory state, every facility being given for every child in the colony being educated—that is, wherever twenty children can be got together, for that is the smallest number for which the government will grant its allowance. Any child not able to pay has only to get a declaration to that effect from a magistrate or minister, and he is taught gratis. They are wanting now to make education compulsory and secular, which may be an improvement. There was a great public meeting about it the other night, and a funny thing happened. One speaker made a very good speech; he spoke with authority. I asked some one, Who is that? and was told that he was a barrister from New Zealand, and a rising man in that colony. He sat down; I was just at his back; he and the man next him began to look at each other; at last the New Zealander put out his hand and said, 'You're Tom Smith,' and Tom said, 'And you're John Johnston.' 'Now,' I said, sticking my head in between them, 'are you very much nearer identification when you have found out that the one of you is Tom Smith and the other John Johnston? I'll clinch the business—you both hail from Quixstar, and I am John Gilbert.' We were all very happy, and at the end of the meeting Smith took us to his hotel, where we were introduced to his wife, and had supper. It is said she is enormously rich; he is a lucky fellow. Couldn't you look out some moneyed ladies for me to pick and choose among when I come home? I mean to try the cuckoo's plan for once, and have no winter in my year, and two summers; look out for me the time the pea puts on the bloom next spring. By the bye, Tom Smith was nearly drowned; he was bathing in the river a morning or two after I first saw him, and took the cramp; I happened to be passing at the time, and pulled him out. His wife has been in an extraordinary state of gratitude. He tells the stale story of seeing all his life before him when he was sinking. When I'm pulled out of the water I'll invent something fresher than that."

This letter was what John sent to his mother to feed her love on, but love is like the cactus order of plants, which can find moisture in a dry and thirsty desert.

November and December are proverbially gloomy months, and they are gloomy, but it is a chastened gloom, a gloom that softens one's mood; they linger among decayed grandeur like people that have seen better days, even the birds—those of them at least that have remained to share their fallen state—respect their misfortunes and hush their songs, except when one by mistake sends out a note and stops short, shocked at its own heedlessness. But for dour, wild, weird gloom there is nothing like a surly January day, with its leaden colors, its sullen inky clouds driven before the wind like a herd of old-world monsters; trees twisting their naked arms in despair; a bare desolate earth, and a bleak desolate sky; yet there is an undertone of vigor in the wind, and a clear freshness—is the young year waking up in a fit of the nightmare? It was on such a day as this that the foundation-stone of Mr. Sinclair's hall ought to have been laid by youthful royalty, if Mr.

Miller had got his own way. If any one supposes Mr. Miller's mood would have been influenced by the weather, any one supposes a laughable thing; but he felt that other people had less wisdom and energy than himself, otherwise, the boy being on the spot, the stone would have been laid with a flourish of trumpets, instead of the occasion slipping past almost wholly unimproved.

The illustrious boy paid his promised visit, however, to Cranstoun Hall, and with his tutor and another gentleman walked the length and breadth of Quixstar, seeing what was to be seen. They did so uninterruptedly, few people being aware of the rank of the visitor. Maddy Fairgrieve, now Jackson, and a happy stepmother, looked in on Mrs. Veitch in the afternoon. "Did you see the Prince?" she asked eagerly.

"Ou ay, I saw him," said Mrs. Veitch; "him and twa gentlemen cam' and stood a gude while lookin' at our midden—it seems the thick o' a battle was there twa three hundred year syne. I forgot a' about it, and wondered what they were looking at; they werena like folk wantin' to buy dung. When Peter cam' in and tell't me it was the Prince, I thought I should hae asked him in to get a drink o' milk or something, but I was that ill wi' the toothache I could not be fashed."

"It's been a cauld day," said Maddy. "I think aye at this time o' the year the wind gangs through ye like a knife; no very gude for the toothache.—And what like was he?"

"Weel, he was muckle like other callants. I dinna think but our Peter looked better than him at his age."

"It's a pity but ye had asked him in," said Maddy.

"Hoot, the like o' him wad get something somewhere. I kent that, or I wad hae asked him in, ill as I was."

"Oh, he wadna starve, I daursay," said Maddy; "but it'll maybe be a while or sic an honor comes your way again."

"Weel, weel, we can live without it. Puir thing, I'se warrant his mother thinks a heap o' him."

"It's likely, or she'll no' be like you."

"Weel, I fancy we're a' ae flesh and blood."

CHAPTER XLV.

NOTHING of its kind could exceed the beauty of Quixstar in May, except perhaps its beauty in June. June might be a degree richer, but oh! May was fresh and vivid and very lovely, especially towards the close of the month, when the leaves had got themselves fully unfolded, and had lost none of their exquisite delicacy of coloring, when the lilac and laburnum were hanging in full cluster in all the gardens, and the fruit of the following autumn was making its first appearance in a cloud of red and white startling into beauty the homely apple and pear trees, and the spring flowers, matchless, in the grace of simplicity, still lingered.

Mr. Kennedy did not appreciate his garden as he might have done. He had it kept in good order, and got a second-hand pleasure out of it. He liked to hear people say, "You have a fine place, or a sweet place, Mr. Kennedy;" but that is a vulgar enjoyment compared with what the man has into whose ear Nature herself whispers.

A lilac-tree stood very near Mr. Kennedy's bedroom window, which had performed its annual miracle of crowning itself with no end of the richest white clusters, drooping slightly with their own weight. It was a miracle that did not attract much attention, not even from the kind of people who don't believe anything but what they understand; and there were people in Quixstar who had reached this point—the point where the fool and the philosopher met.

It was no miracle to Mr. Kennedy how all that fine workmanship, which could stand inspection with the most powerful microscope, that skill in grouping, and chaste purity of color, came there. It was a matter of course, but it was not a matter of course that his property should be destroyed, and one night when the dog began to bark, Mr. Kennedy, thinking some one might be tearing off branches from the trees, opened his window and looked out, meeting the gentle incense from the lilac, which added charm did not strike him either. A man was standing in the shadow of the twilight—hardly twilight, for at that season the day seems to linger and linger for the kiss of the jocund morning before departing forever.

"What do you want?" cried Mr. Kennedy.

"My dear sir," said the stranger, "what could I possibly want at this hour but a bed?"

"Do you take this house for an inn?"

"Yes; a place of spiritual refreshment. The house remains, but the hosts change. The word manse—" here a fit of coughing came on.

"The sooner you go to the inn the better," said Mr. Kennedy.

"I've just come from the inn. I can't get a bed there."

"Why?"

"Because they've washed all their blankets, and they're wet—not a dry rag in the house."

"You can't get a bed here."

"What! My father used to tell me that the manses of Scotland were famous for hospitality. 'Tom,' he used to say, 'whenever you are at a loss throw yourself on the hospitality of the manse.' My father, Dr. Robertson of Hongatonga; you have heard of him, of course—"

Mr. Kennedy said he had not.

"Impossible! The well-known Dr. Robertson, author of a Commentary on the Epistles of Peter. I bet you have the book on your shelves, and I could find it for you!"

"Thank you. No, I don't bet; and as I have said, you can't get a bed here."

"Then let me have a chair—a sofa—anything? My father said, 'Throw yourself on the hospitality of the manse.'"

"You can't get in here."

"And I'm not able to go farther; in my state of health the night air is death," and he had another fit of coughing.

"Get a chair or a sofa in the inn."

"I'll sleep at the foot of this tree rather, and you can let Dr. Robertson know the cause of my death. Mistaken man; he used to say, 'Throw yourself on the hospitality of the manse.'"

Now Mr. Kennedy was hospitable, and he did not like to have the death of any one laid to his door. At the same time he was not inclined to be the victim of an impostor, and he said—

"I know nothing of Dr. Robertson, but if there is such a man I have no proof that you are his son. Seek shelter elsewhere."

"Strange that you should not know of Dr. Robertson of Hongatonga. Why, I should have thought my friend Mr. Gilbert would have mentioned him to you. He often talked to me of you. He used to say, 'Robertson, you may be fortunate in your father, and his Commentary may be good, but if our minister at Quixstar were to publish merely his ordinary discourses few Commentaries could hold the candle to them.'"

"Gilbert—John Gilbert. Do you know him?"

"Intimately—very intimately."

"And he used to speak to you of me?"

"Often, very often. You are no stranger to me, Mr. Kennedy. You see I am not an impostor."

"Well, if I were sure—" Mr. Kennedy began.

"Gae 'way to your bed, Mr. Kennedy," a voice shouted from behind the garden wall, and there was an immediate burst of laughter.

"I'll take the advice," said Mr. Kennedy; "and if you are intimate with John Gilbert, his father and mother will be glad to see you. Make your way to them." And Mr. Kennedy took in his head and shut the window.

And John Gilbert—for it was he—lay down at the foot of the tree, and slept well and soundly, without detriment to his health, which was remarkably good. He had gone to the inn the first thing on his arrival in his native place, and on leaving it had stumbled into the manse garden, his senses not being very acute at the moment. It was not the first time by many that he had slept under the open canopy of heaven. It was well for herself that his mother did not know and could not guess all the outs and ins of his history. In the morning he went to St. Hilda's Lodge and startled the servant who opened the door to his very early visit, by his outlandish and unkempt look, so that she was not at all sure of letting him in; but he got in and made his way to a bedroom, where he effected such a change in his appearance that on his emerging again she was not sure he was the same person she had let in.

"Well, John," said Tom, "you've got back. Have you seen your father and mother yet?"

"No; I wanted to see you first."

"Which means," said Tom, "that you have come home without a penny."

"No, it doesn't. See," he said, "I have more than a penny," and he held up a penny and a halfpenny. "That is the fortune with which I return to my native land; but I'm not going to stay long. Don't be frightened."

"What are you going to do?"

"I am going back to where I came from. Meantime, you must lend me some money."

"I won't lend you money. I'll give you a little."

"Well; so that I get it I don't mind."

"Oh, Jack, you've got home again," said Jane; "and better-looking than ever, I declare. Have you made a fortune? What did my mother say when she saw you?"

"She hasn't seen me yet."

"John!" said Jane, in a tone of reproach.

"Well, I have only arrived, and I thought I would come here and smooth my outward man a little first."

"Have you made money, John?" she asked eagerly.

"Not much. I've told Tom the amount of my fortune quite frankly.

"How much is it, Tom?"

"Just as much as when he went away."

"If I had been you, John," she said, "I would not have come home till I had something to come with. I wonder at you. I would have had more pride."

And this was the outcome of Mrs. Gilbert's visions and anxieties about her children! Why, they were strangers to her, foreign to her very nature!—Jane in her hard respectable worldliness, and John in his careless easy-going vagabondism. Still both loved their mother. It was not that John did not love his father and mother that he did not hurry to them, but that through all he had a sense that he might have been a better son. However, he meant to do wonders yet.

When Jane and he passed the parlor window, Mrs. Gilbert was in her usual seat. She looked up, and a great rush of blood dyed her face and faded out of it again; that was the only sign of extra emotion she gave. After the first surprise and greetings were over, John reclined in an easy chair, and Jane discoursed largely about herself and her concerns. In a little the window was shadowed for a moment by two figures passing, and Jane said, " There's Bell and Effie. It's an early call."

Mrs. Gilbert looked at her son. She was anxious how he might feel in meeting Effie, and hastened to the door to take the girls into another room to save him the shock, or at least to give him time to prepare for it, but Jane cried—

" Bring them here, mamma, they'll like to see Jack."

" Yes," said Jack, as he shook hands; " I was sure you would no sooner know that I was here than you would be across to see me."

" We did not know that you were here," said Bell; " but I am very glad to see you."

" I did not believe you would ever come back," said Effie, without apparent emotion.

" To be sure I've come back. I heard of your wedding and came back to dance at it—for the express purpose. I'm not very intimate with George, but you and I are old friends."

" Oh, George will make you as welcome as I. I really thought that you would be Mr. Wandermere who was to have come home next year."

"I've come home to look for a wife," said John.

"Are ladies scarce where you come from?" asked Effie.

"Far from it; but I have a tinge of patriarchal romance about me. I want a daughter of my own people," said John.

Whatever old-fashioned notions of embarrassment or constraint, or possibly of a fainting-fit occurring at the meeting again, under such altered circumstances, of two who had been ardent lovers, any one present might have had, were thoroughly put to flight by the easy nonchalance of Effie and John.

Bell wondered if she had only dreamed that she had found her sister among the trees, sobbing as if her heart would break; and Mrs. Gilbert thought times had changed since she was young, when broken hearts were an article of firm belief.

"She's a nice little thing, Effie," said John when they were gone; "and she'll have plenty of cash. George is a lucky fellow; but it's always the people who have much that get more. Is there no word of Bell going off?"

"No," said his mother.

"Bell won't be so easily pleased as Effie," said Mary.

"Easily pleased!" said Jane; "George is a capital match. I wish he had chosen you instead of Effie; that's all the ill I wish you, Mary."

"Do you know," said Bell to her sister on the way home, "I was frightened when I heard John Gilbert was home? I did not know how you might feel."

"How I would feel!" said Effie; "how should I feel? I have no feeling in the matter." Then a minute after, "He is amazingly good-looking, and not changed, except for the better."

"It is a pity he is not as good as he is good-looking."

"But he is not bad," said Effie. "No one says he is bad. For his own sake I hope he is not."

Bell thought—" I wonder how she feels. I have not the least idea; but feeling of some kind she must have." Effie's feat of legerdemain in transferring her love so entirely was a thing out of Bell's power.

His son had come home, and Mr. Gilbert, in his school, was not aware of it. On his way home from his daily toil he met Jane and Tom Sinclair, who told him. His eyes instantly lighted up.

"How is he looking?" he asked.

"I never saw him look better," said Jane.

"What has he been doing all this time?"

"A good many things, I fancy," said Tom.

"And he has come back without a farthing," Jane remarked.

Mr. Gilbert's countenance fell, and he said hurriedly, "If he has his health that's everything," and passed on.

Happily parental love is seldom measured by money; and although it grieved and disappointed Mr. Gilbert bitterly that, while other men who had started with John were honorably settled in life and prosperous, his son—his only son—should still be the rolling stone that gathers no moss; yet he was young, and he comforted himself by thinking that he would before long take root and flourish. He went in and welcomed the wanderer with a voice not altogether steady; and when he looked at him he immediately began the old castle-building.

John himself talked of the wonders he was going to do, and smoked and lounged in-doors, and hung about out of doors, and cultivated a close intimacy with his grand-aunt, and was very often at Old Battle House; and patronized St. Hilda's Lodge a good deal, and visited the Smiths and Miss Raeburn, and gave out that he was to leave for the antipodes again in the autumn. Careless as he was, and thoughtless in giving her so much pain, the best thing about John was his love for and belief in his mother. When a boy she had given him a Bible, in which she had written his name. Not having seen it after he left, she hoped he had taken it with him; and when he returned, the first thing she noticed on his dressing-table was this Bible. How it gladdened her heart! Nor was he a hypocrite in this; he carried it about with him from love of his mother.

The first time he met Mr. Kennedy they stood and talked a good while, when just as they were parting, "By the bye, said Mr. Kennedy, "I had a curious nocturnal visit from a friend of yours lately."

"Ay! said John, who was that?"

"Robertson. Do you know any one of the name of Robertson in Hongatonga?"

"Well, yes; a Rev. Dr. Robertson; but it was not him, was it?"

"No, his son."

"Ah, Tom! he's a scamp, and a thorn in his father's side. Yes, I knew he was over. And how did he introduce himself? what did he want?"

"He wanted a night's lodging, and did not bring an introduction. He said he knew you—that you had talked to him of me."

"He has brass enough for anything. Did he stay all night?"

"I never let him in."

"You were wise; no saying when you would have got him out. Poor Tom! it's a pity. He would tell you his father had written a Commentary?"

"Yes; on the Epistles of Peter."

" Ay, that's Tom's sheet-anchor when he's begging. And he would tell you that his father told him to throw himself on the hospitality of the manse?"

" Exactly."

" Ay, that's his story regularly. I wonder he does not tire of it, and invent a change sometimes; I would if I were he."

" Perhaps he hasn't as much brains."

" Ah, Tom doesn't want for brains, if he only made a good use of them."

" That's it," said Mr. Kennedy. " Well I'm glad to find I was right in warning him off; it's very rarely I'm wrong. I had my qualms about it after—he had a bad cough."

" He is subject to a bad cough when it suits him."

" The rascal!—Well, good-bye, Mr. Gilbert. Come in any time you are passing; I would like to hear something of your travels and experience."

CHAPTER XLVI.

THERE was another arrival of an old friend at Quixstar in June—when the east wind was supposed to have retreated to its cave—although every now and then it tried to break out, and whined and showed its teeth—and the south and the west winds to come out and breathe their gentle healing influences over the land—in the person of Mr. Doubleday, who was to be Miss Raeburn's guest during the summer.

Mr. Doubleday had no money, which was bad; and, what was worse, he had no home—his sister, such as she was, being dead. To have no home worthy the name had been his lot for many a day, so that he felt it the less, and Miss Raeburn's kindness the more. Having gone away apparently moribund, he had come back *redivivus*, and Miss Raeburn determined his health should be further confirmed by a summer in the open air. Meantime she was using all the influence within her reach, backed by his own merits—which were not quite unknown—to get him an appointment in some colonial college, where the climate might suit his constitution; and she had great hopes of success.

Bell Sinclair almost danced round him for joy when she saw him return so well; and he, poor man, not having been accustomed to even ordinary kindness, thought this so extraordinary, that the smouldering ashes of the fire within him, blown upon by hope, began once more to flicker up into a kind of blaze. A professorship in a congenial climate, Bell for a wife, and half the globe between them and her mother! Talk of the Elysian fields!—a barren common by comparison!

Miss Raeburn was not one of those people who never doubt the wisdom of their own acts and decisions; and when she saw, as she was not long in seeing, the bent of her guest's thoughts, she felt that her discretion had been at fault. What could she do? There was no pretext on which she could send him away, yet she was exposing him to needless suffering.

"Have you read many novels, Mr. Doubleday?" she said to him one day when they were sitting alone.

"I daresay not; they are hardly in your line."

"Not much, but I used to read them as a boy. I like a good novel yet."

"So do I; nothing better, and I like to watch a novel going on round me if it is a good one."

"Observing people never was my *forte*," said Mr. Doubleday. "It is a gift which, to my loss, I have not."

"Well, I have it a little. I don't know that I could trust to its correctness if much depended on it, but for my own amusement it does very well. At present, for instance, we have a pair and a half of lovers under our eyes pretty frequently."

"A pair and a half!" said Mr. Doubleday.

"Yes; we have Effie and George Raeburn, and we have Bell, and I strongly suspect an invisible half. As the phrase is, her affections are engaged, I have good reason to think."

Mr. Doubleday moved uneasily on his chair—that was all the sign of emotion he gave. The sinking of the heart, the extinction of hope, the blank and pathetic resignation, were invisible even to Miss Raeburn—were known only to divine sympathy.

Miss Raeburn feeling that she had done a good deed in warning him, and hoping that she had not been too long about it, went on—

"I wonder if Effie and George will float away into commonplace comfort without more ado! It looks like it, but I have my own doubts. We shall see."

Mr. Doubleday made no rejoinder.

"Come," she said, "you must not fall into a brown study. Suppose we have a walk?"

"Yes; certainly."

"And we'll have lunch first."

He could not eat, the strain of feeling had given him a sensation of sickness, a choking in his throat. Hope, like a cat, has nine lives. You may throw it out of the window, it will crawl in at the door, and when it does die it dies hard.

When they went out Mr. Doubleday sometimes stood still, and sometimes strode on rapidly, forgetting for the moment that he had a companion; and whom should they meet but Bell and Effie and John Gilbert, who suggested that they might turn back with them, which they did. Bell saw the dazed, wishful look in Mr. Doubleday's face instantly, and without thinking she said—

"What's the matter, Mr. Doubleday?"

"You have seen a ghost, sir! Boswell's Johnson would say," John remarked.

"What like was it?" asked Effie. "Had it a white gown, and eyes like little moons?"

"Oh come, don't let us speak nonsense," said Bell. She and Miss Raeburn seemed naturally to fall behind. Effie and John, with Mr. Doubleday sometimes behind and sometimes before them, but supposed to be in their company, led the way.

"You look a little tired, Tibby," said Miss Raeburn. " Have you had a long walk?"

"Pretty long."

"And has John been with you all the way?"

"No; we met him, and he turned with us just as you did. He is a most unaccountable creature. How such a man can hang about idle so long I don't know. Why, it's four months since he came home. However, he says he is going away soon."

"He is an ornament to the place," said Miss Raeburn. "We'll all miss him when he goes."

"Jane and Tom are very angry at him. It is a great pity he is not as useful as ornamental.—Where has Mr. Doubleday disappeared to?"

All Mr. Doubleday's old feeling with regard to John Gilbert had revived, and it had occurred to him that he was not absolutely compelled to walk before Bell's eyes in the company of her handsome and favored lover, so he had taken another way home.

On reaching her own door Miss Raeburn bade the Sinclairs good-bye, and asked John Gilbert to go in with her to dinner, which he did, not to the delight of her other guest; but one pang more or less, what after all did it signify?

"John," said Miss Raeburn, "before we went out to-day Mr. Doubleday and I were speculating a little as to whether Effie Sinclair's marriage would go on to the end as smoothly as it promises. What think you?"

"I?" said John. "I really don't know. Is there anything to hinder it doing so?"

"I was asking what you thought. I hope not. If there is any such hindrance it should be got out of the way."

Miss Raeburn glanced accidently at Mr. Doubleday, which glance John caught.

"What does Miss Raeburn mean, Mr. Doubleday?" he said. "You are not going to put a stone on the line to upset Miss Effie's marriage, are you?"

"Certainly not," said Mr. Doubleday simply.

"You hear that, Miss Raeburn?" said John. "What is it you are afraid of for Effie? You haven't found that George has a previous engagement he is called on to fulfil?"

"No; I have not found that *George* had a previous engagement, and if any one attempts to break up his present one it will be a cruel thing—very cruel to Effie."

"Are people saying anything of that kind? I have not heard it."

"Neither have I," said Miss Raeburn.

"Then I'll not repeat it," said John. "It would be a pity to set a report of that kind afloat.—They were telling me to-day that the new hall is about finished, and that there is to be some sort of affair at the opening of it. Mr. Doubleday, you'll have to give a speech."

"I'm sorry I can't speak," said Mr. Doubleday.

"But you're not too old to learn."

"No, not too old; but there are other impediments."

"I think of giving a speech myself. My sister and Tom are very angry at the hall being built; but if Mr. Sinclair keeps it in his own hands, and manages it well, it may turn out a very good investment."

"He is not going to do that, though. He is going to hand it over to the town; and, by the way, speaking of investments, is your aunt, old Mrs. Gilbert, thinking of investing in any of the colonies, do you know?"

"How should I know?" said John, with a slight increase of color.

"I thought she might consult you on business matters, and you should advise her strongly against it. She can live comfortably, and ought not to risk loss. I think I must speak to her myself. I could strengthen your advice."

This was Miss Raeburn's way of letting John know that she suspected what he might be about. She could have done better, probably. If a thing is worth speaking of at all, kindly, direct speaking is likely to do more good than a game at side-hitting. However clever, it is apt to put up the quills of human na-¬re.· It says virtually, "You see how acute and dexterous I am. I see through and through you;" it does not say, "I am deeply interested in your welfare, and would like to talk of so-and-so with you," etc.

"By the bye, what has become of the sea-king?" John asked. "I have not seen or heard of him since I came."

"Peter Veitch, you mean?" Miss Raeburn said. "He is at sea; but he is expected home about this time."

"Does he come home every time his ship is in?"

"Not every time; but he is expected at present."

"I used to think Bell Sinclair had a sneaking kindness for him."

"Indeed!" said Miss Raeburn.

"Did you never think so, Mr. Doubleday? You who see so sharply into things, is Bell's·heart still to let, think you?"

"To let!" said Mr. Doubleday, to whose ears the very sound of Bell's name was something sacred; "to let!"

"Yes; you know what I mean—has it got a tenant?"

"Can't you peep in yourself, John, and see?" said Miss Raeburn.

"Well, no. You can't quite makē out Bell at a glance, and I have no time for a protracted siege, which it might be if the place is well garrisoned.—Come, Mr. Doubleday, have you no inkling of the state of affairs?"

Mr. Doubleday said, "I have heard—I have been told that her affections are engaged, but it may be a mistake—it may be all a mistake." As he spoke the last words he kindled to life at the idea. He had all along thought that John Gilbert was the man. Peter Veitch seemed an unlikely substitute.

"Thank you, Mr. Doubleday, thank you for taking such a lively interest in me. If I win Bell you'll go with us to Hongatonga, won't you? But first you and I must find out if there is any chance before I bring up the siege-train."

Miss Raeburn looked pretty steadily at John—she had a sort of feeling that he was performing on her the operation vulgarly known as throwing dust in your eyes. If he was, his face did not betray him in any way.

That evening on his way home he dropped in at Old Battle House. George Raeburn was there also; and they had a little concert, both vocal and instrumental. Mrs. Sinclair remarked that John was a great acquisition—he could do anything, and do anything well; and George echoed her. He had not the slightest tinge of jealousy; not however from the exceeding loyalty of his own nature, for he was keen, and shrewd, and proud, but because George Raeburn's betrothed was above suspicion.

CHAPTER XLVII.

"You are not much given, Mr. Doubleday," resumed Miss Raeburn, as they sat at night by the fire, "to speculate on men and things? You take people, I fancy, to be pretty much what they seem?"

It was at such a time and in such circumstances that Mr. Doubleday shone. Alone with his hostess in an atmosphere that suited him, he was so good, so great even, and so lovable, that had there ever been a person in the wide world sufficiently interested in him to draw him out, he might have been found to have no small conversational talents. But there had not been, and penury had chilled the genial current of his soul, as it has done that of many another besides his.

"You are right," he said. I don't speculate on people as individuals; but neither do I take them for what they seem. I have a kind of instinct that serves me as a guide."

"Like children and dogs, perhaps; but I have seen both children and dogs make great mistakes."

"Oh, I don't think I'm infallible, but my world is not the world of men, so it matters the less."

"And why shouldn't your world be the world of men? On what ground do you claim the right to stand aside?"

"From unfitness."

"Nonsense!"

"It is true. I shrink—"

"Ah, I can believe that you shrink. Well, I don't. I have the necessary amount of impudence when I am abroad in the world to feel myself as clever as other people, and cleverer than some. But there was a time in my life when I could have gone largely into the shrink business, and I understand that kind of thing. There is a way for people, though, afflicted with incurable shrink, to descend into the arena, which I wonder you have never thought of—why not turn author?"

"Compile a school-book — a Latin primer? They exist by the dozen already, better than I could make."

"You know if you are going to wait till you supply a felt want—till there is a vacant nitch for you to fill, you'll be like the man who sat down till the river would flow past and let him over dry-shod. But I didn't mean a school-book. You have read immensely, and you must have thought a great deal. You don't mean to tell me that the thoughts of such a man as you are worth nothing?"

His face flushed—these were perhaps the first words of appreciation and encouragement that had ever fallen on his ear.

"Now," she said, "I've thrown in the acorn; I shall long to see the oak. How proud I shall be!"

"Oaks are long in coming to maturity."

"Oh, but I'll wait a little. If I just see the first tender shoot beginning to appear, I'll be satisfied. Well begun is half ended, you know."

Mr. Doubleday sat in silence for some time—that silence which is the flood-gate of the deeper heart. Appreciation by a person for whom he had a regard—honest, hearty appreciation, without a tinge of pity or patronage in it, was an entire novelty to him. Miss

Raeburn had small idea of the depths in him she had stirred.

"What will you begin with?" she went on. "Not a novel, I imagine. I have sometimes thought I would like to write a novel myself. Couldn't you and I go snacks in writing one?"

"I know," said he, "nobody would read my part of it after it was written."

"I don't see that at all. There is no end to the variety of tastes, and what does not suit one suits another. What do you say to threading up the people round us? I think they would do very well."

"Doesn't a novel need something striking? Are the people here sufficiently outstanding, do you think?"

"Quite sufficiently, if we could make them stand out—that's the difficulty. We might be the better of a bit of scarlet, but we could try to manufacture it for ourselves; and if John Gilbert were dipped in sepia—he is clever and gentlemanly—and made some shades blacker, he would be a very good scoundrel."

"I thought you liked John Gilbert?"

"Yes; I love him. I can't help it. People say you can't love what you don't respect. That must be a mistake. What does your instinct say of him?"

"I never could trust my instinct about him."

"Why not?"

"He caused me so much suffering!"

"Suffering! John Gilbert! How?"

"I imagined—I thought that he and Bell Sinclair—that Bell Sinclair and he were—"

"Were lovers?"

"Yes; and how I have loved her! Oh, how I have loved her—" He stopped as if ashamed, and said in lower tones, "I have never spoken of it, but your sympathy drew me on. Do you think it possible that a woman—such a woman as Bell Sinclair—could love me?"

"I think it possible, and most likely, if she did not love some one else. Bell does that. I'm sure of it; as sure as if she had told me."

"But she did not tell you," he said eagerly; "and you may be mistaken."

"No, Mr. Doubleday; it would be cruel to let you think so, but I am glad you have spoken of it. It is a sorry business to eat one's own heart in silence; and let us be thankful she does not love John. It's a wonder," she went on, half speaking to herself; "it's a wonder—so much of the very best love in this world is wasted. No, not wasted. Such love as yours, Mr. Doubleday, cannot be wasted. The trees shed their leaves only to be enriched by them again, and you'll be richer; your book will be richer, and thereby mankind will be richer through your disappointed love."

Mr. Doubleday smiled a ghastly smile.

"Besides," she went on, "love cannot be disappointed. A woman wanting to marry for a home, or a man for the sake of comfort, may be disappointed, but love cannot. Love goes on loving."

"I know that well," said he wearily.

"Ah," thought Miss Raeburn, as she went to bed, "that is a page for our novel. Poor man, Mr. Doubleday does not seem to have been made for success in any shape. He has been made for something higher and better. Modest merit goes to the wall in this world. Commend me to the Secretary of the Rational Relaxation Society. He'll not stick at trifles," and as Mr. Miller and his doings came up before her she laughed. "I declare," she thought, "we'll put him into our novel too. I'll do Mr. Doubleday, and he'll never recognize himself; and he and Mr. Miller, and Mr. Sinclair and Mr. Kennedy, will contrast like the white and pink and purple and yellow flowers in a ribbon border."

CHAPTER XLVIII.

Mr. Sinclair's hall was nearly finished, and it was a neat, substantial thing, not by any means destitute of ornament either; attached to it was a reading-room, and accommodation for a library, in which a nucleus of books was already placed. In front, close to the street, was a handsome drinking-fountain for man and beast; and the ground round the building and between it and the fountain was laid out in flowers and grass. Mr. Sinclair would have handed over his building to the town quietly, but Mr. Miller knew better, and he was instant in season, and very often, to refined tastes, out of season. Mr. Sinclair disliked "push,"—specially disliked it carried into religious or benevolent movements; but what will you? Even commercially he disliked it. The business into which he had entered, so much against his inclination, had, from a small beginning made by his great-granduncle, struck root and spread gradually and securely. There had been no forcing, and to push like younger houses would have been beneath its dignity. Such a thing as an extra demonstration at the opening of the hall would not have occurred to Mr. Sinclair, but Mr. Miller suggested the wisdom and propriety of a grand opening night.

"They never," he urged, "could have such an opportunity of gathering a meeting. People would come, if only from curiosity, and why not turn curiosity to a good account?"

"Well, well, if it is to do good," said Mr. Sinclair. "It will do an immense deal of good—immense—at least we must hope so, and not lose such an opportunity."

Accordingly Mr. Miller vigorously rushed in where Mr. Sinclair very much disliked to tread; not that the Secretary was a fool, very far from that—he was a really good, energetic, earnest man, clad, it may be, in a rather thickish skin, a species of garment admirably adapted for wear in this world, but not to be had ready-made in any tailor's shop, so far as I am aware. Think of a patent pachyderm overcoat. The man who could invent that would be nearly as blessed as the man who invented sleep. However expensive it might be, I would hasten to present one to Mr. Doubleday, and another to Mr. Gilbert, and expect they would both come to the front ere long sheathed in such a uniform. Neither was Mr. Sinclair an angel, only a somewhat fastidious man. If he objected to any of Mr. Miller's arrangements, Mr. Miller said—

"We must do it, sir. Keep ourselves and our object before the public. It won't do in these days to creep about as if we were ashamed."

"I've been in a fair," said Mr. Sinclair, "where all the showmen tried which could to make the greatest din. The loudest noise attracted most customers."

"Exactly, sir—that's it to a hair. Do all you can to rouse attention—it's the only way. Things have changed since your—" youth he was going to say, but he checked himself and said, "Things are managed differently now from what they once were."

Mr. Miller drew up a placard, headed "Grand Inauguration Soiree," in very tall letters, all the colors of the rainbow, and had it affixed to every dead wall, and every green tree, and dry-stone dike; probably he even stuck one on a cairn among the hills, that the birds of the air might carry the matter, and he did not hesitate to enclose half-a-dozen copies to Mr. Kennedy with compliments, and a polite request that he would intimate the meeting from his pulpit on the following Sunday. Mr. Kennedy was very wroth, thinking that Mr. Sinclair was the author of this audacious and gratuitous insult, whereas that individual knew nothing of the circumstance.

The Secretary was jubilant when Lady Winkworth sent for some dozens of tickets to distribute among her dependants, and declared her intention of being present herself. Her Ladyship took fits of trying to do good—spasmodic they were, and not always productive of benefit, as witness her visits to the laborers' cottages, where in a family of half-a-dozen children it may be supposed that crusts for puddings were not very plentiful, and gigots of mutton unknown, but her benevolent efforts were very sincere.

Decidedly Mr. Miller had a touch of greatness about him, for he could infect others with a portion of his own enthusiasm; for example, he infected Bell Sinclair, who threw herself into the occasion with all her might, and drew with her her sister, Miss Raeburn, Peter Veitch—who had arrived in the nick of time,—John Gilbert, and Mary, and George Raeburn. She did not attempt to enlist Mr. Doubleday; indeed, Miss Raeburn had given her the slightest, faintest, far-awayest hint of the state of matters in that quarter, that Bell might shape her manner a little less affectionately towards Mr. Doubleday—for you see Mr. D. did not know, how should he ? that a free, frank show of interest is no sign of love, but the opposite. These two woman were incapable of discussing such a thing as this fully, far less of making it the subject of a joke. It was a danger that had not occurred to Bell; she loved Mr. Doubleday as Mr. Doubleday, but—well, Miss Raeburn had told him that it was a likely thing she should love him if she did not love some one else; the truth is it was not a likely thing—it was possible, of course, anything is possible, but it was not likely.

When Bell and her corps of volunteers employed themselves for a day or two adorning the hall for the grand occasion, Miss Raeburn seated Mr. Doubleday in state at a desk, that he might begin the projected book.

"What will you call it, think you?" she asked.

"I have been meditating on that. Dreams from the Depths of Dreariness would be descriptive and alliterative."

"Trash!" said Miss Raeburn. "I'm not going to humor you—not too far at least; set to work cheerily, disappointments should only make people braver."

"If that's true I should be the impersonation of bravery by this time."

"If you don't set to work instantly," said she, "I'll get your name put into these flaming placards as one of the speakers on the grand opening night; keep that in mind, and be good."

The hall was large, and there were several workmen present to help with the decorations, but after the general effect was planned the amateur decorators separated to superintend the details. They paired by natural selection, Bell having Captain Veitch as her lieutenant, George, as a matter of course, attending Effie, while Miss Raeburn was left with Mary and John Gilbert. John and Mary looked after the others as they moved away. Mary said, " Effie is very pretty; I don't wonder at George's taste."

"Too pretty for a poor man," said John. "I don't

wonder at his taste, but I wonder prodigiously at hers."

"Do you? Why, what fault have you to George?" Mary asked. Mary had a gentle liking for George Raeburn, which under sunshine would have grown and ripened into love, as surely and imperceptibly as the peach grows and ripens from crude greenness into the soft, delicious fruit, clad in purple velvet shot with green, but this was not to be, it appeared.

"What fault have you?" she said. "I am sure he loves Effie quite as much as if she had not a farthing in the world."

"Quite as much," said John, "and a great deal more. George is not the man to marry the beggar maid."

"I think you are wrong there," said his sister.

"I think so too," said Miss Raeburn. "George is a keen business man, and fond of making money, but he would not marry for it, I am confident."

John shrugged his shoulders. "Deplorable, isn't it, Miss Raeburn, for a poor wretch like me to be left out in the cold? You perceive I was right about Bell and the sea-king? No use bringing up my artillery there."

"I see they are standing speaking together; I don't see anything more at this moment."

"Of course not. It's a great shame; I ought to have had one of them, and would have had if I had not gone away. 'Oh why left I my hame, why did I cross the deep?' What do you suppose people in these circumstances get to say, Miss Raeburn?" looking across to where Bell and Peter were standing. "I can't imagine —it's not the eloquence of silence, you'll observe," and he strolled along the hall, and in a little joined Effie and George.

"George," he said, "Miss Raeburn's compliments,

and she wants your advice as to whether there should be a crown or a star in bay leaves over the platform. I say a star; what sense is there in a crown? unless, indeed, it means to indicate that Rational Relaxations crown a youth of labor with an age of ease; but a star —a star, you see, is the emblem of brilliancy and hope and general excelsiorism, and they should appeal to the young; why, by the time a man is my age it would take a steam-engine to drag him out of his ruts. What say you, Effie—a crown or a star?"

"Oh, a star, by all means a star!"

"Convey our sentiments to Miss Raeburn, will you, George, and your own, and I'll help Effie till you come back?"

George went to the other end of the hall, and had a long confabulation with his aunt and Mary, at the end of which they looked where Effie and John were standing with their backs to them; suddenly Effie turned, and they saw her face.

"Isn't she beautiful when she is so animated?" George said.

"Yes, and she is very animated just now; John must be finding something to say."

"Something amusing, no doubt," said George; "he is not often at a loss."

Effie was saying at this moment to John, certainly with animation, "Go—for any sake go; people are not blind."

"No; but what can they see?—nothing; they can't hear, luckily, and we are not among tell-tale rushes."

"Rushes or not, John Gilbert, go. I'll not have you stay any longer; do go," she ended in a tone of entreaty.

George came up to them. We were wondering

what you were discussing with such interest," he said.

"Miss Raeburn's age," said John. "I was just saying that to see her whisking about at the other end of the hall you might take her for sixteen. I would fall in love with her if I thought I had a chance."

"You might try, said George dryly.

"*Au revoir*, then; keep an eye on us, when you see me sink gracefully on one knee you'll know what I am about."

"He'll go to destruction yet," said George, looking after him.

"Oh no!" cried Effie in sharp, sudden tones.

"You don't like to hear me say so, and I don't like to say it, but think of his father toiling among a pack of unruly children while he hangs about idle. He ought to be flogged. A man of ability, too, for almost any thing."

There was no rejoinder.

By this time Bell and Peter had strayed into the library, which they had all to themselves, and both were to appearance intently occupied in examining it.

"Plenty of room for books here," said Bell.

"Yes."

"If people can be got to read, it is a good habit."

"Yes."

"When kept in its place, and people don't forget their work for it."

"Of course, of course."

"What kind of books do you like best?"

"Oh, any kind. Never mind books," said he. She moved hastily away. Instinctively she felt what was coming, and she was afraid—afraid with that strange kind of fear that is compounded of intense hope and joy.

"Bell," he said bluntly, "you promised not to forget me. Can you marry a sailor?"

She answered, but not to the ear. That was out of her power for the moment, but he understood right well.

"I can hardly believe it's true," he said after a little. "Do you know you have been at sea with me for years?"

"Have I? You would not leave the sea? You like it."

He looked at her anxiously. "It was my first love," he said, "and I cling to it."

"You have not married it, I hope, like the Doges of Venice? for I would not have you commit bigamy."

"So far that I stick to it for better and for worse. Don't tempt me to be unfaithful. You have promised to marry a sailor, and I hold you to it."

"I can bear your absence; but oh, if you were drowned!"

"I'll not be drowned if I can help it. Life is very dear to me, for your sake."

"I'll bear it," she said; "even if you are drowned. I'll live on the past till we meet again."

"I knew it," he said triumphantly; "I knew that I had loved both wisely and well."

"I love, but I did not think about wisdom. However, I hope you are good. Indeed, I believe it," she said simply.

"I try to be so, at least, and you'll help me."

"Rather you'll help me. Do you know I loved you before you—before I thought you cared for me at all —and I was frightened you never would care for me? How miserable I would have been; and how I would have despised myself for making my own misery! When you used to come to uncle for mathematics I strained my ears to hear your voice as you came in and went out. I feel ashamed of it yet."

He listened with eager delight in his face. " Say it again," he said.

" One confession is enough."

" I had the start of you, though ; I loved you when at school, and I never despaired of winning you."

" That's very like you. I believe I have made myself too-cheap."

" I never despaired of winning you when you were out of my sight, but when I came near you—"

" I acted as a scarecrow."

" I was frightened."

" I am glad to hear you can be frightened. I would not have believed it."

" Well, that's all over. I feel as if I were in a dream—"

At this point John Gilbert walked in.

" Well, it's cool, I must say, of you two to shut yourselves in here with your favorite authors, and leave us to toil among bays and laurels, with no hope of wearing any. Were you explaining the Gulf Stream, Captain Veitch, to Miss Sinclair—how is it the great weather-breeder of the North Atlantic ? I would like a little information about it myself."

" I daresay we have stayed too long," said Peter. " Come, we'll go and help you if we can."

" You can't, for we're done ; but it is proposed that we meet here to-morrow to cut bread and butter."

" Bread and butter ? " queried Bell.

" Yes—to add to the bill of fare to-morrow night ; it is thought it will make the thing like a family. A ton of bread and butter wouldn't make me feel like a family, but imaginations differ, so by all means let us meet. The hall holds five hundred. Each will need a loaf—each loaf will need two pounds of butter. Yes, there will be work for the whole of us.—Captain Veitch, you'll bring your cutlass to cut the bread, and I'll bring a few trowels to manage the butter, but mind, Bell and you must not get into the Gulf Stream again."

"Really, John, you must make a speech," said Miss Raeburn.

"If I were not so fatally bashful," said he. "No, no; the bread and butter is my line. I'll stick to it, but you'll get Mr. Doubleday to speak.—By the way, Bell, do you know why he is not here to-day?"

"I suppose it was his own good pleasure to stay at home."

"Ah, you have heard the pretty fiction about the oyster when it gets a wound? It straightway plasters a pearl over it. Well, Mr. Doubleday has begun the pearl business. He is a stricken deer—not that deer make pearls, do they?"

"What puts such nonsense into your head John?" asked Miss Raeburn, laughing.

"My general omniscience. And Bell, Mr. Doubleday has the pen in hand to write a book, to be entitled 'A Rope of Pearls; or the Thoughts of A Doubleday. By a Single Man.'"

"It's a pity, John," said George Raeburn, "that the office of jester is out of date. You might have filled it to some potentate."

"If he who wins laughs, you should be more fitted for that post at present than me," said John.

"I never attempt wit," said George.

"Wherein your wisdom shines out," retorted John.

CHAPTER XLIX.

A SOIREE or tea-meeting is not reckoned a high-class entertainment. Whether Miss Raeburn would have given a page or two of her novel to it cannot be known; but when it has figured in a novel, it has been as a subject for ridicule on account of being vulgar and commonplace. Fastidious people may go to such a thing as expediency compels, but they are either bored or disgusted, or both. And in all conscience the vulgar and the commonplace abound, as they do in every assembly of human beings. The vulgarity exhibited at a garden-party at a nobleman's mansion on the banks of the Thames may be less coarse, but it is not therefore a better article; and the refined individual who gives the light of his countenance to a tea-meeting in the certainty of being bored or disgusted, will be so; he has neither the insight nor the sympathy to know all that is before him. What to him are the lined faces that light up at a joke not worth a smile—the horny hands—the woman fat and frank, her face shining with soap, with a' child by her side and another on her knee, which her husband takes when it gets heavy with sleep—the elderly thin woman with the blank expression, resulting from living alone in one little room—the sharp, ambitious artisan who chafes at being kept down and kept back for want of that education he sees men get who can neither use it nor value it—the giggling girls and the awkward lads, coarse enough, to be sure, but out of whom in a year or two hard toil will take the buoyancy—the decent, pawkie man who, though not refined, sees pretty far into a milestone, and can take the measure of things in his own way? They are nothing to him, for he does not see them. Of course, there is the smug successful tradesman with the unctuous face and the narrow soul; but narrow souls are not confined to one rank. If he had been a few rounds higher up the ladder, his narrowness and self-complacency might have been under a thicker veil, perhaps. Does the refined man know how far he himself is the creature of circumstances, and that circumstances mean divine sovereignty?

Bell went to the hall next forenoon alone. Effie had had enough of it, she said; George had gone to Ironburgh, intending however to be back for the evening's entertainment; and Miss Raeburn stayed at home to look after her guest. On reaching the theatre of operations, Bell saw written in chalk on the fountain the words, "Adam's wine, uncommon fine," and on the door of the hall, " Sinclair's snuff-box will hold us all at a pinch," and she laughed. · Inside the door were Peter Veitch and Mr. Miller talking.

"Ah, Mr Miller," she said, "the mind of the community is waking up already. Have you seen the inscriptions outside?" and she laughed again.

"No," he said, and went out to take a survey.

"The wit," she said to Peter, "is not excessively bright; but when one is very happy, it is so easy to laugh." One can imagine his answer.

"How is it you are alone?" he asked.

She explained.

"We are in luck, then," said he.

15

"Do you call it luck to have all their work to do as well as our own?"

"Decidedly. But I don't see why you should work. Let the people that do the rest manage the bread and butter."

"I could do that; but I want to show my warm interest in the affair, so we'll begin. You can help, if you like."

But he did not help much—he rather hindered.

"I am glad you are awkward at this work," she said.

"Glad! I should think you would rather be sorry."

"No, for I have observed that men good for little household matters are often not good for much else."

"How should that be?"

"Oh, no doubt he is not the perfect man who stands at one end of the line, and he is the perfect man who stands at both ends, and fills and illustrates all between; but we don't have men of that stamp about Quixstar. I should think they are not very plentiful anywhere."

"Then you are not quite blind to my faults?"

"I was not speaking of faults. I know well enough you are not perfect, but you are a good match for me— that is, I think I can match you. I would not like to feel myself inferior."

"The man is the head of the woman," said Peter solemnly.

"The heads are one, and both are either. You'll find that."

"I hope I shall. I find it already, and it's a delightful sensation."

Shortly Effie and John Gilbert walked in.

"I took a remorse of conscience," said Effie, "and came to see if you would really be the better for my help."

"And I," said John, "knew perfectly well you would have fallen into the Gulf Stream again, and came to pick you out."

"Nothing of the kind," said Peter. "Miss Sinclair has been telling me, *apropos* of bread and butter cutting, that men who can help with their wives' work can rarely do their own to purpose. Did you know that?"

"There may be exceptions, of course," said Bell. "Burke could describe a gown he had seen on a fine lady so well that his wife could make one exactly the same from his directions; but Burkes don't grow on every hedge."

"I can't pretend to Bell's range of information," said John, "but I know for certain that hedges often harbor hares."

"Oh, John, that is smart!" said Bell, while they all laughed exuberantly. "I do enjoy being quizzed, when it is so very well done."

"By the way," said John, "may I ask when you sail, Captain Veitch?"

"On the 20th of this month; and I have to leave Quixstar the day after to-morrow, to my grief."

"To all our griefs," said John; "but be thankful you are here for the grand opening occasion. Perhaps you may get some hints you could transfer to the world afloat anent rational relaxations."

The 20th was the day fixed for the wedding of Effie and George.

CHAPTER L.

DAYLIGHT was jostled out of the hall on the night of the inauguration soiree by a brilliant flush of gas, arranged so as to show the building and decorations to the utmost advantage. The place filled rapidly, long before the hour of meeting, for the interest of the public had been well stirred, and curiosity was strong. The Old Battle House party, with the Gilberts, took their seats early; but Peter Veitch, who had that faculty common to great men—if he was not great—of never losing a moment's time, arrived at the precise stroke of the hour, and was rewarded by having to stand during the evening, which was no punishment, for his position commanded a full view of Bell Sinclair's face, and in the seat at the end of which he stood were several members of the Smith family, the one next him being a young lady, who interested and amused him by her remarks on men and things.

Lady Winkworth drove up to the door in a carriage and pair, accompanied by a grandson and Mr. Cranstoun. When Mr. Miller heard this, which he did immediately —for like any other general fighting a battle he had a personal staff flying about to bring him intelligence and do his behests—he determined to have Mr. Cranstoun on the platform. It would sound well in the newspapers that Mr. Cranstoun of Cranstoun Hall was on the platform. Accordingly he waylaid that gentleman, and found no difficulty whatever in carrying his point. Mr. Cranstoun adorned that elevation with his gentlemanly presence and jovial smile. Lady Winkworth, who was an exceedingly stout woman, walking up the middle of the hill leaning on the arm of her grandson, a very tall, slim lad, suggested the idea of a barrel escorted by a pencil-case to Miss Smith, and she suggested it to Captain Veitch.

Great as Mr. Miller in some points undoubtedly was, he failed to originate any new idea in the proceedings of the evening. In the matter of entertainment for an evening, public or private, the inventive faculty of Great Britain seems now threadbare; decidedly she is greater at work than play. But the grosser matter was on this occasion a triumph, and the faces of many of the people as they partook of it proclaimed that. The thin, wan woman who lived in one little room alone, for instance, and sipped her weak beverage with no kindred glance to meet hers, and no cheerful voice to chase the blank expression from her face—why, the brilliant light, the happy-looking company, the profusion of good things, were a fairy tale to her. She could not be merry—she had lost the trick of it—but you saw grave gratification gather on her face. She quaffed the tea as nectar, and from the painfully thrifty habits engendered by necessity, you saw her gather all her crumbs together with her spoon and eat them—at least one person in the assembly saw this and understood it.

Then there was music. Bell Sinclair had sent her piano—a very fine one—and played on it herself, John Gilbert accompanying her on his violin. Most of the audience must have heard a fiddle of some kind before, but many of them had never heard a piano, and when the sweet tones fell on the unaccustomed ears, it seemed like melody escaped from heaven.

"Do you think Miss Sinclair plays well?" asked Miss Smith of Captain Veitch.

"Exquisitely!" he said with enthusiasm. "Exquisitely!"

"Do you really think so? There were several false notes in that last thing she played."

"May be. Not to my ear."

"Ah, your ear cannot be very acute."

Peter Veitch senior, unexpectedly to his son—Mr. Miller had only pressed him into the service after the meeting was convened, not being aware of his gift before—contributed his share to the evening's entertainment. He sang "O' a' the airts the wind can blaw," and "Auld Robin Gray," and when he was vociferously encored he gave "There's nae luck about the house," and he did them well; the pathos and the humor, and the language and the singing, and the somewhat thin, toilworn, undersized man, with the shrewd, good-humored Scotch face, were all the very best of their kind. Some people thought his part the feature of the evening.

A Rev. Dr. Buckram came after Peter, but he seemed to think it was *infra dig.* for him to be there at all, and he was quite unaccustomed to speak at soirees, which seemed to be the case, as his speech was a failure.

Then native talent showed again. A youth with his face at a white heat, and looking dangerously calm, gave his ideas on "The age we live in." The age was marvellous—steam, telegraphs, girdles round the world in forty minutes; newspapers, intelligence, science, onward march, rapid strides, etc., etc., but he wound up by saying "Great as the age was—and since time was evolved from chaos, there never had been a greater—it had two wants: the one, a first-class epic poem; the other, a method of travelling through the air, and he doubted if there was any one in Quickstar capable of writing the one or inventing and organizing the other. But time will show." (Great applause.)

"Now, Captain Veitch," said Miss Smith, "make your way to the front and give us 'Tom Bowling,' or 'Black-Eyed Susan.'"

"Thank you, no; the Veitch family has distinguished itself quite enough for one night. I would rather stay where I am," and he looked down on her with a smile which made her bridle with pleasure, while he was only thinking how well he was placed for seeing Miss Sinclair, and he thought, "Bell is not looking pleased. What can be annoying her?"

Would you believe it? Bell was jealous—actually she was small enough to be jealous. One would not have expected it; but you never can tell how people are to turn up. She saw Peter apparently enjoying himself amazingly, and laughing and talking with Miss Smith, and for the first and last time in her life she was jealous. Probably she is ashamed of it till this day. Peter might have been away for a year, he might have seen her enjoying herself in any company, and he would not have been jealous; he would as soon have doubted that the sun would rise next morning as doubted her; in which, you see, she was not his match.

There were a good many lovers of low degree sprinkled over the hall. What an evening it was for them! Like the flight of the Prophet, it became an era or time to date from—both before and after. Already the finest human associations were beginning to twine round the stone and mortar of Mr. Sinclair's hall.

What an evening too it was for Effie Sinclair! Except the time John Gilbert was playing the fiddle, she had him on her one hand, and George Raeburn on the other. How were her thoughts employed? What were her feelings? She was thinking, "Oh, if John had only George's money and position," and as she looked at George his generally grave face lighted up with a smile of tenderness, and he said—

"Are you tired, Effie? You look a little flushed?"

"Oh, no. I could sit here all night."

"Indeed?" said George.

John on the other side said, "It must be on the 19th, Effie."

"I don't think I can do it, I feel so guilty. If only he knew or suspected, I wouldn't feel so guilty."

"Tell him," said John, "and see what the effect would be. Why should he know it? In fact, it is better for him not to know. It saves his feelings up to the last."

"Oh, John, if I only knew what to do!"

"You know well enough. It's a sin to marry a man you don't love."

"But I do love him a little."

"And me a great deal. Your course is clear."

All this was whispered in the shelter of a speech on Rational Relaxations, by a man from Ironburgh, a member of the Society. He was a man whose hair seemed to have made a complete somersault off his head on to his chin, which it had colonized with great vigor. His head was so bald that, had he lived in the country where eagles were common, one would have dreaded the fate of Æschylus for him, whose death was caused by an eagle mistaking his head for a stone, and dropping a tortoise on it to break the shell. But his face was so overgrown with hair that when he was speaking Miss Smith declared to Peter Veitch that it was like a voice coming out of a bird's nest. He had the good sense to be brief, which was the chief merit of his speech.

It was at this point that Mr. Miller had urged on Mr. Sinclair the propriety of handing over the hall publicly to the town authorities (whoever they might be) assembled in full durbar, but as old Peter Veitch said, "Mr. Sinclair fairly reisted at this." He was firm in his determination to do it quietly in private.

Instead of this ceremony, therefore, Mr. Cranstoun rose and said—

" Our friend Dr. Buckram has told us that he can't speak at a soiree. Now, I am in the position of the man who was asked if he could play the fiddle. He said he didn't know, for he had not tried. Great laughter.) This is my first soiree, and I am heartily glad to be here. I only came by accident, but when you have another, and are at a loss for speakers, if you'll give me timely warning I'll try whether I can make a speech or not, although from what we have seen to-night of native talent I'll need to look to my laurels. Our eloquent townsman says that he doubts none of us will ever write an epic poem—" (Here the youth who had spoken interjected, " A *first-class* epic poem, I said.") "Oh," said Mr. Cranstoun, "I stand corrected. He doubts none of us will ever write a *first-class* epic poem. Now I would not be too sure of that—I would not be at all too sure of that—and who knows but the brain that is to tame the balloon and make it a useful beast of burden is lying hidden among us? (Great applause.) I can't sit down without proposing thanks for the music we have had to-night, both vocal and instrumental. My impression is that we have all been hiding our talents under a bushel, and now that the Rational Relaxation Society is going to give us candlesticks to set them on. I think we have all enjoyed the evening, and I am sure you all agree with me that our best thanks are also due to Mr. Sinclair for giving us this handsome, comfortable hall."

A voice—

> " Wha wad hae thocht it,
> That noses wad hae bocht it? "

Which venerable piece of wit fell as new on the ears of a young generation, and sent a great ripple of laughter all over the hall. Miss Raeburn dived her face into her handkerchief, and was vulgar enough to nudge Mr. Doubleday, but his wits had not been sufficiently alive to catch the joke, so that it served them over the supper-tray afterwards, and Mr. Sinclair felt that

> " Fame is but a wider charter,
> To be mankind's distinguished martyr."

Mr. Cranstoun smiled faintly, waited for silence, and went on as if there had been no interruption. " And I hope we shall have many such happy meetings in it, and that there'll be muckle luck about the house." (Deafing applause.) As he sat down he whispered to Dr. Buckram, " That was a *quid pro quo.*" The anecdote was popped into Dr. Buckram's collections. All his friends must have heard the story beginning, " When I was at Quickstar on one occasion, my friend Sir George Cranstoun—he was Mr. Cranstoun then—" etc., etc.

Every one went away pleased, and Mr. Miller retired a worn-out but a deeply gratified man. He had worked like a horse to bring this affair off successfully, and he had done it. No one but those who have tried it know what a difficult, anxious, toilsome matter it is to get a public meeting into right gearing, and when you think you have got that done you never can tell when or where a belt may give way and cripple the whole concern. It only remained for Mr. Miller to dispatch a list of names to the *Middleburgh and Quickstar Observer* office—whose own reporter had been present—of those to whom he wished copies of that paper sent. He did not forget to pay Mr. Kennedy this attention, and once more that gentleman did not feel in a meek, brotherly frame of mind towards Mr. Sinclair, who was both quite innocent and ignorant in the matter.

CHAPTER LI.

PETER VEITCH called next forenoon at Old Battle House. He had not as yet the right of entrance into that august abode, for, Bell dreading her mother's opposition, they had agreed to keep their secret for a little. He asked for Mr. Sinclair, and was shown into his sitting-room, where he found not Mr. Sinclair, but Bell.

She was free of her uncle's quarters at any time. He had found out her value long ago, and she his, and always the more. There is great truth in that quiet Irishism of Wordsworth's—

"And you must love him, ere to you
He will seem worthy of your love,"

although it reminds one of the problem, Did the hen originate the egg, or the egg the hen? But seeing both are originated, it matters the less.

Peter was completely taken aback by the coolness of her greeting, which she ended by saying, "Uncle won't be in for a little yet."

She was at her old trade of millinery, and her uncle's table was littered with her materials, a state of matters that he did not dislike; he would even, when desirable, give his opinion on a point of taste. Changed times truly!

"I suppose," she said, "you think this work I am at silly. Uncle used to think so; I daresay he thinks so yet."

"What is it you are doing?"

"I'm making a bonnet."

"Isn't that a thing you must have? I don't see how it can be silly to make it."

"Perhaps not silly to make it, but silly to enjoy making it, which I do."

"I would not give much for the work that the worker had no enjoyment in."

"Oh, it may be suitable for *me* to enjoy this kind of thing, but it's immensely below masculine notice."

"I don't think my hands would do it—it's too fine; but I used to make my own clothes—the coarser kind of them—and I enjoy doing that. I like both to look at and to wear a jacket of my own making."

"You mean to say that you learned to be a tailor?" said Bell, laying down her hands and looking at him.

"In a rough way. I don't suppose I'm an ornament to the profession."

"I would like to see you at it; I would remarkably like to see you at it," and she laughed.

"Well, if you'll fix your day and hour to call for me, I'll fish out my materials and let you have that pleasure."

"Well, I *wouldn't* like to see you at it."

"What am I to make of that? You are unreasonable."

"Unreasonable—ridiculous!—You enjoyed yourself last evening, I saw?"

"I did that," said he simply. "It did one's heart good to see so many happy faces."

"Yes, that is always a pleasant sight. How do you like Miss Smith?"

"Very well."

"She is a most delightful creature—so much of the gushing about her."

"The gushing! what's that? That's a phrase that must have come up in my absence. One falls behind, being so much at sea."

"Oh, she laid herself out to entertain you, although she hardly knew you, and she succeeded."

"And that's the 'gushing.' Then I like the gushing remarkably well."

"I don't; I hate it! If there's anything I hate it is the gushing."

"A woman without a temper wouldn't be worth her salt!" exclaimed the sailor, half to himself, with a note of admiration at the end of his sentence.

"You are miraculously impudent," said Bell, with emphasis on the adjective, although she could hardly help laughing, as she rose from her seat and swept all her affairs together, and moved towards the door.

"Don't go," he said; "don't go. Tell me how I have offended. I must leave to-day, and I'll not see you again for—"

At this point the door opened, and Mr. Sinclair entered, with many apologies for being so long of coming. Bell resumed her seat and her work, on which she grew amazingly intent, hardly lifting her eyes; while her uncle and Peter talked. Mr. Sinclair was in good spirits, and inclined to talk. Peter of set purpose tried to let the conversation drag once or twice; he even pulled out his watch and remarked that it was about time for Mr. Sinclair's walk—he hoped he was not detaining him;—all to no end. Mr. Sinclair determined to forego his usual walk in deference to his visitor. You see, he very innocently thought he was of more value to Peter than many nieces. At length Peter had to take his departure. As he shook hands with Bell he looked keenly into her eyes, but they said nothing; so, hurt, vexed, and mystified, he went away.

He was not gone when Bell began to repent. Surely he would come back. He was to leave for Eastburgh early in the evening, but he would have plenty of time, and he would come back. She waited and watched for him all the afternoon, but he did not come. She waited till she could wait no longer; if she did, he would be gone; so, as pride and folly go before a fall, Bell caved in so thoroughly that she resolved to go and see him, if only for a second. There was not much more time now. When she knocked at the cottage door it was opened by Mrs. Veitch.

"Is your son in?" asked Bell.

"Yes; he's just packing up."

"Could I see him for a minute?"

"Surely; come your ways in," and she opened the door at the ben end of the small dwelling.—"Here, Peter," she said, "is Miss Sinclair wanting to see you."

He was stooping fastening the straps of a portmanteau. She had entered softly and shut the door.

"Bell!" he said.

"I couldn't rest, Peter, till I asked you to forget my silliness. Will you?"

"I don't understand in the least," he said; "but I'll never forget your kindness in coming to me—never. I have no time to get out my needles and thimbles—not a moment. It is hard to go." He kissed her—"Till next time," he said; "that won't be long. Don't be anxious. I must go. I'll write the moment I get on board. Stay a little and speak to my mother, will you?" Hurrying into the kitchen, he bade his father and mother goodbye, and was off.

"I'm sure it's very kind o' ye, Miss Sinclair," said

Mrs. Veitch, " to come yoursel' wi' a message frae your uncle." She had jumped to this conclusion in her own mind. " Sirs, there's naething but meetings and partings in this world. Weel, he's aye come back safe yet; but folk can be drowned but ance."

" Weel, weel," said her husband, " it was his ain choice; an' he's gotten weel on, an' behaved himsel'. Let us be thankfu'."

" And a body grows accustomed to things. The first 'way-gaun was the sairest. But be thankfu', Miss Sinclair, that ye're no' conneckit wi' a sailor."

Bell shook hands very tenderly with this pair, all unconscious of the bond between them, or of the depth of her sympathy with them.

At this same time there came to Mr. Doubleday an important missive, no less than his appointment as classical Professor in an Australian college. This, the grand object of his ambition, came with an alloy: he must leave Miss Raeburn and Bell Sinclair, the one, the best and kindest friend he had ever had, and the other —it would be difficult to say what she had been to his bare, meagre, loveless life.

" Now, Mr. Doubleday," said Miss Raeburn, " I see you are thinking that you must leave all your old friends for life. Not at all, people think nothing now of running between this country and Australia; there's Peter Veitch goes and comes every little while, and when you want a change you have only to step into his ship, and he'll bring you to my door, and I know no one I'll be gladder to see enter it."

" I must try to see it in that light; don't think I am ungrateful, Miss Raeburn. I am profoundly thankful to have got such an opening."

" And the book—the *magnum opus*—you're not to

forget it; it will be good work for you at sea. I doubt we'll scarcely be able to carry out our projected novel meantime."

" Oh, write your parts of it, and send them to me, and I'll read them with intense interest, and help you if I can."

"That's very encouraging; well, we'll see. What time are you expected to enter on the duties of your professoriate?"

" By the beginning of January, this letter says."

" And this is September. Then my advice to you is to go with Peter Veitch; he sails on the 20th. I don't wish to hurry you, but it would be a great comfort to me if you were with Peter, and I think a comfort to yourself, and you'll be into the warm region and escape the cold here in the beginning of winter."

" The 20th?—that's about a fortnight."

" Yes, about a fortnight, and you'll have to miss Effie's wedding, but—"

" I wish her all joy, but I don't want to be at her wedding; I would rather not."

Quietly but actively Miss Raeburn went about preparations for her guest's departure; it was a rapid turn-up of affairs after things had lain so long dormant.

Peter Veitch, meeting Mr. Doubleday in Miss Raeburn's garden, said, " So I hear, sir, ye're gaun to tak' a voyage wi' my son?"

" Yes, I am glad to say that is arranged."

" Weel, he has a fine ship, and he's a cautious laddie, and he's aye had gude voyages yet; so I hope ye'll get safe to your journey's end."

" I don't doubt it, if care and skill will do."

" Ay, there's no mony better sailors than Peter. I've often thought I would like to gang the voyage, just to see into things a wee; they tell me it's whiles like a pleasure trip a' the road; but it wad tak' ower muckle time and siller."

"Is it very expensive?" asked Mr. Doubleday, suddenly struck by the idea.

"Gey,—of course it depends on how ye gang; the steerage is no' a very comfortable bit to folk that's been accustomed to peace and quietness."

Mr. Doubleday pondered the subject, and broached it to Miss Raeburn.

"You've nothing to do with that, Mr. Doubleday," said she. "All you have to do is to step on board, and step out again at the other side."

"It is too much. How shall I ever get out of your debt?"

"My dear sir, it is I who am in your debt; one way and another you have given me more real enjoyment than any money could do. How am I to pay you for that?"

"I believe it," he said. "I believe it is a keen enjoyment to help the poor and the needy, but I hope to be able some day to refund at least the money you have given me."

"I'll take it in nuggets then. I've a great desire to clutch gold in the rough,—lumps of gold to have and to hold; civilized little sovereigns give one no sense of barbaric riches at all."

CHAPTER LII.

THE relation between a mother and a grown-up son should be a very tender one; on the part of the mother it generally is so, blended with pride, if the man fulfils the promise of the boy,—with what is it blended if he does not? Mrs. Gilbert had been terribly disappointed in her son, not her pride merely—that would have been comparatively a small matter—nor her heart, but her very soul was wrung. There was no getting at him; time after time she tried it, but he knew everything and agreed with everything. "Why, mother," he said, "you surely don't think I am a profligate, do you? I'm not a bad character; quite the contrary. I can tell you if I had plenty of money I would be very highly esteemed among the children of men, but somehow money has not caught the trick yet of rolling towards me; probably it will some day."

On the morning of the 17th, while they were at breakfast, he said in an off hand way, "I think I'll cross with Peter."

"Cross—where too?" asked his mother.

"Oh, to Melbourne, *en route* to Hongatonga; it is a good season of the year. He sails on the 20th; I have three days yet."

There was a blank silence; this was the first intimation of his intended departure. Mrs. Gilbert was the first to speak.

"Oh, John," she said, "could you not find something to do, and settle down at home?"

"What kind of thing, mother? Would Tom Sinclair take me into his bank, think you? I doubt it," and he laughed.

"What will you do in Australia?" asked his father.

"Well, in the first place, I'm going to test the qualities of a plant that grows in great abundance in some places there. I have a strong idea that it is the very thing to make paper of, in which case I shall clear a fortune by it; and secondly, to have two strings to my bow, I'll buy a pair of sheep and begin flock-master."

"Well," said his father, rising, "I'll have to go, my flock will be waiting for its master. I don't suppose you are in earnest, John, about going on the 20th?"

"Quite in earnest. I've lost enough of time."

"You might have given us longer warning. But what must be, must be, I suppose. Oh, man, if you could but content yourself at home." And Mr. Gilbert went away to his toil with a heavy heart, and trying to make himself believe that his disappointment in his son was less bitter than it was, and trying to put faith in a castle whose foundations were the paper-making plant.

Mrs. Gilbert bethought herself that the reason for John's sudden determination was Effie's marriage;—when it came so near, he found he could not stand it after all, and she respected him for that; that he should feel it so keenly argued well, and she spoke softly and soothingly to him, and hopefully of his future. She and Mary had enough to do getting everything ready for him, having to compress into two days the work that might have been easily accomplished had he given them timely warning; but that was of small consequence, small consequence indeed, compared with the strangled hope, the deadly sinking of the heart at the thought of her first-born, her much-loved and only son, going forth a wanderer on the face of the earth once more. The paper-making plant did not give her the comfort it did to his father; but something might come out of it.

Miss Raeburn meant to see her friend on board the *Golden Hind*—as Peter's ship was called—herself; but when she heard that John Gilbert was going, she naturally supposed he would take Mr. Doubleday in charge, and that she might spare herself the journey. When she proposed this to John, however, it seemed he was not going direct, or there was some impediment which made him decline being Mr. Doubleday's escort; so Miss Raeburn held to her original intention, and was really glad to accompany her guest, even at the cost of being absent from her nephew's wedding. She kept Mr. Doubleday employed one way and another up to the last, avoiding all affecting leave-takings; and on the 19th they left Quixstar on the first stage of his journey towards the antipodes.

This day, the 19th of September, was a day of surpassing loveliness; but no one at Old Battle House had time to remark it particularly, except perhaps Mr. Sinclair, who might be supposed to possess his soul within him in unruffled tranquillity, notwithstanding the notes of preparation for the event to-morrow that sounded on every side, not obtrusively, it is true, but with a kind of muffled hum. In the first place, Effie left the breakfast-table dissolved in sudden tears, and Bell followed hurriedly to comfort her.

"She was always very sensitive," said Mrs. Sinclair to her brother-in-law.

"Poor thing!" said he; "I daresay she feels leaving us all."

"Oh, feels it most acutely; you have no idea. I remember when I was in similar circumstances," etc. etc.

"But, Effie," said Bell, "it's not as if you were going to Australia"—here Effie sobbed more deeply than ever —"like poor Mr. Doubleday. I was sorry for him last night when he said good-bye, although I envy him the voyage, but it will come to an end, and then he will be among strangers, and he is not good at making friends; nobody can see his worth at a glance."

"I daresay he'll do well enough," said Effie; and he had no choice. What a thing it is to be distracted between two courses and not know what to do, and have nobody to speak to!"

"Yes, he has that advantage; his course is clear enough, and it is the best thing he could do, but it is a kind of exile. Now you'll be within two hours of us at any time, and you'll be often here, and we'll be with you."

"Oh, Bell, Bell! don't speak; just let me alone. What's the use of speaking?"

"Very well; if it distresses you, I won't speak. What will you do the time mamma and I are in Eastburgh? If you like I won't go. Mamma could do all that's to be done herself."

"No, no," said Effie eagerly; "go, by all means go. I'll find plenty to do."

"But you are not to tire yourself out. Mind, you are to look as fresh as a daisy to-morrow."

It was commonly thought that Bell ruled the roast at home, the truth being that her strong delicate nature was a kind of slave unconsciously to the weaker natures of her mother and sister—not by any means an uncommon case.

Immediately after Mrs. Sinclair and her eldest daug

ter had set off for Eastburgh, and Mr. Sinclair had gone for his daily walk, a cab drove up to the door of Old Battle House, and Effie descended the stairs in walking dress, entered it and went off to Eastburgh, where she was met by a friend, and jointly they transacted a very important piece of business; then she drove back, leaving the cab about a mile from Quixstar, and meeting her mother and sister at the gate at home.

"Now," said Bell when she saw Effie, "I told you not to tire yourself, and you have done it."

"Have you walked far, my dear?" asked her mother.

"Only about a mile. I shouldn't look tired."

"It's not exactly tired you look," said Bell. "You look a mixture of things,—as if you had something on your mind."

"So she has," said Mrs. Sinclair; "she never was married before."

"Now, Bell," said Effie, "for any sake let me alone. I can't stand much just now. Oh, be good to me."

"Am I ever anything else, I wonder? Why, what is the matter? Something is wrong, surely. Have George and you quarrelled, or what is it?"

Here Effie broke forth into tears again.

"You are worn out," Bell said tenderly. "Lie down and I'll read you to sleep. That's the best thing for you."

"I'm not sleepy. I can't sleep, It's no use trying. —Bell, if I were to do anything you or other people disapproved of, would you run me down or stand up for me?"

"It would depend on the kind of thing. What wicked thing do you propose doing?"

"Ah, not wicked; but people are apt to judge so harshly."

"Nobody would judge you harshly, Effickins. Come, what little sin are you looking at through a magnifying-glass? Get it off your mind, and you'll be easier."

"Oh, it's nothing, nothing at all; but you'll always love me although we are separated?"

"What earthly difference will separation make? Whatever happens, Effickins, we'll never surely forget the days of our youth, nor this Old Battle House, where we have been so happy."

Bell's eyes filled with tears; her sister was very dear to her, and to-morrow the joint volume of their lives would close, never likely to be opened again in this world.

"It is strange," she went on, "how many things are to happen to-morrow: your marriage, and Mr. Doubleday and John Gilbert sailing in the *Golden Hind*, with Peter Veitch for Captain. Why, it looks like yesterday when we were all at school together."

"I wish we were all at school together yet," said Effie.

"Oh, we had our troubles then too. Do you remember how John Gilbert delighted to tease,—how he got hold of your compositions and read them aloud so cleverly?"

"I remember—I remember. I believe he liked me even then."

"Very likely, but I am thankful that it is George Raeburn you are going to marry, not John Gilbert."

Effie turned her face down on the sofa cushion and said no more.

CHAPTER LIII.

THE 20th of September dawned as magnificent a day in point of weather as the preceding, and it is likely it would have done so had a murder been about to be committed in Quixstar instead of a marriage, for the weather does not go out of its way to sympathize with our moods. You may be in an agony of grief or suspense, and the sun will shine as brightly, and the moon sail as calmly through a clear sky as if you had neither feeling nor existence. Great as the age is, the weather does not take much notice of it, and keenly as the age has set itself to watch and note the weather, it has not penetrated very far into its secrets yet. Be that as it may, before the human population of the world was stirring, the sun, having thrown aside a white veil of mist, was smiling on everything great and small.

The marriage hour was fixed for one o'clock, and the Raeburns—father, mother, and four sons, besides the bridegroom—were to arrive shortly before that hour. Mrs. Raeburn was specially pleased with the prospect of this event, the first of its kind in her family, and Effie was a daughter-in-law after her own heart. Mr. Raeburn, with clearer vision than when the case was his own, thought his son had made a poorish choice, but he made no such remark, and he was kind and fatherly to Effie.

Before leaving Ironburgh that day George Raeburn

went over the house he had prepared for his wife and himself, to see that nothing was left undone, and he came to the conclusion that it would be difficult to find fault with it. Effie's taste had been consulted on every point, and he thought she might well be pleased with the result. He loved her tenderly, but he never for a moment forgot that he was doing her an honor in marrying her. He did not consider her his equal, and he had no desire that she should be; but she was very lovable, pretty, and soft and feminine, without the too much stamina which he reckoned her sister had, and would have no will but his, and become in time a reflection of himself—moonlight to his sunlight; while he felt certain that she was sufficiently intelligent and educated to understand and appreciate him.

They sped towards Quixstar. Perhaps Mr. and Mrs. Raeburn thought of that journey long ago when they had taken home their dead—the boy whose life had been laid down on the very threshold; or they thought of their own marriage day, a modest festival that was, compared with what this would be, and a start in the world on a totally different scale. They sped on towards Quixstar. When they got to the station a carriage and Mr. Sinclair's dog-cart were in waiting, but George preferred to walk,—he had plenty of time. "He wants to think of the solemn responsibilities he is undertaking," said one of his brothers, laughing, as they drove off.

Now, while they were on this journey, a very strange thing had happened at Old Battle House. The bride had disappeared! She had gone to the room occupied by her sister and herself immediately after breakfast, and both her mother and sister were with her for some time, then she and Bell went round the garden. When they came in Effie said, "I'm going up-stairs. Don't come to me till it is time to dress. I would like to be alone. Meantime, good-bye," and she laid her arm round Bell's neck, and kissed her.

"You don't want to be alone the whole forenoon surely?" said Bell.

"It won't be long, and I want to collect my thoughts."

"You'll perhaps collect mine too," said Bell. "They are lying all about the room."

"And tie them up with my own? I'll try. I would like to do that. Good-bye."

That was her last word, and no one saw her after.

It was past twelve when Bell went up to her room. The wedding-gown was conspicuous lying flung over the bed, but Effie was nowhere to be seen. Bell went in search of her, for there was no time to lose. She went through the house and grounds without the slightest misgiving, expecting to find her every minute. Then asked the servants if any of them had seen her. No one had seen her. She next went to her mother, who was exceedingly annoyed at Effie's thoughtlessness and actual want of sense in going anywhere at such a time. "And she'll be too late, and have to dress in a hurry, and be out of looks of course," said Mrs. Sinclair.

Ten minutes passed, and Bell went to her uncle. "Do you know," she said, "I can't find Effie?"

Mr. Sinclair was reading composedly. You see he was not going to be married. He looked up, and echoed, "Not find her?"

"No; and I'm getting very anxious, and I don't like to distress mamma. What should we do?"

"Nothing. She'll turn up in good time. I don't know whether a bride can forget her bridegroom, but we have it on good authority that she can't forget her ornaments."

"Oh, uncle, I'm afraid something must have happened, or she never would stay away at such a time as this."

"Nonsense! There is no old chest here for her to get into. Wait till a quarter to one, and if she does not appear by that time we'll see what can be done."

Bell made the round of the premises once more to no purpose, then went up stairs, and listened intently for the footfall of her sister. She sat without moving, staring at the dressing-table, then she rose, and, lifting some little article on it, she saw a letter lying. Hastily she looked at it; it was addressed to herself—in Effie's writing. Her very heart seemed to forget to beat as she read it. This was what Effie had written:—

"MY DEAREST BELL,—I am just going. I can't marry George Raeburn, because John Gilbert and I went before a magistrate yesterday, and declared and signed ourselves married persons. I am his wife. I hope George won't take it very much to heart. I couldn't help it. We are going with the *Golden Hind* to Melbourne, then to Hongatonga. I am glad we are to be with Peter Veitch and Mr. Doubleday too. I shall keep a journal and send it to mamma the moment we land. I hope she will not be very angry. You know John was my first love. If all goes well we will not be long of being back on a visit. I am looking forward to that already before I am gone. Oh, Bell, don't blame me, I could not help it. If you knew how distracted I have felt, you would pity me. Stand up for me with mamma and uncle, will you?—I am ever your loving sister
"EFFIE."

Bell was stupefied. If any one but her sister had

done this thing she would have known how to characterize it, but the pity of it—the pity: the delicately nurtured Effie, on whom the wind had hardly been allowed to blow, thrown on a life of hardship, with a careless, selfish man, without aim or occupation whereby even to maintain her.

"Oh, Effie, Effie, Effie!" burst from Bell's lips in a long cry of tenderness. She stood for a few minutes considering. Could anything be done? could nothing?

She ran down stairs to her uncle. As she passed the dining-room, the door of it was wide open, and she saw the long tables glittering with the wedding feast. Shortly the guests would be arriving.

Mr. Sinclair was walking about his room, proving that he was not quite a Stoic.

"She is gone!" Bell said, with a tone and feeling as if she herself were the guilty person.

"Gone!" said her uncle.

"Read this! she was married yesterday to John Gilbert. Can she be married in that way? Can nothing be done to bring her back?" Bell said all in a breath.

Mr. Sinclair read the note; then looked up and said, "Jilted! How do you mean to tell George Raeburn?" and his face reddened as he spoke.

"I don't know," she said in a dry, hollow voice. "Could no one go after her and bring her back? If I were to start at once I might be in time."

"You, child! No, we could hardly let you run off next. It would do no good; she is married and of age, and the law thinks her able to judge for herself, although I don't."

"Oh, uncle, if you knew how much I love her."

Mr. Sinclair turned hastily away—not from displeasure, as Bell for a moment thought, but because he did not care to show how much he was moved.

"And John Gilbert," Bell went on, "is far more to blame than she is."

"Well, Bell," her uncle said sadly, "the thing is done, and cannot be undone, and I confess my sympathies are with George Raeburn rather than with her, although she is my own niece, and I have loved her, and love her still, I hope."

"Oh, uncle, I am glad to hear you say that."

Mrs. Sinclair refused to believe such a thing. "Effie eloped with John Gilbert! It is simply impossible."

Then when she read the fact in Effie's own writing she grew very angry, though still not really crediting it. "Her first love—hopes I'll not be angry. Why, she must have had it planned for weeks! Where in the world did she learn such a mixture of impudence and cunning? Not from me; all my doings have been above-board since I left the cradle—as open as daylight. Married by a magistrate! was ever the like? The Gilberts must have known it; I should not wonder if Tom's wife did not aid and abet; she was always cunning, and would think it a good stroke for her brother—"

"Oh, mother, I don't believe any of the Gilberts knew more of it than we did. Think of the hard lot Effie has chosen for herself!"

"She deserves it, affronting us all in this way! A highly respectable man of wealth and position like George Raeburn! How are we to look? what are we to say? or what are we to do? I never heard of anything like it! never!"

"I would send at once for Tom, mamma; he and

Jane could break it to George. How grieved I am for George!"

Up to this moment Mrs. Sinclair had spoken as if Effie might come in at any moment—she had not realized the fact. When she did begin to take it in, her anger melted in tears, and Bell had to apply herself to comforting her mother, who refused to be comforted.

By this time the Raeburns had arrived, all but George, and were in their respective rooms dressing for the occasion. Jane and Tom and Mary were in the drawing-room, having come all ready in bridal array. Mr. and Mrs. Gilbert had been asked, but excused themselves: it would have been too painful for Mrs. Gilbert, and Mr. Gilbert had discovered some flaw or shortcoming in the respect that had been shown him in the circumstances. Miss Raeburn was of course absent; but several of the Smiths and other people of the neighborhood were coming, and would soon arrive.

Mr. Sinclair walked up and down his sitting-room. Bell was his favorite, but he had never thought Effie capable of an act like this. Pity for her sister swallowed up other considerations with Bell; and Mrs. Sinclair's grief was mixed up with the question that always bulked largely with her, What will people say?—whereas it was the grievous moral obliquity of the thing that Mr. Sinclair felt. Why, it looked to him as if Effie had neither conscience nor heart. You see Mr. Sinclair's opinions and habits of thinking had been pretty well fixed before the tender period came in. He was apt to think a spade a spade. Effie's youth, inexperience, and impulsive nature, worked on by John Gilbert's fluent tongue and good looks, did not plead for her with him. He was sure she had committed a great sin; but he did not expect she would feel the consequences of her act;

if John had worldly success, as very likely he might have, she would never feel them at all. The people who do reckless, foolish, sinful things are not the people who feel the consequences most deeply; those who would feel the consequences most don't do such things. So thought Mr. Sinclair; and as for what people would say, he did not concern himself. Unquestionably they would say plenty, and not of the pleasantest; but comparatively few persons come and make excessively disagreeable remarks right to your face, although no doubt there is here and there a person with a diabolical taste of that kind.

Mrs. Sinclair went to speak to her son. When she was at the foot of the stairs the house-door opened and George Raeburn entered. Seeing her, he went forward to speak. Involuntarily she put up both hands and waived him off, then turned and ran up the stairs. For once in her life heart and utterance had failed Mrs. Sinclair. She sank on a chair in her daughter's room, and sobbed—

"He'll think I'm mad, and I am not far from it; but I could not face him—I could not do it!"

Her feelings were effectually reached and stirred and wounded. Effie had been her darling, her sensitive darling, since infancy, and behold!

George stood in surprise at the foot of the stairs. He looked up and met Bell's eyes. Uncertain what to do, she had come out of her room, and was looking over the balusters.

"What's the matter with your mother?" he asked.

Bell beckoned him to come up.

"Where's Effie?" he asked. "I can see her for a minute? What ailed your mother just now?"

"Oh, George—"

"Is Effie ill? or what is the matter?"

"Mamma couldn't tell you, and I don't know how I can. Read that," and she put Effie's note into his hand.

His face had grown very white, but as he read, a scowl gathered on it which made it actually black. Bell had read of faces being so transformed, but she had not believed in it till she saw George Raeburn's at that moment.

He looked up—"Is that true?"

"If I could have spared you in any way—" she began.

He flung the paper on the carpet, turned and went down the stairs without uttering a word. By accident possibly he opened the drawing-room door, where Jane, Mary, and Tom were. Tom had seen his uncle, and was just telling the extraordinary news. There was a sudden hush when George went in. Tears were standing in Mary's eyes.

"You have heard the news?" he said with bitter levity. "But why shouldn't we have a wedding, Mary?" and he seized her hand almost roughly. "You'll be the bride. One man is as good as another, it seems, and one woman will be as good as another, I fancy," and he laughed such a laugh as was not good to hear.

"Oh, George," said Mary, "I—my sympathy—"

"Confound your sympathy!" he said sternly, flinging away her hand as roughly as he had taken it, and he immediately left the room and the house, nor did he return. If Mary had not been of a gentle nature, she would have resented this as an insult and unmanly, which it was; but she excused him out of pity, and that it should have been her brother that had robbed him made her all the more lenient, for she had a feeling of guilt in the matter, which she would not have had in any other case.

16*

Tom took on him the disagreeable but necessary duty of dispersing the wedding guests, and they retired making all the different comments on the affair, which will be easily imagined.

When the Sinclairs and the Raeburns sat down alone to dinner on this day—for whatever may pass from our lives that event must go on so long as we have mouths, and food to put in them—it seemed more as if a funeral had gone out of the house than anything else, indeed a party after a funeral has often been a much more lively affair. To use the word "awkwardness" in connection with it, is feeble in the extreme—it was awkward certainly, with the addition that every person present was feeling hurt and mortified to a degree; it was a party that did not linger over the good things of this life; it broke up at the earliest possible moment—every one glad to go.

CHAPTER LIV.

ABOUT the very time that this strange dinner-party at Old Battle House was breaking up, to the relief of all the company, suffering under such a variety of grieved, angry, mortified feeling, Miss Raeburn and Mr. Doubleday went on board the *Golden Hind*, and were received by Captain Veitch, who had been on the lookout for them. They stayed on deck watching the scene —men, women, and children, and every kind of thing coming on board.

"I suppose this bustle is not confusion to you," Miss Raeburn said to Captain Veitch; "there is method in it, is there not?"

"It does not look very methodical," he said, "but by the time we are at sea for a day or two everything will go like clockwork."

"I wish I could go the voyage with you," she said.

"Why not? you might."

"Hardly this time, but when Mr. Doubleday gets well settled I may be tempted to pay him a visit."

"By the by," said the captain, "who has John Gilbert married? It must have been a sudden thing; there was no word of it when I left Quixstar."

"Married! nonsense; I never heard of it," said Miss Raeburn.

"That is curious, and it has not been mentioned in any letter I have had from Quixstar, nevertheless I have it on excellent authority; I had a letter from him yesterday asking me to secure accommodation in this ship for himself and his wife—see, there it is," and he handed it to Miss Raeburn.

"That is most extraordinary," said she; "his own mother did not know till the 17th that he was going with you at all."

"Well, that's all I know about it," said Peter.

"Probably," said Mr. Doubleday, "it is a joke; he is a young man who is fond of jokes."

"I believe that must be the explanation," said Miss Raeburn; "how smart of you to think of it, Mr. Doubleday!"

"If it's a joke, it's a poor one," said Peter; "but we'll not have long to wait for full enlightenment."

"I don't understand it," said Miss Raeburn, "but I am curious to see the ocean bride, if she's not a phantom," and she thought to herself, "It can't be Effie, that at least is an impossibility."

She had hardly thought this when looking up, behold! there advanced towards her John Gilbert with a little cloaked figure clinging to his arm, seen at a glance to be Effie.

"Miss Raeburn," he said gayly, "I am glad to see you here. Allow me to present my wife. She's ower the border and awa' wi' Jock o' Hongatonga, you see."

Mr. Doubleday and Peter Veitch were struck dumb with surprise.

Miss Raeburn did not speak, she only looked at them. Suddenly Effie put her arm round her neck and said, "Oh, Miss Raeburn, I am glad you are here! What a time it has been!"

Miss Raeburn disengaged herself coolly. "Really," she said, "you can hardly expect me to congratulate you."

"Why not?" said John, "we are not conscious of having done anything wrong."

"Then I pity you."

"I appeal to your sense of justice," said he; "she was mine first, and she's mine last, and it's all right."

"Oh take me somewhere, Miss Raeburn," besought Effie, and they went below, where Effie sank on a sofa. "Oh, Miss Raeburn, it looks wrong to other people, I know, but I could not help it," she said, "and don't, please, be hard on us."

"How would you have liked if George had married another woman at the last moment and left you to make the best of it? and George is a very proud man; he'll feel it horribly."

"I hope not. Oh, I hope not," sobbed Effie.

"You may hope as you like, but that does not alter the thing. What kind of day do you suppose they'll have had at Old Battle House?"

"I don't know. I can't believe it was only this morning I left it; it seems like an age."

"Poor thing," thought Miss Raeburn, "it will be a longer age before you get back to it again, which is likely to be your ultimate fate."

Miss Raeburn knew that Effie had done a wicked and a very foolish thing, yet in the bottom of heart she had some sympathy with her. No doubt John was very fascinating, and Miss Raeburn liked to see a girl marry for love rather than for comfort, if only Effie had not played such a wretchedly double part—that was the black feature of it which she could not get over, but of course John was by far the wickeder of the two, for he knew what he was doing, which Effie hardly did. Miss Raeburn stayed with her as long as she could, and still Effie cried, "Oh stay! don't go."

"My child, I must go. I can't go to Australia with you."

"Oh if you could! but I suppose not," she said sadly.

"Then what message have you to send home?"

"Just that I love them—nothing more; and tell Mrs. Gilbert that I'll be as good a wife to her son as I can."

"Poor child," said Miss Raeburn, kissing her, "if I could make your path smooth I would do it."

Effie hid her face in the sofa pillow as Miss Raeburn left the cabin.

It was a harder trial for Miss Raeburn to take leave of Mr. Doubleday. However Effie had acted, she had youth and health and hope, and the husband of her choice (such as he was) by her side, but Mr. Doubleday was lonely and desolate, with uncertain health, and to such her heart went out naturally. She always felt that the prosperous have plenty of friends, which cannot be said of those in adversity, and, as old Peter Veitch sometimes said, "It's no' easy for folk when the wind aye blaws in their face," which hitherto had been Mr. Doubleday's lot. But first she spoke to John Gilbert.

"Be good to that child, John," she said, "now that you have got her; she has given up much for you, and you must learn to settle down into dull respectability for her sake."

"No fear," said he; "I have always been respectable, though not dull, and I'll love my wife as I love myself, and better rather; you can tell George Raeburn that if you like."

"I think it would become you not to speak of George Raeburn after the wrong you have done him."

"I have done him no wrong. She was mine before

she was his. She never was his—never. He thought it, though."

"On what seemed to be very sufficient grounds, but it is no use speaking of it now."

"None whatever. Well, I'll take what care I can of Mr. Doubleday. I declare, when I caught sight of you and him standing together on the deck so couthily, I thought you had just got the start of Effie and me."

"I don't doubt you did, John Gilbert," said she laughing. "You have impudence enough for any one thing under the sun, but I shall feel personally obliged by any attention you show Mr. Doubleday. I hope his health will go on improving, and that he'll be able to look after himself."

She bade Mr. Doubleday good-bye in a short time, and in a few airy, cheerful words, the last of which were, "No idleness, Mr. Doubleday. Mind the *magnum opus*. I and the world are waiting for it."

It was on leaving him she found how much his goodness and simple trust had gained on her. As she drove away she shed tears. If Mr. Doubleday could have known this he would have wondered. He himself reminded you of a dumb animal in suffering. You saw the evidence of it, but there were no tears, and no voice. Of course, one knew quite well that Mr. Doubleday had eternity to be happy in, but this present life is all we have meantime, and oh, there are so many people to whom one could wish a little happiness here and now!

When the pilot went ashore he carried a tremendous array of letters with him. The *Golden Hind* was a floating village in herself, in which every class and interest was represented, except indeed the clergy—there was no clergyman on board—and these were sending their last words to the big world from which they were shut off for a time.

Letters were scattered all over Britain that week dated from on board the *Golden Hind*, many of them no doubt to be read through a mist of tears. Quixstar was not neglected. There was a thick budget addressed to Miss Sinclair, and another to Peter Veitch and his wife, by Captain Veitch. How he found time to write so much, and what he wrote, is a mystery. Mr. Doubleday wrote to Miss Raeburn, his single correspondent. He seemed to find it difficult to express himself; he sighed occasionally. John Gilbert was writing at a table near him, and he cried, "I say, Doubleday, what are you pechin' at? Are you writing to your sweetheart?"

"No," stammered Mr. Doubleday; "I am writing to Miss Raeburn."

"One would think you might write to her without groaning like an engine in want of oil."

"You are blessed with a lively imagination, Mr. Gilbert."

"I don't know if that's a blessing."

Here Effie came to them, and said, "I'm done. I've written two long letters—one to mamma, and one to Bell. I have given Bell your love, Mr. Doubleday, without consulting you—was I right?" She did not wait for an answer to this question, which tugged at the poor man's very heart-strings, but went on: "And here is a little note, John, to put in your letter to your mother."

"Ah, that's right," said John. "I did not think of that."

The consolation these letters could give to Mrs. Gilbert was not great, for, though John was her son, she took the same view of him as Mr. Sinclair did with regard to his niece. He had done a base, dishonorable thing, and Effie's note, kind and gushing as it was, what weight did it carry in the face of the deliberate deception she had practised towards George Raeburn to the very last moment?—a treachery for which there was not the shadow of an excuse. If the thing had been deliberately planned (which, to do the pair justice, it was not) so as most deeply to wound every one concerned, it could not have been done more effectually. But in time Mrs. Gilbert read and re-read these letters, and with the ingenuity of love set herself to make the best of them. After all, they were young, and there was a new element of hope in the fact that John was not at least a solitary wanderer on the face of the earth, but they did not speak much of him in the schoolmaster's house. Somehow the follies and sins of those who are dear to us as our own souls are not things to be talked about. And Effie's marriage, which in the form first proposed would have drawn the Ironburgh and Quixstar connections closer together, as it turned out made a greater dryness among them. The Raeburns, the Gilberts, and the Sinclairs did not see much more of each other than was necessary. George Raeburn lived in his fine house alone. He never referred to his memorable wedding-day, and no one dared ever to speak of it to him, not even his mother. He buried himself in his business, his very soul bidding fair to harden and wither in the process of making money.

Miss Raeburn kept Mr. Doubleday's letter, the third she had had from him since she had known him. Not that it was brilliant by any means. There was no glitter about him, and no conscious fun, and he did not set himself to write a letter; he merely tumbled out his feelings on paper, and that was better than style, or sparkle, or little tricks of manufacture. It was naturalness and honesty and simplicity that were their charm, qualities which Miss Raeburn hoped to see in the *magnum opus* in large measure. She shared the pleasure of reading it with Bell Sinclair, though Bell did not reciprocate by sharing her packet from the *Golden Hind*, which indeed you could hardly expect her to do. But Miss Raeburn was good-natured, and gave Bell every particular concerning that interesting ship, its appearance, accommodation, passengers, confusion, cargo, etc., etc., which a quick-witted person could gather during the short time she had been on board—told her of Effie and John, and Mr. Doubleday and Sir Francis (so she called the captain: the ship being the *Golden Hind*, the commander must needs be Sir Francis Drake, which you will allow is a name that looks a vast deal more elegant in a novel, or even in real life, than Peter)—how they looked, and what they said up to the moment she left them, winding up with, " And, my dear Tibby, I really can't speak too highly of Sir Francis. I think with him and her two other knights Effie is pretty safe, and much better off than she deserves."

CHAPTER LV.

EFFIE was not very well off at that moment. She was lying prostrate with sea-sickness, as were most of the passengers on board the *Golden Hind*. That gallant ship had had something to do holding her own against the Atlantic billows. During the first part of her voyage it blew a perfect hurricane from the south-east, threatening to drive her back on the coast of Spain.

Poor little Effie! If she could have realized this state of matters beforehand it is to be feared John Gilbert would hardly have carried the day. Her heroism was not of a high-pitched tone. Her thoughts would wander to that pretty drawing-room in Ironburgh, every article in which she had chosen with own eyes, and she could have wished herself sitting quietly there instead of tossing madly on the Atlantic. John, who was proof against sea-sickness, devoted himself to her service, only leaving her occasionally to pay some little attention to Mr. Doubleday, who was lying groaning, and dead sick in his berth. He shared his cabin with a gentleman who recognized him and asked when he had left Quixstar. "Eight or nine years ago," said this gentleman, "I was three weeks in Quixstar, and I thought it the dreariest little hole in Christendom. If you are partial to it, excuse me."

"Certainly," said Mr. Doubleday. "I have no remembrance of you."

"No, you can't. I saw you, but likely you never saw me. You were tutor at Old Battle House? So a man called Peter Veitch told me. I painted Peter's house and cow, and got fifteen guineas for the picture. It is in New Zealand now, in Otago—a souvenir of the old country. Well, it's queer where people meet."

"That would be interesting to our captain; he is the son of Peter Veitch."

"Ay, indeed! He was a shrewd canny Scot, Peter. —Heigh-ho! nine years is a great dig out of a man's life. —What's taking you to the other side of the globe?"

"I have got an appointment as classical teacher in a college."

"And I have got an appointment on the staff of a newspaper; and I'm to be 'own correspondent' to a London paper. You and I may do each other good, who knows?"

The *Golden Hind* stood nobly the heavy strain on her timbers caused by the tremendous dash of waves on her weather bows, as she was kept closely hauled to the wind. As soon as Mr. Doubleday was able he made his way to the deck, although he often found it a difficult matter to keep his feet there, feeling like a small helpless feather amid the roar of winds and waves. But he liked to see the operation of putting about the ship when she was to go on another tack; and he was lost in admiration at the coolness and presence of mind the captain showed while giving the necessary orders. For many days the ship ran on a taut bowline, till at last she got under the influence of the north-east trade winds, which bore her quietly into the region of the tropics.

If all the people in a village know each other well, it may be supposed that two hundred and ninety-seven shut into a ship with no imperative occupation, no letters, no newspapers, no rides, no drives, nor even walks, except within very circumscribed limits, will prey pretty fully upon the history, events and circumstances of each other's lives. Of old, ordinary people rarely thought of going a voyage of fifteen thousand miles—at least it was the exception, not the rule. In these latter days ordinary commonplace people contribute their full quota to every ship's company, and there was plenty such on board the *Golden Hind*. But there were some outstanding individuals. Effie and John, for instance, were objects of great interest, because of their romantic marriage. Youth, good looks, and a runaway match will be interesting in all time; and they sat so well on this pair that they "took place when Virtue's steely bones looked bleak in the cold wind," which in a wicked world Virtue's bones have a trick of doing. Neither was Mr. Doubleday what could be called commonplace. What was he about? In lack of external resources (on which, however, happily for himself, he had never been very dependent) was the *magnum opus* progressing? Was he drinking in inspiration from the mighty forces of nature round him? There were an accomplished actor and actress, Fortescue by name, on their way to reap a golden harvest in Kangaroo-land; there were two young *savans* sent out by some society to undertake an exploring expedition; there was the "own correspondent," Mr. Spenser; there was also a plain man of quiet manners and very colonial look; he would have passed muster at once among the ordinary people, but—such a but! It was told, and told with truth, that he had gone out from Ayrshire a raw lad, and had now an income of £30,000 per annum! Think of it and say if the *Golden Hind* did not deserve her name this voyage at least.

"Thirty thousand per an.!" said John Gilbert to his

wife, as they were sitting on the deck with Mr. Doubleday; "I wonder the man is not ashamed of having so much money! Does he not see the injustice of it? Now, if he would give us just one year's income—I wouldn't ask more—we'd go back to Quixstar and set up as gentlefolks for life."

"It would be remarkably nice," said Effie, "but I doubt he won't think of it. Why, life must be like a fairy tale to him; he has only to wish for a thing and get it."

"I don't envy him," said Mr. Doubleday; "it would be a burden to me."

"Ah, but you like to live the life of a mole," said Effie. "I could spend £2500 a month quite well."

"You could spend it: whether you could do it well or not is a different thing."

But this modern instance of success was mightily encouraging to all those on their way to push their fortunes. They buoyantly overlooked the fact that for one great prize Fortune carries in her bag, she has innumerable blanks. And it was well they did so: hope will carry people through much, and melancholy never yet made a man fitter for his work. It was a curious pause this voyage to most of these voyagers. They had let go the business and toil of life on the one shore, and had not got hold of them on the other. Some could make good use of this parenthesis; but most began to weary of what they thought monotony and want of excitement. Want of excitement! if they had only known it, excitement was slowly and surely preparing for them—terror and awful excitement.

CHAPTER LVI.

OF all dangers fire is what a sailor dreads most; and when early one morning it ran through the ship that there was fire in the hold, every pulse stood for a moment, and every cheek grew white, and men looked in each other's faces in silent horror. Some blindly refused to credit it—how could it be? the utmost vigilance had been used to guard against this danger. In the hold —how could it originate there? It was no mistake, however; the captain and the crew had been hard at work most of the night doing all that could be done to conquer the tremendous enemy.

Every one had rushed to the deck, and as they were standing discussing the startling news with all the eagerness and earnestness of a matter of life and death, Captain Veitch waved his hand for attention, and said—

"I depend on every man in the ship to support my authority and keep perfect order—that's the first thing towards our safety. It is possible, and most likely, that we may get the fire under, and there is no immediate danger. We shall make for the coast of America, and we may be pretty near it before—in case of the worst, which I see no reason to dread yet—it is absolutely necessary to take to the boats. The boats will carry us all, and I'll see every one out of the ship before I leave her. We have another chance; a vessel may cross our path. We shall be inconvenienced, and have some anxiety for a time; but I hope we can all submit cheerfully to that," and with a smile the captain ceased speaking, and went about his duties as if there were nothing unusual in the circumstances.

He had the soul of a leader, and never flinched, although he could not take the comfort to himself he had given to others. He felt the fire would conquer; or if they conquered it, it would not be till the ship was damaged beyond remedy. It was possible they might meet another vessel, but only possible on the ground that nothing is impossible; he knew they were out of the track of any vessel, for a sailor knows who and what he is likely to meet with on the ocean, as well as a traveller does who is accustomed to journey over an extended solitary heath.

Every heart was wonderfully lightened of its first alarm, but as the day wore on, hope and despair came up by turns. Where had the ordinary commonplace people disappeared to? Creatures at bay have the commonplace suddenly lashed out of them. The quickening of tremendous emotion had transformed the dullest face there. It seems like a prophecy and a proof of what may be in another state of existence, of the possibilities that lie dormant, to be roused and intensified in a higher life. If Mr. and Mrs. Fortescue wanted any hints in their art, and were able at such a moment to take them in, they had a wonderful opportunity. Mr. Spenser was equal to the occasion, and took brief notes to fill in when he should reach *terra firma*—the scenes were not likely to be forgotten. There was a steerage passenger, a tall woman of thirty, whom from her appearance John Gilbert had called Juno, draped in a black gown that swept the deck in folds, and having a scarlet shawl flung round her shoulders; she had great black eyes, and black hair with a ripple and the sheen of a raven's wing on it; it was swept behind her ears, and hung down her back. She stood on the deck with her hands raised and clasped like some prophetess of doom, and she lifted up her voice and wept. Long and loud she lifted up her voice, and it was deep and powerful, though soft. " O my husband! my husband! my husband! I'll never see him more!" was the burden of her lamentation. Women gathered round her, and lost sight for a minute of their own misery endeavoring to comfort her; but she refused to be comforted; her cry rang on the air again—the waves could not drown it.

John Gilbert was working among the men trying to save the ship, when Captain Veitch said to him, " Go to your wife, will you, and ask her to speak to that poor woman, and soothe her down if she can? It will do herself good."

John had left his wife in charge of Mr. Doubleday. Effie was in terror. How often had she wished herself safe at home, and here was she hemmed in between fire and the deep cruel sea! When John appeared, dirty and begrimed, she took hold of him—" You are not to leave me again," she said; " it is too horrible. We'll sink any moment; and what am I to do?"

" No, Effie; things are not so bad as that yet. The captain says, Would you go to yon woman in the red shawl, and try to calm her? She is doing a world of mischief, exciting the rest of the people."

" What can I do? Oh, if I were only at home with mamma!"

" Come," said Mr. Doubleday, " you'll go and speak to her. I'll go with you."

Effie was hardly the person to pick out for this mission. Very likely the captain was thinking of what Bell could have done in such circumstances when he proposed it.

Effie pulled the woman's shawl to get her attention. "Don't make such a noise," she said; it does no good. Your husband is at least safe—I would be glad if my husband were ashore."

"Would you?" said the woman, with a kind of glare at Effie. "Then you don't love; you don't know what love is. Oh, if I had my husband here I would be content to sink with him in hell!"

"My good woman," said Mr. Doubleday, "you don't know what you are saying, or you would not say it."

"She is mad," said Effie, shrinking away.

Poor Effie! with her flimsy affection, that could be blown now this way, and now that—what understanding could she have of the wild abandonment of a love like this?

This woman was alone—she had no children. But there were women who had gathered their children round them, and crouched in abject despair, weeping silently, while their husbands tried to speak words of hope and safety to them. There was one man who had taken home his family a year before, and was returning to wind up his affairs and go home finally with a fortune. He kept muttering, "And this is to be the end! drowned or suffocated like rats in a hole—like rats in a hole!" There were passengers who had toiled and waited all their lives for a gleam of prosperity, till at last Fortune had fairly kicked them out of their native land. Homeless, friendless, moneyless, they had gathered together a meagre bundle of hopes, to try a start once more in a new country. This seemed a fitting climax to their fate; it was not difficult to crush hope out of these.

But in what better plight was the man with £30,000

per annum? He could not throw a bridge of gold across the waters; Fortune had played into his hands all his life only to turn round now and laugh in his face. But he seemed a man who could meet even such an emergency as this with a brave spirit.

When night came, whether it might have been safe or not, no one thought of leaving the deck. A tarpaulin roof was erected, and under it the little multitude spent the time till morning dawned again; and upon what an array of haggard faces! Features that yesterday were lighted with hope or alive with despair had dulled down into a dreary resignation. A few hours of emotion at such high pressure had done what might have been the work of months in ordinary circumstances.

It was wearing to afternoon of the second day, and it became evident that another night could not be passed in the ship. The captain ordered the boats to be launched and provisioned. It was seen that by the time the whole living freight was embarked they would be sunk nearly to the gunwales, consequently the stock of provisions they could carry could not be great; but what they could take was stowed. Then the last meal that was ever to be eaten on board the *Golden Hind* was served. The captain stood at the head of his company and said —" O God, save us, we perish! In life or in death make us feel that underneath us are the everlasting arms. Look on us sinners; bless this food for the saving of our lives; and grant us mercy, O God, grant us mercy, for the sake of Jesus Christ. Amen."

To not one there was that utterance an empty form. The meal was swallowed, and then they all stood, men, women, and children, waiting till the last moment before they should take to these frail boats. There was no confusion and little noise, for even the children, gathered round the women, had sobbed themselves out. Mrs. Fortescue gazed at these family groups—she had left five little children of her own behind, and this was the bitterness of death to her. That day she had written to them, and made six copies of her letter, which she gave to six different persons, thinking that one would surely reach the hearth she had so lately quitted, if she herself should never reach it more. No stage effect in this—only the great yearning of a mother's love.

"It's of no use," Effie Gilbert said to her husband and Mr. Doubleday, who were standing one on each side of her. "I would rather perish here at once than go to die of cold and hunger in an open boat. I can't stand it. It's too horrible."

"But you must," said John. "It's the only chance, and we can't leave you here."

"Then stay. It was you who brought me here, and you have no right to leave me."

"I'll not leave you, Effie," he said soothingly.

"If my life would save you," said Mr. Doubleday, "how willingly I would give it!"

"But it won't," she wailed. "Oh what a horrible fate! and they'll be all sitting at tea in Quixstar at this moment as if nothing were happening."

"Come, Mrs. Gilbert," said the captain, who passed at that moment, "I know you'll be brave, and set an example to these poor women in the steerage."

But Effie could not be brave in such circumstances. It was not her nature.

Suddenly a great cry was heard of "A sail on the weather quarter!"

Every eye was instantly turned in the direction indicated, but only seafaring organs could make out the distant object. On it came, however; there was no mistake. It could not fail to sight them on that broad ocean, and soon it was seen bearing up to the rescue.

The awful strain was relaxed. Many shouted wildly; many fell to the deck in thanksgiving; mothers clasped their children and were able to sob once more. But the danger was not over. The cabins were filled with dense smoke, and to try to save any property would have been madness. The tongues of flame were darting out, and licking treacherously round and along. The ship was heeling over, and the waves washing into her stern. At any moment she might go down, or the flames might burst along the deck.

Captain Veitch had some difficulty in restoring order after the first ebullition of feeling was over, and he immediately began to tell off the parties as they were to go in the boats when the coming ship should be near enough.

The strange ship proved to be the gunboat *Vulcan* of the African squadron, bound for Rio Janeiro to get a surgeon, her surgeon having died suddenly—died apparently that the lives of all those on board the *Golden Hind* might be saved, as but for this event no sail would have crossed the path of the doomed ship.

The women were to go first, but Effie, who clung to her husband, declared she would not go without him. She would not be reasoned with, but Mrs. Fortescue came up with the woman in the red shawl. "Come, Mrs. Gilbert," she said, "we are to have the privilege of going first, and we must do as we are ordered, and set a good example. Come, I am leaving my husband too."

"And I am going to mine," said Juno, whose spirits from the depths of despair had gone up like quicksilver plunged in boiling water. These three headed the first company. Effie nearly lost her senses looking down the ship's side into the abyss where the boat was swinging and swaying, but Juno descended with sure and agile steps, and, receiving Effie in her arms from the sailors, set her in her place, as she did every woman and child as they were handed down. She was strong in body and spirit, and did a man's work that day. The short voyage was accomplished without accident, but every woman, except Mrs. Fortescue and Juno, fainted as she was lifted on board the *Vulcan*, whose captain and crew lavished every attention they could think of on their unfortunate guests.

There was of course less difficulty in transferring the men, but there was an accident. When midway between the ship and the boat Mr. Doubleday, always short-sighted, missed his footing, and went right down into the trough of the wave. He fell on his back and never uttered a sound. John Gilbert said the expression of his upturned face, off which the spectacles had floated, reminded him of nothing so much as of the look of some cattle he had seen pushed overboard in a Highland loch to find their way to the nearest shore—dumb, meek, astonished resignation was what gleamed from the eyes of the man and of the animals. A sailor standing by with a rope in his hand leaped overboard instantly, and caught Mr. Doubleday as he came to the surface, and they were hauled into the boat apparently not much the worse of the bath.

Captain Veitch was, as he had said he would be, the last man to leave the ship. For two days, and nearly two nights, he had never relaxed his vigilance, nor for a moment lost his self-possession, yet worn out as he was no one would have guessed it either from his speech or bearing, only his face looked stony as he watched, with feelings almost as if she had been a living thing, the *Golden Hind* became a mass of flame and smoke from stem to stern, and then floated away a mere helpless charred wreck on the waters.

CHAPTER LVII.

THE *Vulcan* carried the shipwrecked company to the Cape of Good Hope, and landed them there. Captain Veitch immediately dispatched a letter to his owners, giving full details of the catastrophe. He wrote also to his father and mother, and to Bell Sinclair. To her he said:—

"MY DEAR BELL,—I'll be home rather sooner than I expected. We have had an accident on our voyage. The *Golden Hind* took fire owing to friction in the cargo during the tossing in some gales we had; but we all got comfortably on board another vessel, and we are here in perfect safety. I hope you'll get this before you see the newspapers. They are sure to give an exaggerated account. We had an 'own correspondent' on board, whose business it is to make the most of everything. I daresay if I saw his account of the affair I would not know it. He is a Mr. Spenser, and was once at Quixstar, which made him a relation at once. Most of our passengers are going on to Melbourne with a ship which sails from this port almost immediately. Tell Miss Raeburn I have given Mr. Spenser the charge of Mr. Doubleday for the rest of the voyage, so that she may keep her mind easy. Your sister and her husband are looking well. They are writing too, as every one is. Remember a man is not burned out of his ship twice in the course of his life. I have had no time of late for tailoring.—I am, ever yours, PETER VEITCH.

"*P. S.*—I'll have to wait some time for a vessel home."

This was all Capt. Veitch ever said of his own courage and endurance. He had now arranged for all his passengers being sent on to their destinations, he had dispatched his letters, and at last he fairly gave way, bent his head in his hands, and sobbed like a child.

Effie Gilbert positively refused to go to sea again immediately, and John was quite willing to spend a few weeks at the Cape. He was in no hurry. Certainly there was nothing going wrong at Hongatonga for want of him. However, they and Capt. Veitch accompanied their late fellow-voyagers to the ship in which they hoped to finish their voyage. A few weeks ago they had not known of each other's existence, now they parted as intimate and endeared friends. John issued particular invitations to every one in general to visit him at Hongatonga, and most people seemed to think that at some time or other that embryo city would lie directly in their path. Mr. Doubleday was in good spirits. Perhaps he had got some pages of the *magnum opus* laid out in his mind to his own satisfaction, and the pearl plaster was beginning to take effect.

"Well," he said to Effie, "good-bye. I'll be all prepared to welcome you when you come. You won't be long?"

"I don't know. If I could persuade John, I would rather go home to Quixstar."

"Quixstar!" said Mr. Spenser, shrugging his shoulders, "better fifty years of the fifth quarter of the globe than a cycle of Quixstar. Your husband has more sense."

17*

"Mr. Spenser does not know what Quixstar has been to you and me, Mrs. Gilbert," said Mr. Doubleday.

"Well," said Mr. Spenser, "whether you come or not, Mrs. Gilbert, you'll hear of Mr. Doubleday and me yet. I mean to blow his trumpet furiously in my paper, and he's going to look out fresh and apt classical quotations for me; between us we mean to mould young Australia."

"It will take all your energies," said Peter. "It is a grand work; I wish you well."

"*Au revoir*," cried John Gilbert. Mr. Doubleday stood on the deck and watched them till they were out of sight.

"Now," said Effie, "now, John, you have asked every creature, including Juno, to Hongatonga; I hope I'll never see it. Oh take me home! If I once had my foot on English ground, no power would tempt me into a ship again," and she shuddered.—"I suppose, Peter," she added, "you'll go to sea again just as if nothing had happened!"

"Just," he said. "I like danger; it's the most wholesome and legitimate excitement one can have, and it pushes a man closer to his fellow-creatures and his Creator than any one thing I know."

"It certainly pushes one close enough to one's fellow-creatures," said John—"a shade too close for my taste."

"And," said Peter, "it's purifying; how little selfishness, for instance, we saw in the scene we have passed through."

"Did we? I saw quite enough and to spare," said John.

Now there are two reasons for this difference of opinion. People generally see best what they have eyes to see—none are so quick at detecting selfishness as the selfish—and again, though Peter made no pretensions to extra goodness, and did not pride himself on continually influencing his fellow-creatures, there was that about him which somehow or other made vice, whether big or little, fall back and hide itself in his presence. He had this kind of greatness, and was not conscious of it; if he had been conscious of it, it would have been smallness.

"I would like to see the meeting between Juno and her husband," said Peter.

"Very likely Jupiter will be more surprised than pleased," said John; "the chances are he's little and henpecked, and set off to Australia to be out of her reach—one may have too much of a good thing."

"I would think," said Peter, "that a man who could inspire love like hers—"

"Stuff!" said John; "it's not inspiration, it's outspiration—the woman's nature; Jupiter may be a tall fellow who can hold his own, but, according to the doctrine of probabilities, he's little and henpecked."

"Is it according to the doctrine of probabilities," said Effie, "or is it my fancy, that you are walking as if you were lame?"

"I'm hardly lame," John said; "it's a mere trifle. I ran my foot against a nail coming out of the *Vulcan*, and I feel it a little."

"That's not a good thing," said Peter. "Have you attended to it?"

"Oh, it was a mere nothing, and it is almost healed now."

"I say, Peter," Effie said, "help me to persuade John either to take me home or to stay here. He would be quite as well here as at Hongatonga. I shrink from the sea. I shudder at such horrors. I could risk it only if he would take me home, but to go away to an outlandish place like Hongatonga, I can't do it—don't ask me."

"Do not think of it at all now," said John, "you'll get over the fright and get up your spirits in a week or two, and then you'll be better able to see what's what—there's no hurry, you know."

"If it is only the voyage that frightens you," said Peter, "the likelihood is you would have an uncommonly pleasant voyage."

"Nothing in the shape of a voyage can be pleasant to me," she said.

But she was to have a voyage, and a voyage home too.

It is to be feared that Mrs. John Gilbert's love for her husband was of the fair-weather kind,—it was for better, not for worse; not that she was very selfish, she could not be called that, but her nature was weak; she could not encounter hardship, nor brave danger, nor sacrifice herself; she had no love deep enough for that, and yet in her own measure she loved. Poor thing, it seemed as if all that befell her at this time was like breaking a butterfly on the wheel. The rest and rational relaxation they took in seeing what was to be seen, and making themselves acquainted with the manners and customs of the place, told most beneficially on Effie and Captain Veitch, but John Gilbert was not in his usual high health and spirits. He complained of lassitude, and one evening when they returned from a ride in the country he spoke of having pain about his throat and a stiffness, and seemed depressed and restless.

"You are tired," said his wife.

"Tired! what should I be tired with? it's not that."

"Then what is it? a sore throat? Put something round it and go to bed, that's the best thing, or would you like us to send for a doctor?"

"Yes," he said, "send for a doctor."

Peter was struck with his tones, and when Effie went out of the room he looked at him closely and asked, "John, what is it?"

"I don't know; time will tell. I'll go to bed; help me."

It was evident he was struck down with serious illness of some kind, and Peter's first thought was, "I am glad I am here to help them."

It was an hour or two before a doctor came, and when he did come he had no difficulty in recognizing tetanus, but not a hopeless case at all—not hopeless."

It was well for Effie that she had such a friend as Peter to think and act for her through this terrible time. At his suggestion the landlady of the house kept Mrs. Gilbert with herself, and she only saw her husband occasionally between the paroxysms of suffering. Her love, you see, was of the kind that could be satisfied in knowing he was in the best hands. Oh, if his mother had been there, how she would have encompassed him with her love! Yet after all, what could either of them have done? They could not have lessened his agony, they could only have increased their own.

The doctor might or might not be a skilful man, but he went through the course of remedies with a confidence in himself that knew no abatement, and he and Peter never left the patient. The suffering which in three days will lay a man low who has been in the flush of youth and strength is not small, yet through it all John's mind was as clear and firm as possible. On the second day he could not speak, but he made signs for a pen, and wrote on a scrap of paper these words, "Don't tell my mother yet." Ah, that was the cry of a full heart. No one could read it surely without strong sympathy for mother and son. "Don't tell her *yet*." When was she to be told? When? He wrote again, "Take Effie home." That was all. What the multitude of his thoughts within him were who can tell? He was fully able to think till nearly the very last, when probably the influence of narcotics overpowered him, and on the evening of the third day of his illness he passed away.

Effie's grief was altogether violent and overmastering. Its very violence exhausted it only to come on again after a time with renewed force. She had never encountered either illness or death before, and it seemed an impossibility—an impossibility, and yet there was the awful stillness, and the awful whiteness.

Ten days later, Mrs. Gilbert and Captain Veitch were on their homeward voyage, and John Gilbert was left to sleep the long sleep at the Cape of Good Hope—far from country or kindred. All who had known John, and heard of his strange sudden death, felt as if the world were a chillier place than it had been before, and that they could more easily have spared a better man. There had been so much about him that was lovable, and if only he had lived— But he had not, and his lost possibilities were shut into eternity.

CHAPTER LVIII.

WHEN the late passengers of the *Golden Hind* were afloat once more, and had time to recall all that had passed, it struck one and another of them that but for the coolness and resource of Captain Veitch none of them might have been alive to tell the tale, and it was proposed simultaneously by Mr. Fortescue and Mr. Spenser that an address should be sent to him acknowledging their gratitude, and testifying to his brave, good qualities, signed by all his passengers. This was eagerly entered into from the highest to the lowest. Mr. Spenser then suggested that, as a sort of substance to the shadow, they should subscribe, however little, and send him a sum of money along with the address. This was heartily entered into also; but many of them were poor, and all of them had lost, if not money, their personal effects in the burning of the *Golden Hind*, so that much could not be expected. There was Mr. Walker, the £30,000 a year man, it is true, and he approved also; but he told Mr. Spenser to get his list of subscriptions, and come to him last, and he would give as other people gave. Mr. Spenser shrugged his shoulders, and said to himself that it was a queer world—a conclusion he had not unfrequently arrived at in the course of his life.

Mr. Spenser was wonderfully successful, gratitude not being such a rare growth as cynics would have us believe.

When he applied to Mr. Doubleday — who, poor man, was lying in his berth far from well—he said simply, and without reserve, " I can give you nothing. I am living on charity myself at present, but if I ever have it in my power I'll not forget to acknowledge my debt to Captain Veitch." Mr. Spencer felt small. if he had had money, he would have given it, whether it belonged to himself or not; if he had not had it, he would have given some other reason for not giving it. He held that to seem poor is worse than to be poor. To feel poor, however, is a great deal worse than either. That, and that only, is poverty, a poverty that Mr. Doubleday had never experienced.

Mr. Walker looked over the list of subscriptions, and said, " They have done well. I'll give you mine before we land." When they made the harbor he came to Mr. Spenser as he was standing on the deck with Mr. Doubleday, and said, " There is an order on Liverpool for £1000. Send that with the address to Captain Veitch, let the other people keep their money, and here is £1000 to divide among the steerage passengers. Perhaps you, gentlemen, will take the trouble to see it distributed somewhat equally. I'll be glad to see you at my place any time. That's all. I'm off," and he shook hands, and went ashore immediately.

Mr. Doubleday's face softened, and beamed in the presence of a good action. " That is generous," he said.

" Well," said Mr. Spenser, " I fully expected he would give me the slip. Yes, it is good; but he'll never miss it. Two thousand farthings from either you or me would have been a far bigger gift in proportion, and we would have both missed it. It would have been self-denial, which is true generosity."

" His looks a fabulous income to us," said Mr. Doubleday; "but people who have much have just as much to do with it. Perhaps he is denying himself something, who knows?"

" Well, well, we'll give him the benefit of the doubt, and not knock the bottom out of a good action.—Come, you'll have to help me to apportion it."

Any one who does not believe in gratitude ought to have seen the faces of these steerage passengers, as one by one they got the sum that was to stand between them and starvation in a strange country. Mr. Doubleday had never done anything in his life that gave him more pleasure than acting in this instance as a medium.

When Captain Veitch and Mrs. Gilbert arrived at Liverpool they went first to a hotel, where Effie remained to rest while the captain went to call on the owners of the unfortunate *Golden Hind*, by which, it may be observed, they had lost nothing, the ship being fully insured. They gave him a very hearty reception, and handed to him the address and enclosure from the passengers of the wrecked ship. His face flushed as he read. ".Most extraordinary!" said he, "I did nothing more than my duty—what any man would have done in my place."

"Well, you know, Captain Veitch," said one of the partners of the ship-owning firm, " there are always two ways of doing a duty, and you seem not to have taken the worst. We have another ship building, and nearly ready to launch, which is also to be the *Golden Hind*. It is a very fine ship; if you like to take the command of her, we'll be only too glad to secure your services."

As a matter of course Captain Veitch accepted the offer.

There was a private note from Spenser, giving the particulars of the presentation, and ending with—"So you need have no qualms about the money, for thereby you are not grinding the faces of the poor. Your friend Mr. Doubleday has not been well; I doubt he is a man of a delicate constitution. He is better, however, than he has been, and I hope a few days will set him up again. He and I lodge together, and he is in excellent spirits, looking forward to beginning his work shortly; and I expect before you get this we'll be cheered by the arrival of Mr. and Mrs. Gilbert."

By noon next day Effie and Peter were at the gate of Old Battle House. Mrs. Sinclair and Bell were sitting quietly at work when Effie burst into the familiar room, and flung her arms round her mother's neck, laughing. Actually she had forgotten her widowhood and everything in the one feeling that she was at home and safe once more; but when she saw their grave faces she sank on a sofa and burst into hysterical tears. Her mother and sister set themselves to soothe and comfort her; poor thing, she needed it.

Peter had not followed her. He was as eager to see Bell as she could be; but he could not intrude on such a meeting, so he made his way to Mr. Sinclair's room, where that gentleman was sitting reading. He rose and welcomed Peter with enthusiasm, and put him in his own peculiar chair—that chair which Peter had thought a resting-place of unimaginable luxury, when after cleaning the gravel he had vaulted in at one of the windows, and sank in it by way of a boyish experiment.

"You are quite a hero now, Peter," said Mr. Sinclair.

"It must be in a small way, surely," Peter said.

"One likes modesty, of course, Peter; but I have the idea that it would be an easier thing to go into battle than to command a ship on fire and control all the people."

"I don't know about that; it was not my duty to kill men. But it was a strain, I acknowledge. I had not my clothes off for two days and nights; I must have slept, but when I don't know. I would not like to go through the same thing again."

"I can believe that.—And poor John Gilbert has gone the way of all the earth?"

"Yes."

"And where is Effie? how is she?" asked Mr. Sinclair.

"She is here; I brought her with me. She has stood it wonderfully. I thought at first she would break down altogether, her grief was so violent and so keen."

"Poor thing! poor thing!" said Mr. Sinclair.

"Ay, she has a hard time of it since she left this house," said Peter; "and it was all very new to her."

"And yet," said Mr. Sinclair, "I understand you want to subject another young woman to the same style of hardship?"

"She has told you?"

"Yes, she has told me."

"And you approve?"

"I approve of you, and I approve of you sticking to your business, and I approve of her approving of you; but if a sort of steady-going happiness is her object—"

"It's not her object. She has considered the thing; she can do without happiness, and she'll be very happy —I'm sure of it."

"Well, if she does not want happiness, and can do without it, and is sure to have it, I have nothing more to say. She must make the best of it, and she'll do that. I admire both your taste and your wisdom.—But I must go and see Effie; just sit still for a little, will you?"

In spite of the events of the last three months, and in spite of his philosophical estimate of the place happiness should hold in the theory of a man's life, Peter was at this moment exceedingly happy. Of course there are people who think less of themselves when others think more, who, the more they are praised, know themselves the more unworthy, and have no feeling but that of a whipped cur. Peter was not of that stamp; he was honestly happy without thinking particularly about himself at all—his merits or demerits.

In a minute or two Bell swept in, as majestic as ever; on her face the oxymel expression of joy and grief occasioned by her sister's arrival. Peter was standing in the window farthest away, and was not in view from the door.

"I wonder what uncle sent me here for?" she said to herself.

She did not wonder long. Imagine that meeting. Observe also that Mr. Sinclair was not wholly lost to sympathy with humanity in its more tender phases, and that he could even execute a manœuvre in its behalf—not complicated, it is true, but equivalent perhaps to what in drill is called the goose-step.

"Bell," said Peter, after the first outburst of feeling was fairly over, "a rich man has given me a thousand pounds. He must have known that I wanted money to begin housekeeping with."

"But you didn't; I have plenty."

"Yes, but—"

She laid her hand on his mouth—"Now don't be small; don't take my hero down a few pegs in my estimation. There is to be no question of money or anything else between you and me; we are one and indivisible."

"I was not going to be small; but we'll let the subject rest in the mean time."

"If you would only give up the sea, your thousand pounds would set you agoing as a tailor very well."

"Yes, it would, very well. Do you regret your promise, Bell, to marry a sailor?"

"Not an atom," said she; "but oh, Peter, if you had perished in the *Golden Hind!*"

"Let us be grateful that no one perished."

"And when I thought of that silly quarrel we had the day you went away—it will be a lesson never to quarrel again?"

"What quarrel?"

"Don't you remember? the day after the hall was opened."

"I remember you calling when I had barely time to speak to you; it was an intense pleasure to me, but it takes two people to quarrel, doesn't it? Now I never quarrelled, and to this hour I have not a notion of what offended you."

"Then I won't tell you."

"Not if it is disagreeable to you; but I might mark the rock on my chart and avoid it in future if you were to tell me."

"I'll risk you bumping on it."

"Have you seen the Gilberts lately?"

"I have seen them every day since the sad news came."

"And how are they? how is Mrs. Gilbert?"

"They are well. You know old Mrs. Gilbert, John's aunt, died just before the news came, and was spared that pang—he used to be a kind of idol of hers. She has left all she had to Mr. Gilbert. I like to see money go straight to the right place."

"I am just going to see Mrs. Gilbert; I can give her every particular, and save Effie the pain of doing it. See, I have this to give her," and he showed Bell John's last writing—"Don't tell my mother yet."

"Poor John! that is very touching."

"It is that. I must go, though. I have not been home yet, but I'll go to Mrs. Gilbert first."

"You'll find her very calm. Mrs. Gilbert has the secret of being calm in any circumstances; take her all in all, she is the most perfect woman I know. One thing more—how is Mr. Doubleday?"

"He was looking very well when I saw him last, but he has not been well since; he fell into the sea in going to the *Vulcan*, and he was too long in getting his clothes changed; in the circumstances, that could not be helped, and it may have told on him, but we'll hope he's all right by this time."

Peter, as he expected, found Mrs. Gilbert very calm. He gave her a detailed account of John's illness, softening it as much as possible. She listened intently, but asked few questions; when he gave her John's last writing she did not look at it. She asked most tenderly for Effie, went to the gate with him, and thanked him for his kindness, his great kindness, to her son. When she went in she read the words on the paper; a great cry of anguish escaped her; her feeling was that of the Jewish king, "Would God I had died for thee, my son! my son!" But Mr. Gilbert was coming in; she put the paper away: instinctively even at that moment she felt that if he saw it he would brood over the fact that John had written of her and not of him; neither could she share this sad memento with Mary, for she could not tell her that she was not to speak of it to her father, but Mrs. Gilbert kept it—how carefully she kept it!

Then Peter went home. His father received him with hearty pride, his mother with tearful joy. Shrewd and thrifty, they had a keen enjoyment in hearing of the money that had come to him so unexpectedly. The sum seemed to them a fortune, and comparatively few people have souls sufficiently elevated to be wholly unmoved by a golden shower, expected or unexpected.

"Thirty thousand a year, did ye say, Peter?" his father remarked, "and originally a man frae our ain rank o' life—'od he'll be fair clatty" (tarred and feathered) " wi' siller."

It was graphic—think of it, O ye impecunious hosts, what kind of sensation must it be to be "clatty wi' siller!"

CHAPTER LIX.

A MONTH passed, and the Australian mail came in again. Miss Raeburn had been watching for it,—so, in spite of the fulness of her own life, had Bell Sinclair. Miss Raeburn got a letter addressed in an unknown hand; she opened it with a sickening feeling of dread as to what its contents might be. It was written by Mr. Spenser, and said—

"DEAR MADAM,—Although I am a stranger to you, you are not altogether a stranger to me. When Mr. Doubleday spoke of you I had no difficulty in recalling the fact that I had frequently seen you when I chanced to be in Quixstar, a good many years ago now. I think Mr. Doubleday told me he wrote to you last mail, though only a brief note. He was not given to make himself his subject, but probably he mentioned he had been ill, so that you may not be absolutely unprepared for my sad news. He died yesterday, at a quarter to four in the afternoon. He was never confined to bed, and did not appear to suffer much, or to think himself seriously ill—always speaking spiritedly of his plans for the future. He took great pleasure in the visits of a Mr. Johnston, a native of Quixstar, who is over from New Zealand just now, and whom I met accidentally; he came very frequently to see him, and they had many subjects in common. I discovered that Mr. Johnston is in possession of a picture of mine, which he bought because he recognized the scene, Peter Veitch's cottage in Quixstar. Mr. Doubleday told me with a good deal of enjoyment that John Gilbert and other boys used to call Mr. Johnston's father Old Bloody Politeful as a nickname. He was reading a story, too, which he also enjoyed; it was in some numbers of a magazine lent him by Mr. and Mrs. Fortescue, people with whom we crossed from Liverpool. Mr. Fortescue said to me that Mr. Doubleday had a great man in him, but wanted a prompter. Yesterday at this time he was reading the last number of the magazine I have mentioned. The story was not finished. I said, 'The new number will be here in a few days.' He was lying back in his chair, and he said, 'I would like to see how it ends, but it will end well—stories all end well,' and he gave what seemed a sigh. A few minutes after I looked at him, and he was gone—his story was finished—well, we are certain. Mr. and Mrs. Gilbert have not yet arrived; he looked eagerly forward to seeing them again.—Dear madam, with true sympathy, I am, yours sincerely,

" CHARLES SPENSER."

After reading this Miss Raeburn sat spell-bound for a time; she could not believe it, and yet he had been dead almost two months. She liked sympathy; and, with the letter in her hand, she set off for Old Battle House. As she passed Peter Veitch's cottage, looking as like a picture as ever, she went in and told her news.

" Ay, ay," said the gardener, " and Mr. Doubleday's dead. Weel, he'll wun far'er forrit in the next world than ever he did in this."

Captain Peter went with her to Old Battle House; and without doubt they were all saddened by the intelligence. Miss Raeburn said—

18

"He had no fear of dying. He has told me that many a time he had wished to die, and that if ever I heard of his death I was not to be sorry."

"He was a most modest, unselfish being," said Bell, her eyes filling with tears: "and I am afraid we did not make him so happy here as we might have done."

"As to that," said Mrs. Sinclair, "I have no reflections. I did my duty by him; few people would have had the patience with him that I had. But I am very sorry the poor man has not lived to profit by the situation after so many people taking so much trouble to get it for him."

"It seemed," said Mr. Sinclair, "the post exactly suited for him; but man proposes."

Miss Raeburn went back to her house, feeling that she was the chief mourner. It was fitting that Mr. Doubleday should pass away as unnoticed as he had lived. He had carried the *magnum opus* with him to where he would have scope and verge enough; his early wish was accomplished—he had burst into infinity, and knew even as he was known.

Mrs. Sinclair's love for her favorite daughter triumphed over her anger—even over the sting of the affront which Effie's conduct had subjected her to. She got hot when she thought of it yet—jilting a man in the position of George Raeburn, and going off when the very dinner was on the table and the guests arriving, leaving her to make the best and the worst of it. But Effie had suffered for it; and Mrs. Sinclair took her back into her old place as if she never had left it. In her own private mind Mrs. Sinclair thought it was possible, nay, likely, that George Raeburn would renew his suit. She did not know him. Effie was as clean swept out of his heart as if she had never been there—never. He even imagined that he had forgotten how fiercely his pride had been stung, but he had not, nor ever would.

Mrs. Sinclair had been disappointed in her son's career and marriage; she had been more than disappointed in Effie; and it filled up her measure when Bell had revealed her engagement with Peter Veitch. But there was no help for it—no help. Now that Effie was home, she poured forth her feelings on the subject to her, and got sympathy. Effie's judicious remarks on Bell's folly were edifying.

"It is not," she said, "that I don't like Peter Veitch. I would be very ungrateful if I didn't. But what's the captain of a merchant vessel? I don't suppose many of them get over twenty pounds a month; and no position, no social position whatever. And then the sea! If Bell had only seen what I have seen, it would be the last thing she would do. But it's impossible to make her feel it; people must see with their own eyes to know its horrors."

"Then the connection," said Mrs. Sinclair.

"Oh, well," said Effie, "I don't suppose old Peter and his wife will expect to come here very often."

"I have no idea what such people expect," said Mrs. Sinclair; "but Bell is infatuated enough for anything."

"It's extraordinary," said Effie; "there's nothing so very fascinating about Peter Veitch, I am sure."

"I should say not," said Mrs. Sinclair. "It's pure infatuation; and one may as well try to stop the Eden as to stop it."

Quite as well; and again Mrs. Sinclair had to submit to the inevitable. But she and Effie, to their honor be it said, suppressed their private opinions in consideration of the love they bore to Bell.

Captain Veitch arranged that his marriage trip was

to be the voyage to Australia in the new *Golden Hind*, and the wedding took place exactly a week before the sailing of that vessel. The marriage-party was small, being confined to the immediate relatives on both sides; which was judicious, Mrs. Sinclair said, as the Veitches were not too presentable. She had no other feeling than that Bell was throwing herself away.

As the gardener and his wife walked home he said—

"I think, Jess, ye'll allow that that's ae gude job ower?"

"Weel, Peter, I dinna ken. I'll just hae twa folk on my mind every windy nicht instead o' ane."

CHAPTER LX.

THE elements sympathized with Captain Veitch and his wife—they had a glorious voyage. It was all new to Bell, and with her keen intellect and capacity for enjoyment, and her young life still beaded with the dew of the morning, how could it be otherwise than ecstatic, her lover by her side to explain as far as he could, and, where he could not, to bend with her before the majesty of the mystery?

She kept an " abstract log," whatever that may be, and sometimes rose almost to poetry in her descriptions of sea and sky.

When they doubled the Cape of Good Hope they thought with deep tenderness of him belonging to them who was lying there. Then they got among the most magnificent billows they had encountered—the long majestic roll of these seas, driven and hunted by what sailors call " the brave west winds," and the beauty of their coloring, was a pleasure given a keen edge to by a sense of danger. But then the captain's wife had faith strong and steady in her husband's skill, and an admiration of it profound and enthusiastic.

On the homeward voyage she was quite a sailor, knowing and nautical in the extreme, and had learned to understand her husband's passion for the sea, and to sympathize with it, to his infinite delight. The truth is, it is probable that she was of Norse descent as well as he. In the fourteenth century a Sinclair married the representative of one of the ancient Jarls of Orkney, who, we know, were Scandinavians originally. That Sinclair and that Miss Jarl must, to a certainty, have been among Bell's ancestors; so that there need be no surprise that, under favorable circumstances, the old tastes and tendencies should crop out. There was no drop of the Jarl's blood in Effie or Tom; apparently Bell had got all that could be spared.

When Captain Veitch and his wife returned once more to Quixstar they found Old Battle House prepared and remodelled for their reception. Mrs. Sinclair and Effie were there to greet and install them, but they had taken a genteel house in a genteel quarter of Eastburgh, wishing to mix more in the society of that city than they could do living at the distance of Quixstar, and they removed to it shortly after the arrival of the Veitches. Mr. Sinclair had not frowned upon this plan. There is no doubt he was guilty of favoritism, and to have Bell for an inmate, especially as he would have her so much to himself, was an arrangement that remarkably met his feelings and tastes. Miss Raeburn rejoiced at it too. Bell's marriage was not such a calamity after all, since she was to be in Quixstar still, while her husband would be absent a great part of the year. There are different points of view, certainly.

It was a sharper trial than ever Bell had imagined it would be, when Captain Veitch went away again, but perhaps these partings were compensated for by the appearance every now and then of a new honeymoon in the domestic heavens, and it is likely a sailor and a sailor's wife will be oftener at the foot of God's throne than other people.

Effie enjoyed herself well in Eastburgh. She went

into what John Gilbert would have called the pearl-plaster business. She fell back for occupation on her girlish taste for writing, and she wrote books that got an audience. Some people mentioned the word "genius" to her, and she believed, and was pleased; and others said she had "a turn" for writing, and she believed, and was equally pleased. Possibly the two words had the same meaning in all their mental vocabularies.

She had "a turn,"—that expression hit the mark. The tone of her books was religious and genteel. Religion and gentility is a remarkable mixture, but perhaps not more so than religion and worldliness, or any other of its numerous debasing alloys, but surely more grotesque: imagine the beatitude, "Blessed are the genteel, for they—" But the subject had better be dropped, in case of saying something irreverently strong. Effie had lived for weeks with immensity stretching round her. She had been rescued from a burning ship, she had seen her husband's strong young life extinguished by three days of agony, and the outcome was a mixture of the religious and the genteel! You never can make the stream rise higher than the fountain. Probably her books did little harm. It is even within the bounds of possibility that they did good to the people whose tastes they suited, you never can tell; but there was one good thing they did. Mary Gilbert was visiting her Aunt Raeburn in Ironburgh, and she was reading one day when George came in. When she saw him she blushed vividly, and slipped the book down into her pocket. He saw both the blush and the movement, and wondered what it could mean. Was Mary the good reading a book she was ashamed of? It had a bright green cover, he noticed, and after she was gone he had sufficient curiosity to glance over the books, and he found the green cover. He opened it, and saw on the title-page, "Rosamond Fitz-Herbert; a Tale. By Effie St. Clair Gilbert." He reddened in spite of himself with angry pride. "I see it," he thought, "Mary wanted to spare me. She need not have put herself to the trouble, but *her* feeling was genuine at least, her face showed that." He threw down the book with contempt. This led him to think of Mary, specially to think of her, and the result was a marriage—the most blessed event in his life. It was just in time to save him from growing hard, very hard. She influenced him as the sun does the hoar-frost, smiling it away, and melting by the warmth of his atmosphere what he can't reach with his smile.

Effie Gilbert rejoiced to hear of this marriage, it cleared away entirely any little remaining remorse she had.

And Mrs. Gilbert still sat in the old familiar window-seat. The garden and the flowers and the water were all there as of old, but her children, the pretty girls and the clever, handsome boy,—yes, they were there too as in a dream. The future had become the past, that future into which she had so often peered with longing anxiety. She still has Cowper on her table, and between the leaves of it are her son's last words. How often she looks at them, how often!

Bell admired her sister's books. It was her one weakness—or strength—to see no fault in those she loved. Her husband, she was aware, did not share her admiration. Once when she was reading a contemptuous notice of one of Effie's productions he watched her face gather into an expression of grieved indignant feeling, that, it must be allowed, amused him.

"I wish I had written this book," he said.

"Do you? said she eagerly. "You think so much of it. I was sure the newspaper had made a mistake. It must have been some other book they were thinking of when they wrote that."

Peter smiled. He said, "If I had seen about a book of mine such an expression as was on your face a minute ago, it would have made up to me for all the wicked reviews in Christendom. How do you think 'Mary Wilson; a Tale. By Mrs. Peter Veitch,' would take? I much doubt the young lady would eschew it, but, without a joke, I think you should publish your log. I always grudge nobody having the enjoyment of it but a trio like your uncle, Miss Raeburn and myself."

"Now," said she, "if you mean that, you are just in as great a blunder about me as you think I am in about Effie. Nobody would care a pin-point for my log."

"I think differently," said he.

After all, what a thing love is! Stung by the world, we rush to its shelter as lunatics to their padded room, and there we fall softly, and get healed of our hurts. Pity the wretches who have no such retreat! Not that this remark has any bearing on Effie St. Clair Gilbert; she had lived in a padded room all her days, and continued to do so.

Bell could not get the flame of enthusiasm to kindle up in her uncle either with regard to Effie's works. When she introduced the subject, he had a trick of going off to something quite foreign to it, as when she brought under his notice the mistaken review she had seen, he said—

"Ay!—By the way, when I was out I met that woman who used to be here, Maddy—what's her name? Her child has been ill, it seems, and I could hardly get away from her. She told me how 'it grat and pu'd up

18*

its wee feetie,' always putting an emphasis on the *wee*, as if the child had two pairs of feet, and drew up the smaller ones. She talks tremendously, yon woman."

Bell laughed heartily at her uncle's logical rendering of motherly endearments, and thought, "Maddy must have grown weak as other women, and weaker than some, or she would hardly have entertained uncle with her bairn's ailments."

And time slipped on in Quixstar. The Rational Relaxation Society continued its labors with encouraging success. The hall was found so generally useful that the town wondered how it had ever got on without it. Mr. Kennedy and Mr. Sinclair made some faint adumbration towards cordiality. One wonders if people feel ashamed of having quarrelled, after the heat of the occasion is by? But they cannot blot out what has been said, nor undo what has been done; they can't put their feelings exactly where they were, nor call in the evil effect of their deed. These men could not prevent people in Quixstar saying, " Ay, ministers are nae better than other folk;" or, " Presented a hall to the town! he built it to spite the minister." Religion and philanthropy don't by any means look at their best under these circumstances. But the peculiar blindness of the two men began to wear off, and in time the restoration of sight may be complete.

One day Miss Raeburn in passing went in to call on old Peter Veitch and his wife, and found them engaged in a way that made them look slightly caught. Peter was at one end of the table and Mrs. Veitch at the other; standing on a chair at the side was the heir-apparent, two and a half years old; the gardener was sending a hoop—*girr*, the little Captain called it (he followed his grandfather's nomenclature)—along the table to his wife, and she sent it back, Peter the Third trying to catch it as it passed. Which of the three faces looked most delighted could hardly be said. The boy was in extraordinary glee, crying, "Do it 'gain, g'an'pa! g'an'ma, do it 'gain!" his whole little person and face in a glow of mirth and motion.

"Miss Raeburn, ye'll think there's nae fules like auld fules," said Mrs. Veitch, by way of apology for being detected in such high-jinks.

"Go on, said Miss Raeburn; go on. I like to see the play."

It was a study for an artist, and Miss Raeburn was a bit of an artist. It touched her feelings, too, as a human being and a woman. As the boy's mother came in, she said—

"Tibbie, you and I are not needed here. Come, we'll take a little walk and come back."

Bell kissed her son, which he thought a most absurd interruption of the business of life he was so intent on; and as Miss Raeburn and she went out at the door, they heard the ringing music, "Do it 'gain, g'an'pa!"

THE END.

www.ingramcontent.com/pod-product-compliance
Lightning Source LLC
Chambersburg PA
CBHW030548300426
44111CB00009B/903